T0397141

Doubting the Divine in Early Modern Europe

In this book, George McClure examines the intellectual tradition of challenges to religious and literary authority in the early modern era. He explores the hidden history of unbelief through the lens of Momus, the Greek god of criticism and mockery. Surveying his revival in Italy, France, Spain, Germany, the Netherlands, and England, McClure shows how Momus became a code for religious doubt in an age when such writings remained dangerous for authors. Momus ("Blame") emerged as a persistent and subversive critic of divine governance and, at times, divinity itself. As an emblem or as an epithet for agnosticism or atheism, he was invoked by writers such as Leon Battista Alberti, Anton Francesco Doni, Giordano Bruno, Luther, and possibly, in veiled form, by Milton in his depiction of Lucifer. The critic of gods also acted, in sometimes related fashion, as a critic of texts, leading the army of Moderns in Swift's *Battle of the Books*, and offering a heretical archetype for the literary critic.

George McClure is Professor of History at the University of Alabama, where he has taught since 1986. He is the author of *Sorrow and Consolation in Italian Humanism*, which won the Marraro Prize of the Society for Italian Historical Studies, *The Culture of Profession in Late Renaissance Italy*, and *Parlour Games and the Public Life of Women in Renaissance Italy*, which received Honorable Mention for Best Book Prize of the Society for the Study of Early Modern Women.

Doubting the Divine in Early Modern Europe

The Revival of Momus, the Agnostic God

GEORGE McCLURE
University of Alabama

CAMBRIDGE
UNIVERSITY PRESS

University Printing House, Cambridge CB2 8BS, United Kingdom

One Liberty Plaza, 20th Floor, New York, NY 10006, USA

477 Williamstown Road, Port Melbourne, VIC 3207, Australia

314–321, 3rd Floor, Plot 3, Splendor Forum, Jasola District Centre,
New Delhi – 110025, India

79 Anson Road, #06-04/06, Singapore 079906

Cambridge University Press is part of the University of Cambridge.

It furthers the University's mission by disseminating knowledge in the pursuit of
education, learning, and research at the highest international levels of excellence.

www.cambridge.org
Information on this title: www.cambridge.org/9781108470278
DOI: 10.1017/9781108636636

© George McClure 2018

This publication is in copyright. Subject to statutory exception
and to the provisions of relevant collective licensing agreements,
no reproduction of any part may take place without the written
permission of Cambridge University Press.

First published 2018

Printed in the United Kingdom by Clays, St Ives plc

A catalogue record for this publication is available from the British Library.

Library of Congress Cataloging-in-Publication Data
Names: McClure, George W., 1951– author.
Title: Doubting the divine in early modern Europe : the revival of
Momus, the Agnostic god / George McClure.
Description: New York: Cambridge University Press, 2018. |
Includes bibliographical references.
Identifiers: LCCN 2018003781 | ISBN 9781108470278 (hardback)
Subjects: LCSH: Agnosticism – Europe. | Momus (Greek deity)
Classification: LCC BL2747.2.M33 2018 | DDC 211/.7094–dc23
LC record available at https://lccn.loc.gov/2018003781

ISBN 978-1-108-47027-8 Hardback

Cambridge University Press has no responsibility for the persistence or accuracy
of URLs for external or third-party internet websites referred to in this publication
and does not guarantee that any content on such websites is, or will remain,
accurate or appropriate.

Contents

Preface		*page* vii
1	The Classical Tradition	1
2	Renaissance Antihero: Leon Battista Alberti's *Momus*, the Novel	34
3	Momus and the Reformation	82
4	The Execution of Giordano Bruno	123
5	Milton's Lucifer	144
6	God of Modern Criticks	181
7	Conclusion: Momus and Modernism	226
Bibliography		243
Index		263

Preface

Why did the relatively obscure and uncelebrated Greek god Momus ("Blame") come to have such an enduring and sometimes subversive history in Western culture? Certainly, this pesky god of criticism and mockery – expelled from heaven for his mischief – stirred up trouble both in this world and the one above. From his birth in Hesiod in the eighth century BCE he has had a persistent presence: among classical fabulists and satirists, Renaissance humanists, Reformation heretics, seventeenth- and eighteenth-century literary critics, nineteenth-century Bohemians, twentieth-century existentialists, and contemporary Mardi Gras revelers. Focusing on his reincarnations in the early modern period in Italy, France, Spain, Germany, England, and Holland, this book examines how Momus became a medium for dangerous challenges to religious belief and a literary trope for challenges to literary and intellectual authority – and shows how at times these two roles intersected. The study argues that in this period Momus simultaneously signaled the emergence of the Agnostic in the theological realm while reifying the Critic in the literary realm. Understanding this dual role sheds new light on the hidden, or coded, history of unbelief, traces the connections between theological and literary doubt, and explains why such connections coalesced in an era of growing secularization.

In his many epiphanies in Western culture the protean Momus sometimes resembled the transgressive Prometheus, sometimes

vii

the rebellious Lucifer, sometimes the brazen Adversary in Job, sometimes the naughty Pasquino of the Renaissance pasquinade, and sometimes the insolent court jester. Although his skeptical stance and mordant tongue could target various authorities, it was his assault on his own tribe (the gods) that was the most controversial – whether it be explicitly the Greek pantheon of Olympian gods in the ancient period or implicitly the Judeo-Christian God in the early modern era. Momus's vocation of apostasy could have serious consequences for the writers he inspired: for Lucian, whose Momus may have clinched his reputation as an atheist, and for Giordano Bruno, whose use of him likely contributed to his execution for heresy in 1600. In other cases, Momus made his entrance more quietly, like Sandburg's fog, "on little cat feet." Rousting this stealthier Momus as he peeks around doors and from under beds offers new insight into the covert ways in which writers explored the possibility of unbelief.

Momus's birth was a rather unceremonial one announced by Hesiod in the *Theogony* 211, where he is named as one of the many children of Night, along with such entities as Doom, Fate, Death, and Distress. His persona, however, remained largely undefined until enlivened by Aesop, who ensured that "Blame" would be more than an abstraction and would persist as a personified god. He did so by assigning Momus his first controversial act: to judge a contest between Zeus, Poseidon, and Athena as to who could create the most beautiful thing. Momus, however, found fault with all three creations: Poseidon's bull, for not having horns beneath his eyes so that he could see to hit his target; Athena's house for mortals, for not being portable; Zeus's man, for not having a grill over his heart so that his true sentiments could be seen. This fable, the most cited of all of Aesop's Momus tales, established him as a saucy critic of the greater gods. Equally important, his insightful critique of ever-dissembling mortals indirectly reveals what would be Momus's own distinctive feature as one who does *not* conceal his heart, who speaks truth to power, and who is arguably the creator of *parrhesia* (frank speech).

Preface

Aesop's use of Momus as a divine critic – challenging, as Leslie Kurke argues, *mythos* with *logos* – was more fully realized centuries later by the second-century CE satirist Lucian, who included the god in nine of his dialogues. In two of these, Momus plays a major part and poses a radical challenge to the Greek pantheon, exposing the flawed justice of the gods, the ambiguous and incompetent oracles of Apollo, and the many "aliens" and unworthy demigods who have entered the pantheon. He assails Zeus's consorting with mortal women as starting a trend that produced such gods, and he extends his reproach to attack the array of Hellenistic, Egyptian, and mystery-religion gods, as well as the philosophical, conceptual gods such as Virtue, Destiny, and others. Momus's attack, though in the guise of protecting the reputation of the pantheon, satirically exposes it as questionable and mocks all belief with an assertion of religious relativism. Lucian's Momus dialogues display most dramatically the Greek tradition of *parrhesia*, a truth-telling that explains Aesop's vague allusion to Momus's departure from the Olympian court.

When Momus reappeared in the Italian Renaissance, Leon Battista Alberti honored him with his own epic, in which he extends Lucian's episodic portrait to a full biography. In the first Latin novel of the Renaissance, *Momus* (*c.* 1450), he explains exactly why Momus was kicked out of heaven, how he roiled both the divine and human worlds with his antics, and how he was victimized and largely ignored by Jupiter and other gods. Alberti's story simultaneously makes of Momus a hero (for his *parrhesia*) and an antihero (for cynically becoming a dissembler to match the norms of a decadent culture). Alberti frames his epic as a political allegory of the wayward prince or pope – and certainly that is one layer of its meaning. In fact, however, he may have had a more important target. He uses the persona of Momus (with whom he pairs another figure clearly intended as Alberti's alter ego) to pose doubts about the divine governance of the Christian world in the guise of a naughty god who does so in the safer setting of pagan theology. Hints of unbelief – influenced by the recent recovery of Hermetic and Lucretian texts in Italy – occur in all four books of *Momus*. As a proud and

x *Preface*

envious troublemaker – and yet heroically tragic figure chained to a rock as an explicit analogue to Prometheus – Momus is endowed by Alberti with both cosmic agency and tormented interiority that likely inspired a later, more famous divine rebel.

Because Alberti preceded the Reformation – and because he identified his work as an allegory concerning political rule rather than divine rule – his *Momus* did not immediately stir the attention of the censors. In the next century, however, Momus's persona became more suspect as a closet heretical or blasphemous voice. A Spanish translation of Alberti's epic in 1553 purged various passages and took pains to allegorize entire sections that could be read as heterodox or anti-religious. An angry Luther labeled the satirical Erasmus as a "true Momus, mocking all religion and Christ," even though Erasmus – probably with clear intention – did *not* include the Momus dialogues among his thirty-six translations of Lucian. Other satirists and writers both in Italy and France used the Momus model or Momus voice for challenging the divine. Most dramatically, Giordano Bruno's *Expulsion of the Triumphant Beast* (1584) deploys the god to blasphemously mock the Eucharist and the dual nature of Christ. Worse, his Momus depicts Neptune's son Orion as a Christ-like figure who can walk on water and perform miracles, and he recommends that he be sent to earth to convince mortals that white is black and Nature a "whorish prostitute." No wonder this treatise was explicitly cited as the work that confirmed Bruno as an atheist in the lead-up to his trial and execution.

In the seventeenth century, the Momus story interpenetrated with the Lucifer legend: Lucifer giving theological depth to Momus's expulsion from the heavens, and Momus offering secular plausibility to Lucifer's fall. These unacknowledged borrowings would culminate in *Paradise Lost*. While in Italy in 1638–39, Milton spent considerable time in Florence and Rome. Textual evidence suggests that he may have had occasion to read Alberti's *Momus*, whether in one of the two 1520 Latin editions or the 1568 Italian translation. Further, according to Milton's daughter via Voltaire, he saw a performance of Giovan Battista Andreini's *Adam*. This play itself revealed the influence of the Momus story in Andreini's *Dialogo fra Momo e la Verità* and inspired Milton's early conception of *Paradise Lost* in two skeletal dramas of the early 1640s entitled "Paradise Lost" and "Adam Unparadiz'd." Coincidentally (more likely, than causally), a few years after the initial version of *Paradise Lost* appeared, Baruch Spinoza also noted the similarities between Momus and Lucifer, as he argued that the Satan figure in the Book of Job was in fact Momus.

Gradually Momus's theological relevance began to wane, and his identity became more wedded to intellectual and literary criticism. Jonathan Swift, in particular, was emblematic of this shift, as Momus was a figure in the "Digression on Criticks" in his *Tale of a Tub* and the leader of the Moderns in his *Battel of the Books*. Some theological resonance of Momus the Agnostic remained, but the transition to Momus the Critic gained momentum. By the eighteenth century, he became increasingly a figure resembling an Epicurean bon vivant, buffoon, and court jester. Even here, however, he attached to the counter-cultural sentiments of Henri Murger's Bohemians, who, as immortalized by Puccini, made the Café Momus one of their chief gathering places. In the late nineteenth century he made his way to America in Mardi Gras celebrations, in which the Momus Krewe continues to this day to have a presence in parades. For all of this softening in the modern era, however, a residue of theological mystery may have remained in at least one case, as Kafka appears to have intended him as a perverse version of divine mediator in the Absurdist tale of *The Castle*. Perhaps the distance between Alberti and Kafka is not so great if Momus is understood as the coded message of unbelief in the early modern era. From Aesop onward Momus has signaled the revolt against authority – whether divine, literary, or even political. His starring moment in the early modern era when both the religious Agnostic and the literary Critic began to take shape – in the likes of Alberti, Anton Francesco Doni, Tomaso Garzoni, Bruno, Milton, Swift, and Spinoza – suggests that the god of criticism and "frank speech" played a significant role in heralding the modern world.

As a reception study, this book proceeds on two fronts simultaneously. On the one hand, it is a diachronic study that traces a trope from the classical world to the modern era. Here the goal is to examine how Momus authors spoke to one another across time, largely sustaining his generally arch attitude but transforming the targets of his bile and derision. On the other hand, the book aims to offer a synchronic analysis of the thought of various writers within the context of their particular time and body of work. In this sense, the question is why did these particular authors resurrect Momus, and how did they do so in the context of their other writings and intellectual influences?

Because the core of this book is about Momus's use as a vehicle for religious doubt, let me offer a few clarifications and caveats. First, by religious doubt, I mean two things: doubt about divine justice or governance; and, more radically, doubt about belief itself. Sometimes these two forms of skepticism overlap, sometimes not. In any case, I make no claims to pronounce with any certainty on any author's personal belief. I would not presume to do this in regard to my familiars, much less in figures from a different time and religious climate. I hope, however, that readers will keep two points in mind. The humorous depiction of religion does not necessarily signal unbelief. Conversely, expressions of orthodoxy do not necessarily certify belief – especially in the Renaissance and early modern era, when overt declarations of agnosticism or atheism were still quite dangerous. Such professions could lose one his position, if a cleric; or his life, if, like Bruno, he went a step too far. Momus's use as trope for religious satire may in fact inhabit the middle zone between these extremes, offering a writer a means to safely air, disguise, or exorcise religious doubt. Certainly, Aesop and especially Lucian offered a template for humorous challenges to religious authority that had an enduring appeal, even when the target shifted from pagan gods to the God of Alberti or Spinoza. My study attempts to show how Momus reveals the range of religious humor in the early modern period, when his invocation could signal a moderate questioning of divine justice or a radical, and necessarily coded, assault on Christianity or theism.

Preface xiii

Aside from being a reception study, this book is even more a work of intellectual history. In examining Momus as a metonym for religious uncertainty, it enters the sometimes contentious debate over the currency of unbelief prior to the Enlightenment. Lucien Febvre famously threw down the gauntlet for this historiographical contest in his 1942 *The Problem of Unbelief in the Sixteenth Century*, an overheated rejection of Abel Lefranc's characterization of Rabelais's "atheism" in the preface to his 1922 edition of *Pantagruel*. More recently, this debate has been reinvigorated with a series of studies regarding the reintroduction of Lucretius' *De rerum natura* in Italy in 1417, including most notably Stephen Greenblatt's 2011 *The Swerve*. My study engages this question by showing how the appearance of Momus in fifteenth-, sixteenth-, and seventeenth-century writers – sometimes in conjunction with a new reading of Lucretian materialism – adds further evidence for the view that unbelief may have been more common in the Renaissance than Febvre allowed. At the same time, the book examines how the challenge to divine authority intersected with the assault on literary authority, as some writers used Momus to defend or embody the critique of literary tradition. In this nexus Momus became something of an emblem for a modernism that bespoke both secularism in the face of the divine, and revolt in the face of literary and cultural convention.

I am grateful to the anonymous readers for Cambridge University Press for their thoughtful and helpful comments. I would also like to thank Beatrice Rehl of the Press for shepherding the book in its early stages and Eilidh Burrett and Mary Bongiovi for their help in later phases. I am especially grateful to Christopher Feeney for his most helpful and careful copy-editing of the manuscript. My greatest debt is to my wife Jennifer, who gave me sage advice on substantive issues throughout the project and applied her keen eye to stylistic matters in the writing phase. She has been a friendly Momus (or Moma) in all of my scholarly projects, a *dea ex machina* delivering needed criticism before the end of the play. To her I lovingly dedicate this book.

I

The Classical Tradition

You never know how your children will turn out. Such was the case of the birth and life of Night's child Momus ("Blame") in the ancient world. Hesiod rather unceremoniously recorded the birth in his *Theogony* 211–25, where Night (herself the product of primeval Chaos and Erebus) gave birth to a string of largely gloomy children: hateful Doom, black Fate, Death, Blame, Woe, Nemesis, Strife, and others. But we learn no more of Night's Momus in Hesiod's mythography. What exactly did he mean by Blame, whom he paired with "painful Woe"?[1] The course of Momus's career in the ancient world reveals that he (and he does appear as male) variously kept company with envy, irrepressible criticism, and heresy, and had some parallels with the heroic rebel Prometheus. Charting his path from Hesiod to Lucian tells us how and why the classical world "needed" such a god.

The gods of Hesiod represented the universe of conditions, perceptions, fears, and hopes that attended mortal life. These included a mix of the realms of natural forces (Ocean, Earth, Night, Day, Zeus's thunderbolt), the cultural (Muses), the theological (Fates), the moral (Deceit), the physical (Sleep, Eros), the social (Friendship, Strife, Murder, Quarrels), and the political (endless battles of Zeus, Cronus, Typhoeus). Homer and, later, the dramatists added more anthropomorphic delineation

---

[1] Hesiod, 1936, 95.

2 *Doubting the Divine in Early Modern Europe*

to the pantheon of the twelve Olympian gods, their demigod pretenders, and their intercourse (in all senses) with mortals. The Olympian gods, as patrons of various arts and natural forces – Apollo of poetry and the sun, for instance – simply elevated human endeavor or demystified natural occurrences. But what of a personified god of Blame? What does he explain or exorcise? Envy – and, if so, envy of what? Skepticism – and, if so, skepticism of what?

We can find some clues in the un-personified presence of "momus" in language itself. In his discussion of the poetry of praise and blame, Gregory Nagy charts some oppositional uses of *momos* and *aineo* (praise). As the germ of epideictic rhetoric, this binary would normally mean praise of the worthy, and blame of the unworthy: in effect, literature's template for prescriptive morality. Yet "blame" can also be applied to the worthy, and this is where Momus starts to come to life. Pindar, in his *Olympian Ode* 6:74–75 in honor of Hagesias of Syracuse's victory in the mule chariot race, writes that *momos* (reproach) may issue from the envy (*phthonos*) regarding the winners of the contest. Bacchylides' *Ode* 13, celebrating victory in the Pancratium (Greek version of ultimate fighting), similarly urges that the "grip of envy" should be cast aside and recognizes that "mincing blame / dogs every work."[2] When personified, Momus will assume both roles: at times a reasonable, skeptical challenge to the unworthy; at other times an unreasonable, resentful assault of the worthy. The latter perhaps will take precedence as Momus often seems to embody the upstart who challenges higher authorities. And when he does this with a kernel of truth he broaches the satirical *lèse-majesté* of the court jester or renegade courtier.

Momus's first substantive appearance as a personality came in Aesop's fables, the provenance of which is murky. A freed Thracian slave of the sixth century BCE, Aesop has a dim and somewhat legendary biography. He apparently did not write his prose tales; only later in the fourth century BCE did a figure,

[2] Nagy, 1979, 222–24; Pindar, 1937, 63; Bacchylides, 1998, 41.

The Classical Tradition

Demetrius of Phaleron, compile them in a rhetorical handbook that is no longer extant. This compilation was, however, available to the later poets Phaedrus, who identified himself as the "Freedman of Augustus," and Babrius, from the late first or second century CE. These writers versified the tales into Latin and Greek respectively to elevate the "lowly" prose into a "higher" literary form.[3] The single-most influential Momus story among the ancients is found in Babrius 59. Although the gods in question sometimes vary in its iteration, this is certainly the Ur-Momus tale in subsequent literature:

Zeus and Poseidon, so they say, together with Athena, strove to see which one among them might create a thing of beauty. Zeus made man, pre-eminent of living creatures, Pallas a house for men, and Poseidon a bull. To judge these things Momus was chosen, for he was still living with the gods. Since it was his nature to hate them all, he proceeded accordingly. The first fault he found, right away, was with the bull, because his horns had not been placed beneath his eyes, that he might see where he struck. As for man, the trouble was, he had no windows in his breast, nor could it be opened up, so that what he plotted would be visible to his neighbor. The house, too, was a failure, so he judged, because it did not have iron wheels on its foundations, and could not go from place to place with its owners when they went away from town.

[What does this story tell us? Strive to create something, and let not Envy be the judge. Nothing whatever is entirely pleasing to the fault-finder.][4]

This fable lays out several legacies of the Momus meme. First, his primary target is aesthetic: namely, the creation of beauty. In this case, the gods attempt to create something beautiful in all the realms of the animal, human, and built world. Like Paris, in another famous beauty contest, Momus was deputed to judge. His status is vaguely defined: he is at the time "still living with the gods," implying his subsequent exile and his likely subaltern status. Certainly, he was not one of the big twelve Olympians – a slight that may partly explain why "it was his nature to hate (*echthrainon*) them." Momus was appointed to say which

---

[3] Ben Edwin Perry's Introduction in Babrius and Phaedrus, 1975, xi–cii; Kurke, 2011, 43–44.
[4] Babrius and Phaedrus, 1975, 75–77.

creation was most beautiful and yet subverted divine intention by ruling that none was truly beautiful. The epimythium, or moral, which was probably added later, suggests that Envy (*phthonon*) is the inevitable nemesis of all who try to create. And yet Momus's criticisms are all legitimate or at least plausible: the bull's horns are a bit inconveniently situated; man's true intentions should be more transparent; in fact, mobile homes and RVs (sadly) were eventually invented. So maybe this fable is not just about unwarranted Envy. Maybe it is about unvarnished Truth.[5] The criticism of humans in this regard is doubly meaningful. Not only does it speak to the universal propensity to dissimulation and artifice. It also implicitly announces Momus's own role in the world as one who does *not* conceal his heart or mince his words. He will be the bane of both gods, who presume to craft the perfect creation, and humans, who hide their true beliefs and intentions. Hovering between the divine and human worlds, Momus will be a subversive force in both, and Fable 59 will endure as the classic Momus *locus*.

We can never know for certain which of Babrius' fables were original to Aesop and which were interpolations of Demetrius of Phaleron or of Babrius himself. The affront to the gods, however, seems to befit the character of Aesop. In her remarkable *Aesopic Conversations*, Leslie Kurke views the Aesopic tradition in the context of the "little tradition" (popular culture) of the Greek world, "mediating" and sometimes challenging elite culture.[6] Thus, even the *Life of Aesop* had no clear, stable text or author, although various accounts of his life current by the mid fifth century BCE share many details. He was a slave bought by the philosopher Xanthus of Samos, and was freed and

---

[5] As for divine design flaws in the creation of humans, cf. Babrius 66, which disparages Prometheus for hanging on man two wallets: in the front, one containing the faults of other mortals; in the back, a bigger one containing one's own faults: obviously, a recipe for humans' lack of self-knowledge (Babrius and Phaedrus, 1975, 83).

[6] She cites Peter Burke's application of Robert Redfield's distinction between "little" and "great" traditions to early modern culture – including his revision of Redfield that elites could also participate in popular culture, but not vice versa (Kurke, 2011, 7–8; Burke, 1978, 23–29; Redfield, 1956, 69–72).

eventually ended up in Delphi. There he insulted the Delphians for their slavish worship of Apollo, for which he was framed for theft and forced to leap to his death.[7] He was, in short, a low-born contrarian who challenged the most cherished feature of Greek religion: Apollo and his oracle. His fables, furthermore, represent another assault on tradition. As Kurke argues, they represent part of the movement from poetry to prose, which might parallel the transition from *mythos* to *logos* in Greek culture.[8]

Indeed, aside from Babrius 59 several other fables ridicule or debunk the gods. Babrius 68 brings Apollo up short. When he boasts that no one, not even Zeus, can shoot an arrow farther than he, Zeus bounds in one leap to the destination of Apollo's arrow that reached the westward garden of the Hesperides at the end of the world; declaring that Apollo has nowhere left to shoot, Zeus declares victory.[9] Aside from this unflattering tale about Apollo, Aesop elsewhere accused the Delphians of being parasitically dependent upon the sacrifices pilgrims make to Apollo's oracle. Such transgressions, along with his preference of the Muses to Apollo as the true patrons of literature, cast him as a somewhat heretical figure, leading to the Delphians' persecution of him.[10] But Apollo is not the only target of the fables. Babrius 3 has Hermes complaining to a sculptor, who has fashioned his image for sale as a gravestone or an idol: "So then, my fate is being weighed in your balances: it remains to be seen whether you will make me a corpse or a god."[11] Clearly, the fable inverts the hierarchy of the god and his sculptor. Tales of Zeus are likewise cynical. In Babrius 142, when oak trees complain that they live only to be cut down, Zeus callously remarks that they themselves provide the wood for the axes that destroy them. Even worse is Babrius 127, in which Zeus tells Hermes to write down all the misdeeds of men, so he can punish them, but

[7] Kurke, 2011, 4–5, 16–22.
[8] Kurke, 2011, 15.
[9] Babrius and Phaedrus, 1975, 84–85.
[10] Kurke, 2011, 59–74, esp. 62–64, 66, and 72.
[11] Babrius and Phaedrus, 1975, 43.

6 *Doubting the Divine in Early Modern Europe*

then fails in his duty: "since the shards lie heaped up one upon another awaiting the time when he can examine them, some are late to fall into the hands of Zeus, others more prompt. We must not, therefore, be surprised if some evil doers who are quick to commit crimes are late to suffer for them."[12] Such a fable ventures beyond the realm of idle insult of the Olympians into the more serious territory of theodicy.

Whether Hermes' herm, Apollo's embarrassment, Zeus's negligence in administering justice, or Momus's criticisms in Babrius 59, these fables reveal an Aesop who shows little respect for divine culture. Possibly, he even held the beastly realm in higher regard. Certainly, the predominance of animals over gods in the collection is another measure of privileging "low" wisdom over "high." One index of the collected *Aesopica* contains fifty-five tales involving wolves and thirty-four on asses or donkeys, as compared to three on Apollo.[13] More to the point, one of Aesop's gods, the subaltern Momus, challenges the creations of his betters in critiques that are playful but also, in the case of mankind's deceits, true. Aesop's Momus thus fits into a larger scheme of opposing low truth to high, prose to poetry, animals to gods, and *logos* to *mythos*. Aesop brought Hesiod's vague Momus to life as the critic of gods' creations and man's faults.

Momus's status as unrivaled Critic was assured by the fourth century BCE, when Plato attests to his authority. In the *Republic* 6:487, he both affirms Momus's role as a critic and ties his judgment to the highest standards of Socratic *logos*. Having parsed the difference between opinion and knowledge, as represented by non-philosophers and philosophers, Socrates defines the qualities of such a philosopher who must then assume the reins of state. He asks Glaucon: "Is there any fault, then, that you can find with a pursuit [philosophy] which a man could not properly practice unless he were by nature of good memory, quick apprehension, magnificent, gracious, friendly, and akin to truth, justice, bravery, and sobriety?" Glaucon

---

[12] Babrius and Phaedrus, 1975, 165.
[13] Babrius and Phaedrus, 1975, 613–30.

The Classical Tradition

answers: "Momus himself could not find fault with such a combination."[14] The judgment of Momus is thus equated with the wisdom of Socrates. Momus in this instance is not a vindictive, unreasonable critic, but rather the gold standard of logic.

Consider the fate of Socrates, which was akin to that of Aesop: death for his heretical stance toward the traditional worship of the gods. We might ponder whether Socrates himself, as a tireless and annoying critic of his fellow Athenians, was a type of Momus figure. Even in his professed devotion to Apollo in the *Apology*, he displays a rational doubt of the truth of the Delphic oracle that proclaimed that no one was wiser than he. He explains his whole life of questioning the politicians, poets, and craftsmen of Athens as a testing of the truth – or true meaning – of the oracle. And although he eventually proved the oracle to be ironically true – he was wiser than all these others for recognizing his own ignorance – this testing of the oracle did constitute a potential challenge of *logos* to the *mythos* of oracular prophecy.[15]

If Plato elevated Momus to the station of philosophical arbiter, most other classical references characterized him as uber-critic in more purely aesthetic realms, which resonates with his critique of the gods' beautiful creations in Babrius 59. The creative efforts of the gods, however, were readily transferred to the efforts of mortals, where Momus could be invoked as the canon

---

[14] Plato, 1961, 723.

[15] Kurke, 2011, 308, compares Socrates' self-description as a vexing "gadfly" (to the Athenians) to Aesop's "stance as challenger, debunker, and parodist of traditional wisdom." More generally, on Plato's ties to Aesop in regard to the development of mimetic prose (in contrast to high poetry) and low, plain speech (in contrast to the stylized speech of the Sophists), see Kurke, 2011, 241–64, and 325–60, esp. at 330. As Kurke suggests (2011, 251–55), Socrates' link to Aesop appears in the beginning of the *Phaedo*, when he is seen translating Aesop's fables into verse. Informed by a dream that he is to practice the "arts" – and wondering if philosophy indeed counted as one – he piously seeks on his deathbed to fulfill the will of the gods by composing hymns to Apollo and versifying Aesop (*Phaedo* 60d–61b). In both cases, philosophy and prose are opposed to theology and verse. While ostensibly a pious act, this deathbed gesture reinforces the possibility that Socrates' mission of philosophical *logos* and doubt may have been at odds with the traditional truths and literary medium of the divine.

8   *Doubting the Divine in Early Modern Europe*

of perfection in the realm of art or literature. An anonymous poem in the *Greek Anthology*, a compilation of classical and Byzantine poetry, praises the sculpture of Praxiteles as meeting the standards of Momus. Likewise, in the fourth century CE, the Greek writer Libanius claims that Julian (the Apostate) had a degree of virtue unassailable even by Momus.[16] More often, however, the appearances of the god are rather grudging or outright nasty. In the *Greek Anthology* two anonymous poems are devoted to him: one depicting him as quarrelsome and an envious foe of all that is good; another castigating his "poisonous jaws" as he bites into his targets.[17] Yet a third in that collection by Philippus of Thessalonica characterizes pedantic grammarians as the companions of Momus.[18] It is in this literary realm that he had a particularly prominent presence.

Momus's role in the ancient literary world is best illustrated by the fourth-century BCE Alexandrian poet Callimachus. In his *Hymn to Apollo*, he reveals the links between poetry and piety, and between envy and criticism, that foreshadow the complicated ties between literary criticism and heresy that will accompany Momus in various incarnations in Western culture. As god of prophecy and poetry (among other pursuits) and as deity of classical Greece's most important cult center, Apollo is an emblem of the divine status of poetry. Beginning with Hesiod's *Theogony*, poetry had served as the medium for theology, but it was the figure of Apollo who expressly joined the labor of the poet to a religious act. Those poets inspired by Apollo are his theologians and priests. In his *Hymn to Apollo* Callimachus exults that "Apollo will honor / my chorus: it sings to his liking."[19] But this gift is a product of divine election: "Not on everyone, but only on the noble / shines Apollo's light. He who has seen the god / is great, he who hasn't is of no account."[20] His hymn praises Apollo's other roles as patron of prophecy,

---

[16] *Greek Anthology V*, 315; Libanius, 1969, 93–95.
[17] *Greek Anthology V*, 317–19.
[18] *Greek Anthology IV*, 219.
[19] Callimachus, 2001, 24.
[20] Callimachus, 2001, 24.

The Classical Tradition

archery, medicine, pastures, and then ends on a defiant note. Those who would diminish such lyric poetry as inferior to the grander epic genre, take heed. Apollo will put you in your place: Envy (*Phthonos*) whispered into Apollo's ear:

> "I don't like a poet who doesn't sing
> Like the sea." Apollo kicked
> Envy aside and said: "The Assyrian river
> Rolls a massive stream, but it's mainly
> Silt and garbage that it sweeps along. The bees
> Bring water to Deo not from every source
> But where it bubbles up pure and undefiled
> From a holy spring, its very essence."
> Farewell, Lord! Let Criticism (*Momos*)
> go where Envy's gone![21]

Callimachus defends the special "nectar" of his poetry against the indiscriminate flood of literature (the Assyrian River) which carries everything in its current. In his *Aitia* 1, he similarly promotes his more original, minor-scale poetry over a "monotonous / uninterrupted poem featuring kings / and heroes in thousands of verses," although there it is he as a poet, not Apollo, who chides his critics, saying "To hell with you, then, / spiteful brood of Jealousy: from now on / we'll judge poetry by the art, / not by the mile."[22] Callimachus' *Hymn to Apollo* is simultaneously an act of homage to the god of poetry (a religious act) and a defense of his own poetic style (an aesthetic claim). In terms of the latter, the nemesis is Envy, who is given equal stature with Momus – both assailed as unworthy foes rejected by Apollo. Certainly, this equation of Envy and Momus recalls the moral attached to Babrius 59: "Strive to create something, and let not Envy be the judge. Nothing whatever is entirely pleasing to the fault-finder." In fact, however, in Aesop's fable, the criticism of

---

[21] Callimachus, 2001, 27.

[22] Callimachus, 2001, 62–63. The religious dimension (proper worship) and the aesthetic one (originality) are also revealed: "my own / Lykian Apollo said to me: / 'Make your sacrifice / as fat as you can, poet, but keep / your Muse on slender rations. And see that you go / where no hackneys plod: avoid the ruts / carved in the boulevard, even if it means / driving along a narrower path'" (63).

the gods' creations had some satirical truth. The libelous tagline of Envy was presumably added later, but it clearly stuck. For Callimachus, Momus's complaints are purely the result of Envy and are deemed unworthy by Apollo himself. Momus's linkage to envy will be a steady one in his many invocations, especially as the literary function increasingly overtakes his theological symbolism in the early modern period.

And yet the theological dimension is inseparable from the literary one in Callimachus. Poetry of and to Apollo is a religious gesture, a somewhat priestly act. This nexus will inform the connection between heresy and criticism: challenging the poet (as priest) can constitute a challenge to the gods. This heretical dimension is emphasized by the fact that Momus and Envy are both excluded from the divine pantheon.[23] They themselves, as subaltern deities, are forever keen to confront their betters. And this moves the context of envy from the mortal sphere of poets to the divine sphere of the gods. This challenge will be the particular province of Lucian's use of Momus.

Lucian of Samosata (born *c.* 125 CE) makes use of Momus more than any other ancient writer. There is good reason for this, as Lucian's works represent a synthesis and culmination of several classical streams in which Momus could wade: satire, Cynicism, Epicureanism, frank speech (*parrhesia*), doubt (*apistia*), and religious unbelief. As for the last, Lucian was rather catholic in his attacks on religion, which embraced not only the traditional pantheon of Greek gods, but also the more recent Eastern deities, abstract deities (of which Momus as "Blame" was obviously one), and even Christianity. Such a wide range of targets could win him friends and foes, depending on whose ox was being gored. Certainly, some Christians would be able to find common cause with his ridicule of the Olympian gods and all the attendant practices of their worship.[24] Yet, others,

[23] Giangrande, 1992, 62, who confirms that the last line of the *Hymn to Apollo* indeed should read "*Phthonos*" (envy) rather than "*Phthoros*" (decay).

[24] Weinbrot, 2005, 63. Caster, 1937, 188–90, systematically compares the attacks on the myths of the Greek gods in the second-century CE *Apology* of Aristides of Athens to those found in Lucian's works.

The Classical Tradition

who focused on his occasional depiction of the Christians, saw him as a dangerous enemy. A comment in Lactantius' *Divine Institutes* 1.9.8, which despite its dubious status as a possible interpolation would be quite influential, alluded to Lucian as one "who spared neither gods nor men."[25] But the most destructive appraisals of his reputation emerged later in the Byzantine East, beginning in the tenth century with Greek theologians such as Arethas of Caesarea.[26] Its culmination came in a scathing biography in the *Suda* λ 683, where Lucian is identified as being

nicknamed blasphemer or slanderer, or better to say godless (*atheos*), because in his dialogues he ridiculed the things said about the divine. He lived in the time of the Emperor Trajan and later. Early in his career this man was a lawyer in Syrian Antioch, but, after proving unsuccessful at this, he turned to writing and wrote endlessly. The story goes that he was killed by dogs, because he turned his savagery against truth; for in his *Life of Peregrinus* he attacked Christianity and – the scoundrel – slandered Christ himself. Wherefore he paid sufficiently for his rage in this life, but in the life to come he will inherit with Satan a share of the eternal fire.[27]

Although the comments about Christians in the *Passing of Peregrinus* would be particularly offensive to Christian readers, Arethas of Caesarea and other Byzantine clerics also reviled Lucian's lampoon of the Olympians in works such as *Zeus Rants*, in which Momus plays the starring role.[28]

---

[25] Lactantius, 2003, 77; on the passage's questioned authenticity see ibid., note 58 and Jones, 1986, 22n88.

[26] Baldwin, 1913, 7–8, 100–2.

[27] "Lucian." *Suda* Online. Trans. Akihiko Watanabe. May 5, 1999. www.stoa. org/sol-entries/lambda/683. On the intellectual context of this abusive entry and on the sketchy details of Lucian's itinerant career as a sophist (which may have included legal oratory) and administrative official in Egypt, see Baldwin, 1913, 7–20, 97–102. On Lucian's career, also see Jones, 1986, 6–23; Bowersock, 1969, 114–16. On the impact of the *Suda* on Lucian's reputation, also see Lauvergnat-Gagnière, 1988, 12–14.

[28] Baldwin, 1913, 100–2. Opinions differ on the best translation for *Zeus tragoedus*, most scholars defaulting to this untranslated designation, some preferring *Zeus the Tragic Actor*, and some following A. M. Harmon's *Zeus Rants* in the 1915 Loeb edition (which I will use, as I think that it best captures the spirit of the dialogue).

12 Doubting the Divine in Early Modern Europe

Momus appears in nine of Lucian's dialogues: substantially in two, in which he appears as an interlocutor; and seven others, in which he is variously invoked as the archetype of the critic, especially in regard to the famous Aesop story of Babrius 59.[29] In these minor appearances Momus represents the voice of criticism in several arenas: philosophical, historical, literary, and theological. This range speaks to his expansive role as a skeptic and cynic in regard to all conventional wisdom and traditional culture. A devotee of Menippus, who appears as a character in several of his dialogues, Lucian is closely aligned with the Cynics – and yet he even assails the Cynics in several of his dialogues.[30] In short, no target is off-limits. He assails the philosophers in several dialogues: in serial fashion in *Philosophers for Sale*, in which the gods parade philosophers of the various schools (Pythagorean, Cynic, Stoic, Peripatetic, etc.) before buyers who literally purchase their worthless wares. The aggrieved schools fight back in a subsequent dialogue, *The Dead Come to Life, or The Fisherman*: here Lucian assumes the persona of Parrhesiades (Frankness) when the philosophers put him on trial for his assaults. Ironically, Diogenes the Cynic is appointed prosecutor of this most cynical of Menippean critics (though, tellingly, Menippus is absent from the trial).[31] Diogenes, especially insulted for having been sold for a lowly two obols, charges that Lucian has used the philosophers' "Dialogue, our serving man" against them.[32] And so it was: the Cynic Lucian attacked even the Cynic founder with *parrhesia*, thus turning the (dia)-*logos* of reason back onto itself – just as Aesop had

---

[29] Caster, 1937, 208n41.

[30] In the *Icaromenippus*, Menippus journeys to the heavens, and in the *Menippus* he reports on his visit to the underworld; he is also in several of the *Dialogues of the Dead* (Lucian, 1913–67, 7:9–53). For his attacks on Cynics (or Cynic posers), see the *Passing of Peregrinus*, the *Runaways*, and *Philosophers for Sale* 7–11). On the paradox of Lucian's maligning the Cynics with whom he is aligned, see Branham, 2010, 247. On Menippean influence and Lucian's use of Menippus as a character, see Branham, 2010, 14–28.

[31] *Dead Come to Life, or The Fisherman* 23, 26.

[32] *Dead Come to Life, or The Fisherman* 26; Lucian, 1913–67, 3:43.

The Classical Tradition

done in regard to the *mythos* of the gods. In a sense, Lucian was truly loyal to the iconoclasm that characterized the Cynic (and skeptical Academic) schools, but in combating the Cynics themselves, he staked his claim to refusing all systematic schools of thought – or exposing all to the harsh truth of frank criticism and ridicule. Here the motive could simply have been the triumph of satire and comic dialogue, which is how some scholars read (and, I think, minimize) Lucian. Or it could also signal something more. Whether here as a persona – or more commonly as a rhetorical stance or descriptor – "*parrhesia*" appears often in Lucian's works. In both dialogues in which Momus appears as an interlocutor, he explicitly declares his desire to dare address his fellow gods with *parrhesia* (at *Zeus Rants* 19 and *Parliament of the Gods* 2).[33] What was Lucian's Momus signaling by this intention?

In his insightful lectures recorded in *Fearless Speech*, Foucault noted that *parrhesia* could be defined fundamentally in opposition to rhetoric: as frank, undisguised speech shorn of all dissimulation. For him a key ingredient of frank speech was speaking truth to power, although he shows that it could also indicate the prerogatives of free speech in a democratic state such as Athens. He traces the origins of the term to Euripides, in whose works the word appears in both contexts.[34] As the world of the independent polis eventually yielded to that of Hellenistic monarchies, Foucault argues, the political context of *parrhesia* shifted to that of ruler–subject (or monarch–courtier), which activated that feature of frank speech that demonstrated the courage and danger of speaking truth to power.[35] In general, this

---

[33] Lucian also devotes a treatise to another "frank-speaker," Demonax, who "commit[ted] himself unreservedly to liberty and free speech [*parrhesia*]," and because he refused to offer sacrifices to Athena or to be initiated in the Eleusinian mysteries was indicted for heresy in the manner of Socrates (though he escaped punishment). Lucian, 1913–67, 1:144–45, 148–51.

[34] For instance, in *Ion*, in which Ion seeks the rights of *parrhesia* in Athens and his mother Creusa upbraids Apollo for his rape of her; in the *Phoenician Women*, in which Polyneices bewails his loss of *parrhesia* as an exile; in the *Electra*, in which Electra speaks freely in accusing Clytemnestra of the wrongfulness of her murder of Agamemnon (Foucault, 2001, 27–74).

[35] Foucault, 2001, 22–23.

14 *Doubting the Divine in Early Modern Europe*

facet of *parrhesia* relies on the inequality of the principals in literary depictions – whether subjects to their rulers or, in Lucian's case, subaltern gods to the Olympian Twelve. Oddly, Foucault leaves Lucian out of the discussion, except to cite him as critical of Cynics in certain works and as employing as a character Parrhesiades in *The Dead Come to Life, or The Fisherman*.[36] Nor does he ever cite the Momus trope, even though this figure – especially as incarnated by Lucian – embodies the more daring face of *parrhesia* in the ancient tradition.[37]

Momus's most dramatic appearance in Lucian comes in *Zeus Rants*, a dialogue in which Zeus frets that mortals do not believe in the gods.[38] Zeus has overheard an unfinished debate between two mortals – the Stoic Timocles and the Epicurean Damis – and worries that the latter, a full-throated "god-hater" (*theos echthre*) and "god-fighter" (*theomache*), is getting the better of the argument.[39] He has Hermes assemble the gods to decide how to proceed in order to ensure that the pious Timocles will eventually prevail when the debate continues. When Hermes calls for the gods to offer up advice, no one comes forward – except Momus, who scorns the others' silence and asks that he may be permitted to speak frankly (*meta parrhesias*).[40] Zeus, allowing that such frankness will be for their collective good, sanctions Momus's most vocal debut in Western culture.

Momus warns that his comments will come "straight from the heart,"[41] a promise made all the more relevant by Lucian's citing elsewhere (in *Hermotimus* 20) Aesop's story of Momus's criticism

---

[36] Foucault, 2001, 11, 116–17.

[37] For other scholars, who see Lucian's role as a purveyor of Cynic *parrhesia*, see Bosman, 2012; Branham, 1989, at 29, 32–34, 59.

[38] For treatments of Lucian's use of Momus in *Zeus Rants* and *Parliament of the Gods*, see Caster, 1937, 208–11, 340–45, who rightly characterizes Momus as "un dieu qui ne croit pas aux dieux" (209); Jones, 1986, 33–45; Branham, 1989, 163–77.

[39] For these epithets of the Epicurean Damis, see *Zeus Rants* 43, 45.

[40] *Zeus Rants* 19. Lucian depicts Momus's self-perception as a courageous figure by having him cite a line from the *Iliad* 7.99, where Menelaus berates the Greek warriors for their fear in facing Hector. Momus thus becomes Achilles.

[41] *Zeus Rants* 19; Lucian, 1913–67, 2:119.

The Classical Tradition

that mortals were made without grills over their chests to reveal their true sentiments. Momus's own heartfelt feelings are a *tour de force* of "tough love" for his fellow gods. He assails the essential features of traditional belief, starting with a flawed theodicy:

I quite expected that we should wind up in this helpless plight and that we should have a crop of sophists like this [the Epicurean Damis], who get from ourselves the justification for their temerity; and I vow by Themis that it is not right to be angry either at Epicurus or at his associates and successors in doctrine if they have formed such an idea [Damis' atheism] of us. Why, what could one expect them to think when they see such confusion in life, and see that the good men among them are neglected and waste away in poverty and illness and bondage while scoundrelly, pestilential fellows are highly honored and have enormous wealth and lord it over their betters, and that temple-robbers are not punished but escape, while men who are guiltless of all wrong-doing sometimes die by the cross or the scourge?[42]

He then mocks the ambiguity of oracles, citing, for one, the famous story of the deceptive prophecy Croesus received from the oracles at Delphi and Amphiaraus that his crossing the river Halys would succeed in destroying a great empire – his own, it turned out, not the Persians' (Herodotus 1.52–53). Next, he cites the poets' tales of the gods' many dalliances, misadventures, and spats: all tales of worldly vicissitude that clearly belie the gods' claims to heavenly contentment and invulnerability. Is it any wonder, he asks, that mortals put little stock in our status and our providence?[43]

Then in a withering bit of irony about the very composition of the divine pantheon, Momus asks the gods to feel free to consider these matters truthfully since there are no humans present to hear – except for the half-mortal newcomers among their numbers: Heracles, Dionysus, Ganymede, and Asclepius! This issue of the proper boundaries of the pantheon – in regard to

---

[42] *Zeus Rants* 19; Lucian, 1913–67, 2:119–20. Cf. Cicero's *De natura deorum*, where the critique of Stoic Providence comes not from the Epicurean speaker but the Academic skeptic, Gaius Cotta (probably Cicero's voice), at *De natura deorum* 3.32–39.

[43] *Zeus Rants* 19–20.

16   *Doubting the Divine in Early Modern Europe*

demigods, abstract gods, and foreign gods – would be the subject of another Momus dialogue. But for now, Momus returns to the problem of the divine disregard for justice – that would let marauders lay waste and allow monsters free rein – to argue that mortals have no reason to think otherwise than the godless Epicurean Damis does:

> If you would have me speak the truth, we sit here considering just one question, whether anybody is slaying victims and burning incense at our altars; everything else drifts with the current, swept aimlessly along. Therefore we are getting and shall continue to get no more than we deserve when men gradually begin to crane their necks upward and find out that it does no good to sacrifice to us and hold processions. Then in a little while you shall see the Epicuruses and Metrodoruses [Epicurus' chief disciple] and Damises laughing at us, and our pleaders overpowered and silenced by them. So it is for the rest of you to check and remedy all this, you who carried it so far. To me, being only Momus, it does not make much difference if I am to be unhonored, for even in bygone days I was not one of those in honor, while you are still fortunate and enjoy your sacrifices.[44]

Momus thus proclaims his status as a subaltern god, an outsider, who perhaps for that reason is well situated (and well motivated) to tell the Olympians about their failed governance, false prophecies, embarrassing behavior, dubious membership, and sad reliance on sacrifices from mortals. Lucian has promoted Momus from the episodic critic of Aesop's fables to the spokesman for unbelief.

Poor hapless Zeus, now regretting that he granted Momus the license of *parrhesiasmenos*, proclaims Momus's speech so much nonsense, dismisses him as one who is always "harsh and fault-finding," and calls for others to advise.[45] When Poseidon recommends a quick thunderbolt to take Damis out of the picture, Zeus protests that that would be a cheap victory – even, indeed if he has that power vis-à-vis Fate (this is the subject of another dialogue, *Zeus Refuted*). When Apollo ventures to speak, Momus gamely baits him into making a prophecy as to

---

[44] *Zeus Rants* 22; Lucian, 1913–67, 2:123.
[45] *Zeus Rants* 19, 23; Lucian, 1913–67, 2:118, 125.

The Classical Tradition

who will win the debate between Timocles and Damis. Apollo complies with an absurdly vague *verse* prophecy, which Momus greets with laughter. When Zeus asks what the oracle means, Momus says that it is very clear: namely, that Apollo is an impostor (*gohes*) and all who believe in him are fools.[46] This encounter enacts Momus's earlier criticism that Apollo's oracles are worthless. In fact, it goes further to indict the god as an impostor in the same language Lucian uses to expose a charlatan in his lengthy *Alexander the False Prophet*.[47] Like Aesop, then, Momus (as Lucian) was no respecter of Greece's holiest fount of oracular truth. And like Aesop, Lucian challenges the poetic tradition of divine truth with prose criticism. In fact, Lucian derisively opens the dialogue with Hermes, Aphrodite, and Zeus speaking in verse, and elsewhere has the gods aspiring to make proclamations in pompous, vague verse (Hermes at *Zeus Rants* 6 and *Hermagoras* at 33) as if their *divinity* is affirmed by their *poetry*. Or, conversely, as if their status as impostors is exposed by their verse. While these bits could reinforce the view that Lucian is primarily a parodist toying with earlier literary *forms* (here of heroic verse) rather than a satirist critiquing substantive *beliefs*,[48] it is equally possible that the two interpretations could coexist. Lucian's efforts as a satirist should not be underplayed, especially if part of his strategy was to overtly oppose the *logos* of prose to the *mythos* of Homeric poetry.

When Hermes enters to report that Damis and Timocles are squaring off again, the gods listen in to find Damis routing his opponent. He even uses the same argument Momus had delivered earlier regarding the deceptive oracle given Croesus about his planned invasion of the Persian Empire.[49] Damis the Epicurean is thus fully the mortal counterpart to Momus, the

---

[46] *Zeus Rants* 31.

[47] In *Alexander the False Prophet* 1, Lucian identifies Alexander as a "*gohes*" (Lucian, 1913–67, 4:174).

[48] On the distinction and overlap between parody and satire, and Lucian's falling more in the category of the former, see Branham, 1989, 127–35, 167–77.

[49] *Zeus Rants* 43.

18   *Doubting the Divine in Early Modern Europe*

frank-speaking god. The Epicurean–Stoic debate recalls features of that between an Epicurean, Stoic, and Academic in Cicero's *De natura deorum*. When Timocles asserts that the orderly motions of the sun and moon and the structure of nature necessarily evince a divine providence, Damis counters with an Epicurean assertion of randomness.[50] Damis also disputes the existence of a judicious providential ruler by detailing the disparities between mortals' qualities and their deserts, the unworthy triumphing and the worthy languishing.[51] As for the behavior of the gods, Damis draws many stories from the *Iliad* regarding their atrocious conduct.[52] And when Timocles suggests that Euripides depicts the gods punishing evildoers and the impious, Damis makes a telling observation about the difference between fettered and unfettered opinion:

I assure you when Euripides, following his own devices, says what he thinks without being under any constraint imposed by the requirements of his plays, you will hear him speaking frankly (*parrhesiasdomenou*) then:

> Dost see on high this boundless sweep of air
> That lappeth earth about in yielding arms?
> Hold this to be Zeus, and believe it God.[53]

And Lucian follows this Euripidean fragment with another line (from another lost Euripides play) that similarly professed unbelief:

---

[50] *Zeus Rants* 36–38; Lucian, 1913–67, 2:149n1; cf. *De natura deorum* 2.19ff.; 1.15.51–55; 1.23.65ff.; Lucretius, *De rerum natura* 1.1021–51; 2.216–93, 1090–174.

[51] *Zeus Rants* 47–49; on this refutation of Stoic theodicy, cf. the Stoic argument and Academic refutation in *De natura deorum* 2.65.164–2.66–167; 3.32–39.

[52] *Zeus Rants* 39–40.

[53] Lucian, 1913–67, 2:153. This fragment 386 is from a lost play and cited by Cicero in *De natura deorum* 2.25.65, where the Stoic Balbus quotes it as an example of the popular derivation of the gods from natural forces. For Lucian, however, it is clearly meant as an example of Euripides' frank belief in nature rather than the traditional gods, much as Aristophanes' Socrates "heretically" affirms in the *Clouds* 246–426 (Aristophanes, 1924, 1:284–307).

> 'Twas Zeus, whoever Zeus is, for I know
> Him not, except by hearsay.[54]

According to Plutarch, this line from the lost *Melanippe the Wise* caused such a stir that Euripides felt compelled to change it in another iteration of the play to read:

> Zeus, as the voice of truth declares.[55]

Lucian, like Plutarch, thus recognized Euripides as one writer who felt somewhat constrained in expressing his heterodox views. Damis' invocation of Euripides is congruent with his identification with Momus. Damis, Momus, and Euripides (on whom, more later) form a triad of unbelief and *parrhesia* in Lucian's works.

Finally, the Stoic Timocles appeals to positivist, universalist arguments in his brief for theism. Most nonsensically he argues: "If there are altars, there are also gods; but there are altars, *ergo* there are also gods."[56] As absurd as it is, this syllogism does suggest a truth about the power of ritual and custom. So also does Timocles' similar argument that the universality of belief and religious ritual among all peoples proves the existence of the gods. Lucian uses this last point to set up Damis' assertion that the very plurality of gods and forms of worship simply points up the tenuous nature of religious truth:

Thank you kindly, Timocles, for reminding me what the nations believe. From that you can discern particularly well that there is nothing in the theory of the gods, for the confusion is great, and some believe one thing, some another. The Scythians offer sacrifice to a scimitar, the Thracians to Zamolxis, a runaway slave who came to them from Samos, the Phrygians to Men, the Ethiopians to Day, the Cyllenians to Phales, the Assyrians to a dove, the Persians to fire, and Egyptians to water.[57]

And on it goes. At this point, Momus chimes in: "Didn't I tell you, gods, that all this would come out and be thoroughly looked into?"[58] Other interventions by Momus during Damis' demolition

---

[54] Lucian, 1913–67, 2:153.
[55] Plutarch, *Moralia* 755 B–C; Plutarch, 1927–2004, 9:347–49.
[56] Lucian, 1913–67, 2:167.
[57] Lucian, 1913–67, 2:155.
[58] Lucian, 1913–67, 2:155.

20 *Doubting the Divine in Early Modern Europe*

of Timocles similarly suggest his complete anticipation of (or, really, agreement with) the arguments of the Epicurean atheist, including Damis' declaration that, in effect, Zeus is dead, since the Cretans testify to his gravesite.[59] As Momus and Zeus overhear this obituary of the king of the gods, Momus archly notes that "I knew far in advance that the fellow would say that" and then, faux innocently, asks "But why have you become so pale, Zeus, and why do you tremble till your teeth chatter?"[60] Lucian's picture here of a pitifully frightened king of the gods – comic as it is – might be his most searing assault on Greek religion.[61] That the debate between Damis and Timocles is so one-sidedly a victory for Epicurean "atheism" is clear to Zeus, who at the end of the dialogue wishes that he had a spokesman like Damis on his side. Perhaps, though, more vexing is who he has *at* his side: Damis' divine counterpart, the frank-speaking Momus.

In *Zeus Rants*, when Hermes calls together an assembly of the gods, the attendees included the major Olympians – several of whom fought over seating priority based on the material or workmanship of their statues – but also various foreign gods (Bendis, Anubis, Attis, and Mithras) as well as the dubious demigods (Dionysus, Heracles, Ganymede, and Asclepius).[62] The porous boundaries of this Greek pantheon were the subject of another dialogue in which Momus is the principal player. In the *Parliament of the Gods* an assembly is convened to deal with complaints that too many aliens have intruded into the divine ranks. The first to speak is Momus, who asks permission to speak

[59] *Zeus Rants* 44–46, 50.
[60] Lucian, 1913–67, 2:159.
[61] As for the use of the term "Epicurean atheism" here, as Stephen Greenblatt (2011, 71) and Ada Palmer (2014, 9–11) assert, Epicurus did not explicitly deny the existence of the gods (though Cicero claims that he did not do so only to avoid censure), but claimed that they had no interest in human affairs. He apparently saw the gods simply as other atomic entities, and in this sense I think that it is fair to call Epicurean materialism "atheistic" relative to the traditional pantheon, the gods toward whom Damis was deemed a "god-hater" and "god-fighter."
[62] *Zeus Rants* 8, 21. Lucian classifies Dionysus among the suspect demigods, although he was sometimes included among the Twelve; cf. Hansen, 2004, 250.

The Classical Tradition

frankly and reveals something about his own innate tendencies as a critic:

I beg you, Zeus, to let me speak frankly (*meta parrhesias*), for I could not do otherwise. Everybody knows how free of speech I am, and I am disinclined to hush up anything at all that is ill done. I criticize everybody and express my views openly, without either fearing anyone or concealing my opinion out of respect, so that most people think me vexatious and meddling by nature; they call me a regular public prosecutor.[63]

He then attacks these pretenders for daring to attend the gods' assemblies as peers and even bring their attendants along to feast with the real gods and receive sacrifices.

When Zeus asks Momus to be specific – to name names – Momus again welcomes the royal license for his *parrhesia*, and he indicts Dionysus, the half-human god of Lydian stock, womanish affect, and drunken demeanor.[64] There are other demigods Momus could have named such as Heracles and Asclepius – whom Zeus subsequently warns Momus dare not mention – but there may be special meaning in his leading with Dionysus, as this takes us back to Euripides. Arguably, the most vicious *implied* attack on the gods in classical Greek tragedy is the *Bacchae*, in which Dionysus storms into Thebes to orchestrate the murder of the doubting Pentheus at the hands of his crazed Bacchic mother. This may have been what Timocles was referring to when he argued in *Zeus Rants* that Euripides depicts the gods as justly punishing the impious.[65] Ostensibly, of course, the play is about the necessity of acknowledging the divine in no matter what attenuated or decadent form. Given the perversity of Dionysus' actions in the play, however, one can certainly find a much darker subtext, especially since Euripides expressed heterodox thoughts elsewhere, as Lucian notes in *Zeus Rants*. Indeed, the rationalist, sophistic Pentheus (Dionysus' mortal cousin) is identified in the play as a "god-fighter" (*theomache*), the same term

[63] *Parliament of the Gods* 2; Lucian, 1913–67, 5:421.
[64] *Parliament of the Gods* 4.
[65] *Zeus Rants* 41; Lucian, 1913–67, 2:52–53.

22   *Doubting the Divine in Early Modern Europe*

applied to Damis in *Zeus Rants* 45.[66] When Dionysus assumes human form to appear as a disciple of Dionysus in Thebes, Pentheus labels him an impostor (*gohes*, line 234), a label that obviously applied both to the disciple and to the god himself. Lucian's Momus applies this same term to Apollo in *Zeus Rants*, as he also invoked it to label the impostor in *Alexander the False Prophet*. Lucian uses the figure of Momus in the *Parliament of the Gods* to forthrightly do what Euripides could only cautiously do: condemn Dionysus as an example of a fraudulent god. This act of *parrhesia* by Lucian in the second century CE made overt the implied act of *parrhesia* by Euripides (via Pentheus) in the fifth century BCE. Although Foucault focuses on the *parrhesia* requested by the herdsman to report the wild behavior of the Bacchic women,[67] the real *parrhesia* in this play is Pentheus' denial of Dionysus' divinity. Lucian, at a further remove from the theological monopoly of the Olympian gods, is perhaps freer to accost this pantheon, and Momus is his spokesman to do so.

From Dionysus, Momus moves further up the shaky ladder of *lèse-majesté* in the *Parliament* when he attacks Zeus. In a nice bit of *praeteritio*, he says that he will not mention that some would charge Zeus with being an alien – assigning him both an origin and a tomb in Crete – or that he is in fact a changeling. No, he will not go that far (though, of course, he does), but he does blame Zeus for filling the heavens with demigods resulting from his philandering with mortal women. Here again Dionysus is cited as one such figure who is undeservedly hailed as a god, while his mortal cousins, one of whom was Pentheus, suffered unhappy fates.[68] From the demigods, Momus then proceeds to mock the soup of alien gods and mystery religions of the Hellenistic world: the Phrygian Attis, Corybas, and Sabazius; the Thracian Zamolxis, a slave from Samos elevated to a god; the Persian mystery god Mithras; the Egyptian gods Anubis and Apis; and the syncretic Zeus Ammon (who, Momus teases,

---

[66] *Bacchae*, line 45; Euripides, 2002, 14–15.
[67] *Bacchae*, lines 664–744; Foucault, 2001, 31–32.
[68] *Parliament of the Gods* 7.

The Classical Tradition

should truly have embarrassed Zeus with his accretion of the ram's horns).[69] At the lower reaches of the divine, Momus next attacks the oracular charlatans Trophonius and Amphilochus and the cults surrounding heroes such as Hector and Polydamas. Finally, at the level of the most ephemeral, he mocks "beings not to be found among us and unable to exist at all as realities": namely, abstractions such as Virtue, Nature, Destiny, and Chance.[70] As one of these abstractions ("Blame"), Momus wisely omits himself from this list of non-entities. Noting that many in the divine assembly are already irked by his "*parrhesia*," he will end, even though he could go on. The dialogue ends with Momus reading a proclamation that a committee of gods – four from the Olympian Twelve and three from the era of Cronus – will review credentials of all the gods, expel the fraudulent (whose altars will be converted to graves), and forbid the philosophers from deifying their meaningless abstractions.

As the champion of a divine purge – supposedly undertaken to protect the honor of the gods – Momus is, in fact, just a literary vehicle for Lucian to mock the divine realm. In the *Parliament*, as in *Zeus Rants,* Momus diminishes the gods in every possible way. He questions their behavior, their justice, their prophecies, their incoherent pluralism, their insecurity, their materialism (in the statues vying for priority seating), and their banal worldliness (in forming a credentialing committee, which as we in the modern university know, is the true measure of status anxiety).[71]

Was Lucian at heart an atheist? An agnostic? Or simply a professional parodist and satirist? We cannot know, though his readers have offered diverse opinions, some of which may give a clue as to how and why his elaboration of Momus re-appeared in later settings. Some scholars have de-emphasized the content of his dialogues in favor of their form. That is, Lucian was most truly a literary prankster, riffing on earlier traditions of

---

[69] *Parliament of the Gods* 9–10.
[70] *Parliament of the Gods* 13; Lucian, 1913–67, 5:435.
[71] On the scene involving the statues of the gods and the materialist meanings, see Branham, 1989, 168–71.

24 *Doubting the Divine in Early Modern Europe*

epic poetry, tragedy, and comedy: a rhetorician of the Second Sophistic entertaining audiences with light-hearted banter on familiar literary traditions, and devising innovative combinations of narrative, dialogue, and pamphleteering. In this view, there is no deeper philosophical ideology or theological position underlying his works – unless it is a nihilistic mockery of all schools, beliefs, and practices equally.[72] Others, however, see him as "second-century Voltaire," offering serious commentary on the religion of his day. This view, in turn, is countered by those who deny that his works represent a truly historical reaction to the contemporary religious climate, as he makes no mention of Serapis.[73] Instead, he is merely looking far back in religious time and mocking a theology long ago left behind.[74]

Not surprisingly, Enlightenment writers saw him in the tradition of Rabelais, but one who was able to flout religion in his day more freely for living in a more latitudinarian era. Such was the argument posed by George Lyttelton, who composed an encounter between Lucian and Rabelais in his *Dialogues of the Dead* (1760). Here Rabelais regrets that he did not have the freedom of Lucian to mock religion without fear of persecution:

You, Lucian, had no need to use so much caution. Your heathen priests desired only a sacrifice now and then from an epicurean, as a mark of conformity; and kindly allowed him to make as free as he pleased, in

---

[72] On this view and its attenuation, see Robinson, 1979, 1–63, esp. at 43–45; Caster, 1937, 383–84, 387; Branham, 1989, esp. at 13.

[73] Hewitt, 1924; Oliver, 1980 (who reads the *Parliament of the Gods* not as a religious statement but as a refiguring of Marcus Aurelius' attempt to restore the old lineage requirements for membership in the Areopagus in Athens – an intriguing argument, but one that is not exclusive of the religious critique, in my view); Caster, 1937, 341–42, 383–84, Robinson, 1979, 49–50. On Lucian's not being a "second-century Voltaire," see Lauvergnat-Gagnière, 1988, 22–23.

[74] Branham, 1989, 128–29 rejects this view; Baldwin, 1913, 104, similarly denies that Lucian was a "flogger of dead horses" and argues that the traditional Greek religion was still ensconced, as does Jones, 1986, 35. I think that Lucian's comments were pertinent to his time, in that he sought to put the final nail in the coffin of traditional Greek theology and did so in the context of the exceptional religious pluralism (and therefore religious relativism) of the Hellenistic era.

The Classical Tradition

conversation or writings with the whole tribe of Gods and Goddesses, from the thundering Jupiter and the scolding Juno, down to the Dog Anubis and the fragrant dame Cloacina [goddess of the sewers].[75]

Lyttelton may have been correct in his reading, both identifying Lucian with Epicureanism and his age with exceptional religious pluralism.

Lyttelton's dialogue suggests that we should take Lucian – and in particular his Momus – somewhat seriously. So many other of Lucian's pieces assail religion that to read the Momus dialogues solely as entertainment belies his systematic assault on religious convention. Some of these dialogues dealt with easily parodied practices, but some with more serious theological quandaries. The most important in the latter category is *Zeus Refuted*, in which a figure Cyniscus (or "Puppy," a stand-in for a dog-like Cynic) queries Zeus as to how the gods could exercise providence over the affairs of mortals if there exist powerful forces of Fate and Destiny.[76] If the Fates spin the threads of our life and/or if Destiny dictates inevitability, what is the power and function of the gods? What good are the sacrifices that mortals offer to the gods? What rationale for just deserts exists – whether in the gods' providence or in Destiny's rule – when the wicked prevail and the good suffer? How can Minos reward or punish souls after death, if it is necessity that controls all of our actions? Almost anticipating sixteenth-century critiques of Calvinist views of predestination, Cyniscus asks "if Minos were to judge justly, he would punish Destiny instead of Sisyphus and

[75] Dialogue 22, "Lucian–Rabelais," in Lyttelton, 1797, 176. This same sentiment occurs in another Enlightenment dialogue, this one by Voltaire in his "Conversation de Lucien, Érasme, et Rabelais dans les Champs Élysées," in which it is Erasmus who envies Lucian for living in a less perilous time for satire: "Il y avait une énorme difference entre les gens ridicules de votre temps et ceux du mien: vous n'aviez affaire qu'à des dieux qu'on jouait sur le théâtre, et à des philosophes qui avaient encore moins de credit que les dieux; mais, moi, j'étais entouré de fanatiques, et j'avais besoin d'une grande circonspection pour n'être pas brûlé par les uns ou assassiné par les autres" (Voltaire, 1939, 146–47).

[76] On this treatise as an example of Lucian's "literary Cynicism," see Bosman, 2012.

26   *Doubting the Divine in Early Modern Europe*

Fate instead of Tantalus, for what wrong did they do in obeying orders?"[77] These are hardly the questions of mere comedy: they are the imponderables that challenge any theological system, whether polytheistic or monotheistic.

Beyond the finer points of theology, however, Lucian also assails religion in almost all of its institutional and ritual manifestations. Forsaking the cover of dialogue he delivers a diatribe (literally), *On Sacrifices*, which is a thoroughgoing assault on religious practices.[78] He debunks the folly of a public that offers religious sacrifices, gods who are vengeful or benevolent in return for lacking or receiving such tributes, the temples in which rites are performed, the victims offered up, and the images and statues that are mistaken for the gods themselves. Even worse, he rehearses the depravity of such gods who receive these gifts: for instance, a philandering and incestuous Zeus who unfairly bound Prometheus on the Caucasus Mountains (the subject of another dialogue) and crippled Haphaestus by tossing him from the heavens ... and so on.[79] All politics being local, he also explains how separate states lay claim to particular gods, much as Aesop assailed the Delphians in regard to Apollo. Most scandalously, he reports yet again the embarrassing fact that the Cretans claim both Zeus's birthplace and his grave. But it is not just Zeus who is dead to Lucian, as he closes the harangue by mocking the religious customs of the Scythians, Assyrians, Phrygians, Lydians, and Egyptians.

If the genre of the diatribe moves us closer to Lucian's undisguised voice, two other narratives do so even more, as they include first-person testimony regarding religious hoaxes. In *Alexander the False Prophet*, which Lucian addressed to an

[77] *Zeus Refuted* 18; Lucian, 1913–67, 2:87.
[78] On the centrality of the *Sacrifices* as a template for many other of Lucian's works, see Caster, 1937, 181–82.
[79] *Sacrifices* 4–7; Lucian, 1913–67, 3:158–63. As for the vindictiveness of the gods, in the *On the Syrian Goddess* 19–21, Lucian (to whom this work is dubiously attributed) depicts the malice of Hera, who in anger at Stratonice (wife of the Assyrian King) for not building a temple to her, created a scenario in which an upright man castrates himself so that he not violate Stratonice, who falls in love with him (Lucian, 1913–67, 4:364–69).

Epicurean friend named Celsus,[80] he produced a lengthy account of a figure, Alexander of Abonoteichus (in Paphlogonia), who posed as a prophet of Asclepius. Lucian describes how he perpetrated his fraud of offering prophetic answers to sealed questions. Whereas Aesop attacked the Delphians for exploiting their cult site, Lucian exposes in detail the creation of a fake cult site. Alexander buried and unearthed bronze tablets that indicated that Apollo and his son Asclepius would soon decamp to Abonoteichus; fashioned a fake linen snake as an incarnation of Asclepius; then for a fee offered prophetic answers to sealed questions and prescribed remedies for ailments (truly, the first snake-oil salesman). Lucian reports his own attempt to expose him, and Alexander's ensuing attempt to have him drowned at sea.[81] He also depicts Alexander as a particular enemy of Epicurus, whom Lucian praises as an antipodal model of "straight thinking, truthfulness, and frankness (*parrhesia*)."[82] Even those scholars who claim that Lucian is more entertainer than historian admit that *Alexander* attests to a tangible engagement with contemporary religion – and not just for laughs.[83]

---

[80] This is probably not the Celsus, author of the *True Doctrine*, to which Origen responded (on this debate see Origen, 1965, xxiv–xxvi), though it is interesting to note some similarities in Celsus' *True Doctrine* (as excerpted by Origen) and Lucian's writings. For instance, Origen says that Celsus "thinks that 'because we [Christians] worship a man who was arrested and died, we behave like the Getae who reverence Zamolxis, and the Cilicians who worship Mopsus, the Arcarnanians Amphilochus, the Thebans Amphiaraus, and the Lebadians Trophonius'" (Origen, 1965, 151, bold in original). Lucian, via Momus, similarly attacks Zamolxis, Amphilochus, and Trophonius in *Zeus Rants* 9, 12; and via Menippus mocks Amphilochus and Trophonius in the *Dialogues of the Dead* (Lucian, 1913–67, 7:50–53).

[81] On his own encounter with Alexander, see *Alexander the False Prophet* 53–57.

[82] *Alexander the False Prophet* 47; Lucian, 1913–67, 4:235. On the *Alexander* in the tradition of Epicurean *parrhesia*, see the introduction to the *On Frank Criticism* of Philodemus (*c.* 110–40 BCE) at Philodemus, 1998, 7.

[83] See, for instance, Robinson, 1979, 57–61, who concedes the historical qualities in this treatise and the *Passing of Peregrinus*, but also contends that both works also contain fictional components. On these two works, also see Caster, 1938; Jones, 1986, 117–48.

28 Doubting the Divine in Early Modern Europe

So also did another work, the *Passing of Peregrinus*. This exposé, which mocks the Cynics, proves that Lucian was no strict adherent to any philosophical way of life, even though his attacks on convention loosely put him in the Cynic school. Most importantly for Lucian's legacy, this work would be the most damning one in the view of later Christian readers. The treatise deals with the martyrdom of a Cynic zealot (or poser) named Peregrinus, who, inspired by the practices of the Brahmins, orchestrated a self-immolation at Olympia in 165 BCE following the Olympic games. In his account Lucian depicts this figure as a grandstanding phony, who was mainly interested in his fame. Clearly, Lucian sees him in the same vein as Alexander, though as a fraud seeking glory rather than fees. At one point in his travels Peregrinus encountered Christians, joined up with them, and quickly became a type of second Christ for them:

It was then that he learned the wondrous lore of the Christians, by associating with their priests and scribes in Palestine. And – how else could it be? – in a trice he made them all look like children; for he was a prophet, cult-leader, head of the synagogue, and everything, all by himself. He interpreted and explained some of their books and even composed many, and they revered him as a god, made use of him as a lawgiver, and set him down as a protector, next after that other, to be sure, whom they still worship, the man who was crucified in Palestine because he introduced this new cult into the world.[84]

Lucian then recounts how the Christians tended to him in prison, supplying him with a stream of revenue; because their "crucified sophist" had taught them to hold all property in common, he snipes, any "charlatan" (*gohes*) can readily exploit them.[85] That such a figure as Peregrinus would be readily embraced by the Christians and revered as another god and cult leader akin to Christ certainly implies that the Christians were vulnerable to impostors. In fact, Lucian almost equates Peregrinus and Christ.[86] In any case, for Lucian, whether as a Greek Cynic,

---

[84] *Passing of Peregrinus* 11; Lucian, 1913–67, 5:13.
[85] *Passing of Peregrinus* 13; Lucian, 1913–67, 5:14–15.
[86] Although Lucian calls Peregrinus a Christ-like protector and religious leader to the Christians at *Passing* 11, at 12 he says that they saw him merely as "the new

The Classical Tradition

Brahmin martyr or Palestinian Christ, a figure such as Peregrinus is an impostor not unlike Alexander the false prophet. He says that when he laughed at the pyre of Peregrinus, he "narrowly missed getting torn limb from limb ... by the Cynics just as Actaeon was by his dogs or his cousin Pentheus by the Maenads."[87] Lucian thus equates himself with Euripides' disbelieving Pentheus, who showed such contempt for Dionysus, an impostor god by Momus's account. Lucian's fear of being torn apart may have fueled the later tradition that he and Euripides died (like Actaeon) by being torn apart by dogs.[88] Such is the result of his doubts concerning gods, prophets, and martyrs.

Lucian's assault on religion is so pervasive and, at times, so trenchant, that it cannot be relegated to the ranks of mere literary play. Certainly he is in part an entertainer parodying earlier treatments of the gods in epic poetry, drama, and comedy. He may also be translating into new (prose) performative formats some of the comic play involving religion that could be found in the Old Comedy of Aristophanes.[89] But there is more at stake

---

Socrates" (Lucian, 1913–67, 5:13). Still, there was much that later Christians could condemn in this account. Later in the treatise Lucian comments that when he embellished the telling of the story for simpletons he added that at the moment of Peregrinus' immolation there was an earthquake and a vulture winging its way to heaven giving a farewell statement (*Passing* 39), a tale later repeated back to Lucian by a bystander who also claimed that after the cremation Peregrinus appeared in white clothing (*Passing* 40). Both the earthquake and the resurrection story could have inflamed later Christian readers.

[87] *Passing of Peregrinus* 2; Lucian, 1913–67, 5:5.

[88] Jones, 1986, 21. That the passage in *Passing of Peregrinus* 2 (concerning Actaeon's dogs) may have been the seed for the later tradition for Lucian's fate is noted in "Lucian," *Suda* Online. Trans. Akihiko Watanabe. May 5 1999. www.stoa.org/sol-entries/lambda 683, note 3. Also, it should not be forgotten that the term Cynic derives from "dog" (Foucault, 2001, 122), which may have inspired such an ironic fate for a disbelieving Cynic.

[89] There can be found parodies of religious ritual, for instance, in the *Lysistrata* 181–237, when she and her rebellious companions swear a religious oath and slaughter a jar of wine to consummate it; or depictions of atheism in the *Clouds* 246–426, when Socrates denies the existence of Zeus. But these are either minor scenes (in the first case) or depictions of public (mis)perceptions of philosophy (in the second) that lack the sustained assaults on religion itself found in Lucian. Branham, 1989, 174, argues that the encounter between Damis and Timocles has the tone of the comic agon rather than

30   *Doubting the Divine in Early Modern Europe*

here. Why else would he expand his religious net to include the religious practices of the Phrygians, Scythians, Thracians, Egyptians, Indians, and Persians? Why expose contemporary prophets and holy men like Alexander and Peregrinus? More importantly, why does he lay out in such persuasive fashion so many serious arguments of theodicy, anthropomorphism, materialism, syncretism, ritualism, and providentialism: issues that go to the core of religious belief? It is, moreover, his greatest mark as an ironist that he enlists a god, Momus, to be the conveyor of *parrhesia* in two of the most caustic assaults. In deploying Momus in this way in *Zeus Rants* and *Parliament of the Gods*, Lucian fully invests him with the aura of agnosticism or even atheism. The light-hearted critiques of the gods' creations that Aesop conferred upon Momus have been turned into serious critiques of the gods themselves and all their properties, powers, and prophecies.

Scholars have not fully recognized the role of Lucian's Momus as a forceful and consequential embodiment of *parrhesia* in the ancient world. Foucault rightly closes his lectures on frank speech by identifying it as one of the signal features of the "critical" tradition in Western thought. He is correct, though he misses its most potent exemplar in Lucian. In fact, Lucian's Momus should be viewed in the context of several currents of rationalism that culminated in his Late Antique writings. Beginning in the fourth century BCE with Palaephatus, a genre emerged entitled *Peri apiston* (On Incredible Things), which attempted to take Greek myths and "rationalize" them by speculating on their origins in some type of reality. In Lucian's era, Pausanias in his travelogue *Periegesis* (*c.* 155–175/80 CE) exposed or explained myths associated with certain places. Lucian did something similar, though with a huge dollop of Cynic mockery.[90] His interest in rational scrutiny, moreover, extended beyond myth to history. He devoted an entire diatribe

---

the substance of the Platonic debate. I disagree: Lucian's Momus and Damis offer substantive and mutually reinforcing challenges to religion that incorporate serious arguments from Epicurean and Academic (or Skeptic) thought.

[90] On the rationalizing of myth, see Veyne, 1988, and Hawes, 2014.

The Classical Tradition

to *How to Write History*, excoriating hacks and flatterers, and insisting that the historian

> should be ... fearless, incorruptible, free, a friend of free expression [*parrhesia*] and the truth, intent, as the comic poet says, on calling a fig a fig and trough a trough, giving nothing to hatred or to friendship, sparing no one, showing neither pity nor shame nor obsequiousness, an impartial judge, well disposed to all men up to the point of not giving one side more than its due, in his books a stranger and a man without a country, independent, subject to no sovereign, not reckoning what this or that man will think, but stating the facts.[91]

Parrhesia, then, is the tool of the trade of the historian, as it was for Momus in speaking to the gods.[92] What Lucian mandated for heavenly matters, he prescribed for earthly ones as well. This manual for writing history was a serious one – and another indication that Lucian's writings sought to rationalize both the theological and historical realms.

Frank speech vs. flattery; *logos* vs. *mythos*; prose vs. poetry: these are the binaries of Lucian's corpus and his Momus. Should we add a final one: unbelief vs. belief? To some degree this is an imponderable, given that there were layers of belief (in the gods) and unbelief (in their Homeric depictions) common in the ancient world. As Paul Veyne has shown regarding the Greek world, intellectuals sometimes were torn between their own skepticism and the need to conform to some degree to popular beliefs. As he argues, "the learned respected popular ideas on myth and ... they themselves were split between two principles: the rejection of the marvelous and the conviction that legends had a true basis."[93] The weight of social pressure should not be disregarded. In his *De natura deorum* Cicero's interlocutors reveal that even Epicurus simulated belief in the gods for reasons of social necessity.[94] And despite Cicero's own notable doubts as

---

[91] *How to Write History* 41; Lucian, 1913–67, 6:57.
[92] He repeats the criterion of *parrhesia* at *How to Write History* 44; Lucian, 1913–67, 6:58.
[93] Veyne, 1988, 56–57.
[94] *De natura deorum* 1.44.123; Cicero, 1951, 118–21; and at 3.1.3; Cicero, 1951, 286–89.

32 *Doubting the Divine in Early Modern Europe*

expressed in Cotta's critique of Stoic belief in Book 3, even he, like Cotta, defaulted to a vague probabilism linked perhaps to the religious underpinning of the Roman state – or even more likely to his own position in the college of augurs, to which he alludes in Book 1.[95] It is revealing that even he could refer to Diagoras' epithet as the "Atheist" only in the Greek rather than in Latin, as if he needed some remove from the term.[96] And yet, as Cicero noted, the ancient world clearly spawned notions of both agnosticism in Protagoras and atheism in Diagoras.[97] Certainly, Lucian was heir to these views, as he was to the general debate on belief and unbelief so thoroughly laid out in Cicero's dialogue. Indeed, Lucian cites some of the same arguments that Cicero's Academic Cotta does in Book 3: challenging the Stoic tenets that gods oversee the natural order, that deified moral abstractions are really gods, and that divine providence oversees the affairs of mortals.[98] Lucian, of course, differs in that he uses a god, Momus, to assert some of these doubts rather insultingly to Zeus himself. Furthermore, Lucian pairs Momus with Damis, a voice of Epicureanism, clearly the most atheistic school in ancient thought. Whereas the Epicurean interlocutor, Gaius Velleius, received relatively little space in Cicero's treatise,[99] Damis is the chief foe of the Stoic in *Zeus Rants* – and a more full-throated "god-hater" and "god-fighter" than the Epicurean spokesman in Cicero's dialogue. Like Lucretius, who celebrated Epicurus as the first great foe of religion and saw religion as the enemy of mankind (*De rerum natura* 1.62–126), Damis is an unalloyed atheist in *Zeus Rants* and one who, in both Momus's and Zeus's minds, unequivocally wins the day.[100]

---

[95] See respectively, *De natura deorum* 3.1.5; Cicero, 1951, 288–91; and 1.6.14; Cicero, 1951, 16 (and note therein)–17.

[96] *De natura deorum* 1.23.63; Cicero, 1951, 60; also at 3.37.89; Cicero, 1951, 374.

[97] *De natura deorum* 1.2; Cicero, 1951, 4–5.

[98] Caster, 1937, 343; Jones, 1986, 35.

[99] *De natura deorum* 1.8.18–1.20.56.

[100] Whereas Bosman, 2012, 787, 794–95, would loosely situate Lucian among Cynics, and Lauvergnat-Gagnière, 1988, 23–24, classify him as a skeptic, Caster, 1937, 103–6, 206–8, places him closest to the Epicurean camp.

The Classical Tradition

Why could Lucian safely present such a thorough assault on religion, especially one offered in oral performances reliant on the interests and support of audiences?[101] An answer, explaining the attitudes of both author and listeners, may be found in the particular moment of his writing: a time of a religious pluralism that pitted a culturally descending Greek pantheon next to an array of Near Eastern, Egyptian, Indian, and even Christian forces. He becomes a second-century entertaining ethnographer of religion who is more skeptical than Herodotus – who was, for instance, uncritical of the oracle given Croesus – and as clever and cynical as Menippus. As for himself, he is akin to that ideal historian in his *How to Write History*, who is frank-speaking and "without a country." An itinerant sophist whose travels ranged from cites in Asia Minor, Macedonia, Egypt, and Gaul, to Athens and Rome, he lived in a world in which the civic reasons for worshipping Greek gods – whose local cults were a matter of civic duty in the era of the independent *poleis* – were no longer extant.[102] As a Syrian living in an era of Roman domination, he did not share Cicero's innate (or coerced) desire to accede to religious tradition as an act of Roman *pietas*. Stateless, it was easier to be godless. Whatever the confluence of political, philosophical, and personal factors, Lucian shaped the Momus of Hesiod and Aesop into the most iconoclastic god of the ancient world.

---

[101] On Lucian's works as oral performances, see Jones, 1986, 14–15; Robinson, 1979, 3–8, 61.

[102] Robinson, 1979, 46–47; on the reconstruction of his travels from comments in his works, see Jones, 1986, 6–23.

2

Renaissance Antihero: Leon Battista Alberti's *Momus*, the Novel

After his flurry of activity in Lucian, Momus was dormant for centuries. The Romans almost completely ignored him. I find only two references to him in all of the classical Latin corpus, both from Cicero: one in *Letters to Atticus* 5.20.6, in which he is cited by his Greek name as the symbol of exacting standards; the other in the *De natura deorum* 3.17.44, where he appears in his Latin equivalence as "Querela" in a list of the many children of Erebus and Night. In both cases, he is silent. Given the Roman propensity to cherish the collective over the individual, and considering the ties between religion and the Roman state – as exemplified in the key virtue of *pietas* – it is no mystery that the Romans would avoid this god. This is not to say that frank speech and invective were absent, as Cicero's vitriolic *Philippics against Antony* famously demonstrate, but attacking one's political opponent was quite another matter from affronting religious authority in Lucianic fashion. Lateral *vituperatio* is one thing; vertical *parrhesia* quite another.[1] If the tenth-century Byzantine theologians and *Suda* are any indication, Momus's submergence

---

[1] A notable exception might be the cheeky religious satire, *Apocolocyntosis*, the Pumpkinification (or apotheosis) of the emperor Claudius, attributed to Seneca. While deriding the recent custom of deifying emperors, this work is more an assault on Claudius than on traditional religion itself, although P. T. Eden does classify it as Menippean satire and notes some of its similarities with Lucian's *The Parliament of the Gods*, in which Momus challenges the porous boundaries of the pantheon (Seneca, 1984, 9, 13–15).

could also in part have been owing to Lucian's atheistic reputation, which derived in part from the Momus dialogues. In any case, whether for being so minor in stature or so disagreeable in nature, Momus seems to have had no presence in the medieval perpetuation of the classical gods, whom Christians adopted for cultural, allegorical, or astrological reasons.[2]

Not surprisingly, Momus makes his reappearance in the early humanist Boccaccio's massive encyclopedia *On the Genealogy of the Pagan Gods*, though under his Latin form of "Querela," which Boccaccio drew from Cicero's *De natura deorum*. Clearly, Boccaccio had nothing to rely on but Cicero's bare listing of him here, so he proposes to improvise as to what this god of Grievance was like: he embodies a

sickness of a mind not in harmony with itself, and from there it extends to a demented heart, whether because an injudicious man insists that he is missing what is owed to him, or because he can hardly bear not being given what he hopes for, or because he is not able to get what he wants. And so, deprived of mental lucidity, he thinks his sin belongs to someone else. For this reason the lascivious lover complains, as does he who is desirous of gold, as does he who is avid for honors, as does he who is thirsty for blood, and many others, weeping about an evil they introduce themselves but which prudent people are able to reject.[3]

While correct in surmising some of the features of envy and resentment that traditionally accompanied Momus, Boccaccio clearly adds other unseemly personality traits – avarice, ambition, bloodthirstiness – and does not envision any positive attributes, such as perceptive skepticism or demanding rationalism. Perhaps this is partly owing to Boccaccio's identification of Querela's parent, Erebus (whom he equates with Tartarus) as the Serpent in Eden.[4]

This association of Momus's parent with the Fall points us in the right direction of decoding Momus's greatest literary elaboration a century later in Leon Battista Alberti's epic novel, *Momus*. The conflation of the biblical with the classical is a key to a

[2] Seznec, 1953.
[3] Boccaccio, 2011, 147.
[4] Boccaccio, 2011, 114–23, 134–35.

36   *Doubting the Divine in Early Modern Europe*

reading of the *Momus* that places it in a theologically fraught, heterodox light. Investing his antihero with cosmic dimensions of independence, rebellion, and mischief, Alberti takes Momus beyond Lucian's frank-speaker and closet agnostic to a figure capable of leading "men, gods, and the whole machinery of the world into utter calamity."[5] He becomes a Luciferian figure, who as I later will show, very likely inspired Milton's own antihero.[6] The story of how Alberti creates the first antihero in the Italian Renaissance's first Latin novel is one that entails a blending of new currents in humanist thought (Epicurean and Hermetic), the critique of court life (papal and princely) in fifteenth-century Italy, and the personal trials of the figure whom Burckhardt famously lionized as the "universal man" of the Renaissance.[7] Why would Alberti be the figure to give Momus his fullest incarnation and biography? How did he extend Lucian's use of him (especially in *Zeus Rants*) to create a potentially radical critique of theism?

Alberti (1404–72) was tied to some of the most dynamic elements in the society and culture of Renaissance Italy. The illegitimate scion of a major merchant family, he was a product of the ruling social and economic class of fifteenth-century Italian urban society. A practicing architect and theorist of painting, sculpture, and architecture, he was linked to the artistic circle of figures such as Brunelleschi, Donatello, Ghiberti, and Masaccio – and to the creative spirit of Florence's cultural environment. A student at the school of Gasparino Barzizza in Padua and an author of various literary works, he was ensconced in

---

[5] I will be citing the superb 2003 edition and translation by Virginia Brown and Sarah Knight; here, at 93.

[6] Thus, my reading of the work will de-emphasize the more customarily stressed political meaning and focus on its religious implications in the vein of treatments by Stefano Simoncini and Christine Smith, both of whom, for instance, broach the Lucifer-Momus parallel (Simoncini, 1998, 408, 433; C. Smith, 2004, 167–68), as did I in my review of Knight and Brown's edition of the *Momus* for H-Italy in 2005. For a thorough and useful survey of Momus's appearance from Alberti to Bruno, see Simoncini, 1998.

[7] Burckhardt, 1990, 101–4. On *Momus* as the first Latin novel of the Renaissance, see Marsh, 1998, 123.

Renaissance Antihero

the humanist revival of classical learning and its application to the contemporary moral, social, and political setting. Long a secretary at the papal court and a recipient of various church benefices, he was part of the institutional network of the church in Rome and even an advisor to Pope Nicholas V. A whirlwind of accomplishment and man of many parts, he was an architect (designing, among other things, Mantua's Sant'Andrea and the facades of Florence's Santa Maria Novella and Palazzo Rucellai), gymnast, musician, painter, sculptor, theorist, and scholar. He composed several comedies and satirical works: a forged "classical" comedy, the *Philodoxeos*; Aesopic fables and light-hearted "dinner-time" dialogues, the *Apologi centum* and *Intercenales*; a mock praise of the fly, *Musca*; a funeral oration for his dog, *Canis*; a novel regarding a renegade, *Momus*. He wrote on architectural and artistic theory (*De re aedificatoria*, *Della pittura*, *Della statua*), various areas of moral philosophy (*Della famiglia*, *Theogenius*, *Profugiorum ab erumna*, *De iciarchia*), mathematics (*Ludi matematici*), cartography (*Descriptio urbis Romae*), horses (*De equo animante*), love (*Amator*, *Deifira*), and grammar (producing the first Italian grammar in his *Regule lingue florentine*).[8] This enormous productivity (and this just a partial list) issued from a figure beset with misfortune, including his family's exile from Florence, his illegitimate birth, illness, his father's death during his first year at university, mistreatment by relatives, and a bleakness concerning his circumstances.[9] But rather than being an ironic counterpart to a difficult life,

[8] On Albert's life, see Mancini, 1971; Gadol, 1969, esp. 3–11; Grafton, 2000; Santinello, 1962. The earliest biography, which Burckhardt particularly draws on, is the fifteenth-century *Vita anonyma*, which most scholars rightly believe to be Alberti's own work (see, e.g., Watkins, 1957; Fubini and Gallorini, 1972; Grafton, 2000, 18; but for the contrary opinion, see Gadol, 1969, 11n16). Certainly, it voices some of the same themes found in Alberti's other works, such as the contempt for sloth ("Hinc neque otio aut ignavia tenebatur, neque in agendis rebus satietate usquam afficiebatur," in edition in Fubini and Gallorini, 1972, 68), the notion of assiduous study and zealous investigations, the account of bitter family relations, and the idea that human talent is capable of creating something "almost divine" (*prope divinus*) (77).

[9] On Alberti's hardships, see the *Vita anonyma*, trans. in Watkins, 1989, at 8–9; Garin, 1975, 168; Watkins in Alberti, 2004, 4–5; Santinello, 1962, 27.

38   *Doubting the Divine in Early Modern Europe*

his impressive *vita* may have been in fact an understandable product of it. An intense sense of isolation and alienation may have been the engine of productivity as well as the reason for his eventual invocation of the troublesome god Momus.

After the loss of his father when at the University of Bologna studying canon and civil law, which was followed by the death of his guardian uncle, Alberti was at the mercy of cousins who cheated him out of some of his inheritance. Thus, although well begun on an elite educational track, he found himself vulnerable. A work that he wrote shortly after his university days, the *De commodis litterarum atque incommodis* (On the Advantages and Disadvantages of Letters), clearly reflects his doubts about his prospects for a future in a learned profession and how such a career would measure up against the merchant life of his family. He portrays in great detail the contrast between the tangible social, economic, and psychological hardships of the academic life and the wholly intangible moral and cultural rewards. Reflecting the mentality of a bourgeois investor (or even actuarial accountant) handicapping the future yield of an education, he offers a precise calculation of the odds for success. Only 300 out of 1,000 university students will live to age 40 when their education is complete; only 100 of that 300 will survive war, illness, and other misfortunes; only 10 of that 100 will be talented enough to be successful; only 3 of that 10 will have the perseverance to thrive economically – and those only in the notarial art, law, or medicine, professions that often occasion moral compromises.[10]

More revealing, however, was the hovering bourgeois work ethic in the opening sentence of the treatise, addressed to his brother Carlo, in which he says that their father Lorenzo urged that they "never be idle (*ociosi*)."[11] He says that whereas Carlo mixed the literary with practical pursuits, he has pursued letters exclusively, finding in them a bulwark against the difficulties of life. He then, argues, however, that his literary endeavors should not only profit himself psychologically, but also should meet the

[10] Alberti, 1971, 92–101; McClure, 2004, 11, 225–26n56.
[11] Alberti, 1971, 42.

expectations of his friends that *daily* he show some "fruit of his vigils," something from "my labor and assiduity of studies."[12] This treatise, simultaneously a response to a request from his family and a tangible product of his studies, fulfilled Alberti's need to make literary work in some way as visible and "productive" as the practical work pursued by his brother and others in the family. Translating this literary productivity into a career would be a taller order. In his dialogue *On the Family*, the first three books of which were written in 1433–34, he praises the merchant profession as a better choice than either letters or the military as a refuge against the travails of fortune and one that guarantees a mind "never servile, always free."[13] As it turned out, the path Alberti took would place him forever in the debt of others (whether princes or popes) or in the grip of an institution (the Church) for which he had little or no vocation. This relative sense of failure vis-à-vis the merchant legacy of his family joined with an obsession with trying to honor somehow the practical, "active" values of that family in other ways.

In the early 1430s Alberti obtained a position many humanists of his ilk held, as an abbreviator (or secretary) in the Papal Curia. This brought him into contact with like-minded humanists such as Poggio Bracciolini, Lapo da Castiglionchio, and others with whom he shared an interest in the classical world and the study of ancient texts circulating at the Curia or in Florence, where he accompanied the papal entourage for the Council of Ferrara-Florence.[14] From this setting two seemingly contradictory paths emerged: one, the secular and even arch pursuits of humanists at the Curia that prompted Poggio's collection of jokes (*facetiae*); the other, Alberti's appointment by Nicholas V to church benefices outside of Florence and in the Florentine cathedral.[15] Like other humanists such as Petrarch, Alberti used the Church as a life-line for letters. By taking minor orders as a cleric to hold benefices (after receiving a papal dispensation regarding his

---

[12] Alberti, 1971, 42.
[13] Alberti, 2004, 177–78.
[14] On the humanist culture at the Curia, see Celenza, 1999.
[15] For the joke-book, see Bracciolini, 1879, 1983; McClure, 2004, 30–31.

40   *Doubting the Divine in Early Modern Europe*

illegitimacy), these sinecures, together with the secretarial position he held until 1464, provided a partial livelihood. This arm of support would be supplemented with patronage by various princes, such as Leonello d'Este of Ferrara, Ludovico Gonzaga of Mantua, and Federico da Montefeltro of Urbino.[16] He was, in a word, forever in the service of the Church and princes. His merchant ideal of a life "never servile, always free" would be hard won for one whose circumstances dictated dependence. That resentful sense of dependence as a courtier would animate the rebellious spirit of Alberti's Momus.

Still, Alberti did find a way to honor his merchant father's advice and to console himself for the vicissitudes of fortune: incessant creative work. As many scholars have noted, the themes of work and sloth punctuate Alberti's thought from the *De commodis litterarum atque incommodis* of the 1420s to the *De iciarchia* of the 1460s. As Joan Gadol rightly pointed out, words such as *adoperarsi* and *esercitarsi* vs. *ozio* (or *otium*) and *pigrizia* fill his writings.[17] In the dialogue *On the Family*, Alberti presents a forceful articulation of this ethos in the voice of his uncle Lionardo, with whom he lived while studying in Padua:

Idleness is not only useless and generally despised in young men, but a positive burden and danger to the family ... Who has ever dreamed he might reach any grace or dignity without hard work in the noblest arts, without assiduous efforts, without plenty of sweat poured out in many and strenuous exertions? Certainly a man who would wish for the favor of princes and fame must avoid and resist idleness and inertia just as he would do major and hateful enemies.[18]

Man's activism seeks out the social realm – as "Plato ... declared that men were born to serve their fellow men, and that we owe a part of ourselves to our country, a part to our kinsmen, and a part to our friends" – and this, no doubt, was one spur for

[16] Gadol, 1969, 3–10; Grafton, 2000, 8–9, 189–224.
[17] Gadol, 1969, 225–39; Saitta 1949–51, 1:393–424; Garin, 1965, 64; Watkins in Alberti, 2004, 11; for his use of "pigrizia" (indolence), see Alberti, 1969, 252.
[18] Alberti, 2004, 132.

Alberti's decision to write serious moral works in the vernacular for the benefit of a wider audience.[19] Human dynamism also extends to exploring and conquering nature, as "man alone stands erect ... as though made by nature herself to gaze upon and know the paths and bodies in the heavens." He even invokes the famous declaration of Protagoras that "man is the means and measure of all things."[20]

Alberti's vibrant praise of human dignity and intellectual power certainly embodies part of the Renaissance humanist *topos* on the dignity of humankind developed by figures such as Petrarch, Giannozzo Manetti, and Pico della Mirandola.[21] But the stress on ceaseless productivity, as Joan Gadol argues, has roots in the ethos of his bourgeois family. Thus, long ago, Werner Sombart in *The Quintessence of Capitalism* situated Alberti as an early exemplar of a capitalistic, "middle-class ethic," a figure in the same vein as Daniel Defoe and Benjamin Franklin.[22] Understandably, Max Weber, who famously linked the triumph of capitalism to Protestantism, found this reading of Alberti incorrect.[23] Yet, the sentiments on work, frugality, and the careful marshalling of time that Alberti identified with his family in the *Della famiglia* and the *De commodis letterarum*, suggest that Sombart has the better of the argument.[24] Perhaps it does not require Protestant theology

---

[19] Alberti, 2004, 134. On his decision to write in a more accessible *volgare*, see the preface to the third book of the *Della famiglia*, ibid., 153 and the dedicatory letter in the *Theogenius* to Leonello d'Este at Alberti, 1954, 55–56.

[20] Alberti, 2004, 134.

[21] On the theme of the dignity of humankind in humanist thought, see Trinkaus, 1970. On Alberti's turning this theme of human power to negative ends, see Garin, 1975, 147–50, 161–62.

[22] Sombart, 1915, 103–21; Gadol, 1969, 225–27; Saitta, 1949–51, 1:409.

[23] Weber, 1958, 194–98n12, disputes Sombart's comparison of Franklin and Alberti.

[24] The merchant character Giannozzo Alberti in the third book of the *Della famiglia* urges thriftiness (*masserizia*) in the use of time (Alberti, 2004, 171–72); in the second book Lionardo declares that "The opposite of prodigality, the opposite of neglect, are carefulness and conscientiousness, in short, thriftiness [*masserizia*]. Thriftiness is the means to preserve wealth" (144, with slight alteration).

42   *Doubting the Divine in Early Modern Europe*

to champion a vocation of secular work, especially from one such as Alberti, who continually mocked the clergy and, in *Momus*, the gods for their indolence. Given Alberti's profiting from benefices that required little or nothing from him, it is no surprise that he may have drawn a work ethic from the lore of his merchant family, which, as he boasted in the *Della famiglia*, at one point supplied one thirty-second of the Florentine tax base.[25] And although Alberti's work would be creative rather than commercial, he nonetheless sought to make it comparably useful, social, and tangible: thus his decision to write in the vernacular; thus, in all likelihood, his preference for architecture, the most visible and grandiose of the design arts.

Whether for his bourgeois work ethic or for his more general determination to vanquish *fortuna* with *virtù*, Alberti is a fitting emblem for the centuries-long debate on secularism in Renaissance humanism. Beginning with Burckhardt and his successor, John Addington Symonds, the classical interests of the humanists were thought to inevitably signal a high degree of irreligion or even paganism.[26] A pushback against such overstated views emerged in the twentieth century with scholars such as Giuseppe Toffanin and Charles Trinkaus, who explored the religious dimension of humanism.[27] Lucien Febvre, in his zeal to exonerate the naughty Rabelais, even insisted unpersuasively that "unbelief" was a virtual impossibility before the seventeenth century – largely for want of a proper philosophical foundation and scientific method.[28] More recently, the pendulum has

---

[25] Alberti, 2004, 143.

[26] Burckhardt, 1990, 312–51; Symonds refers to the humanists' "deep internal irreligiousness" and argues that "the study of the classics and the effort to assimilate the spirit of the ancients, undermined their Christianity without substituting the religion or the ethics of the old world" (Symonds, 1967, 379, 381). He declares that Alberti, "though frequently approaching the subject of religion, never dilates upon it, and in no place declares himself a Christian. His creed is that of the Roman moralists – a belief in the benignant Maker of the Universe, an intellectual and unsubstantial theism" (Symonds, 1898, 1:179).

[27] Toffanin, 1954; Trinkaus, 1970.

[28] Febvre, 1982; and for a critique of his famous 1942 *The Problem of Unbelief in the Sixteenth Century*, see Wootton, 1988. Febvre's book presents ample

Renaissance Antihero

43

begun to swing back, as scholars such as Alison Brown, Stephen Greenblatt, and Ada Palmer have traced the heterodox currents flowing from the reintroduction of Epicurean thought in fifteenth-century Italy.[29] In her study of the marginalia of readers of Lucretius' text, Palmer traces Epicurean currents that she defines as "proto-atheistic" – such as unordered atomism, the denial of Providence, and the mortality of the soul – rather than a fully formed atheism.[30] The historiographical verdict need not be as simple as that between belief and unbelief – and, in any case, such matters can rarely be proven in regard to the dead (or the living).[31] Still, Alberti's *Momus* is a novel that encapsulates the debate, albeit cryptically, in at least one humanist's case in mid-fifteenth-century Italy.

evidence to contradict his thesis regarding the near impossibility of unbelief in the sixteenth century. See, for instance, his treatment of Etienne Dolet (esp. Jean Visagier's comments upon him at Febvre, 1982, 56); Guillaume Postel's attacks on atheists (107); Nicholas Bourbon's attacks on the same (92); Calvin's assault on unbelievers (130); and his comments on Bonaventura Des Périers's *Cymbalum mundi*, to which he will devote a discrete book also published in 1942 (see my Chapter 3). In the end, Febvre can only assert that Rabelais was not an atheist – or viewed as one – by the time of the publication of the *Pantagruel* in 1532 – and admits that Euhemerism may have had its advocates by mid-century. Febvre apparently does not recognize that Lucretian views of materialism may have been enough of a naturalist foundation to support agnostic or atheistic views.

[29] Brown, 2010, esp. at viii–x, discusses this debate; Greenblatt, 2011; Palmer, 2014; and more generally, on the seeds of unbelief prior to the Enlightenment, also see Davidson, 1992; Vasoli, 1980; Gauna, 1992; Muir, 2007; McClure, 2010.

[30] See her precise definition of Epicureanism, the problematic elastic use of "atheism" as simply a polemical epithet, and her six categories of "proto-atheism," which she identifies as "a label for talking about other ideas that may facilitate atheism without attacking belief directly" (Palmer, 2014, 1–42, esp. at 25). She cites one telling example of the range of unbelief imaginable in the fifteenth century from Marsilio Ficino's *Philebus Commentary*, in which Ficino can easily envision the classical range from atheism, to agnosticism, to the denial of divine Providence: "Quare impietatis causa de religione male sentiunt, quoniam vel, ut Diagoras, Deum negant; vel, ut Protagoras, sitne an non Deus dubitant; vel, ut Democritus et Epicurus, Dei providentiam negant" (Palmer, 2014, 31, 273n92; Ficino, 1975, 233).

[31] Brown, 2010, ix–x.

44   *Doubting the Divine in Early Modern Europe*

Written at the mid-point in Alberti's life, probably between 1443 and the mid 1450s, *Momus* needs to be read in the context of earlier circumstances in Alberti's life and related currents in his thought.[32] In contrast to the image of Alberti as the Renaissance man exemplifying human capability and confidence, Eugenio Garin in the 1970s was the first to argue for a much darker Alberti, a figure unhappy with features of his own life, pessimistic about the human condition in general, and skeptical of the existence of a rational world order.[33] From his university days Alberti had begun to use satire to ease his woes and vent his spleen. A classical comedy written in Bologna in 1426, the *Philodoxeos*, was meant to console himself and teach that "the studious and industrious man, not less than the wealthy and fortunate one is able to obtain glory."[34] In the later 1430s he collected his *Intercenales* (Dinner Pieces), which were Lucianic dialogues and Aesopic fables that often reflected the hardships of his life and voiced cynical views on various segments of society.[35] His dialogue *Erumna* (Affliction) bewails his family's exile and, worse, his mistreatment by his family. A long rumination on fortune, the dialogue ends with Fortune's concession that the

---

[32] Mancini believes that Alberti first conceived the idea of the *Momus* upon his return to Rome in late 1443 with Eugenius IV; as for a *terminus post quem* for the completion, in late 1450 and 1451 Francesco Filelfo writes a poem and letters to Alberti, wanting to learn more about the work (which was rumored to be about him) (Mancini, 1971, 260–70; Alberti, 2003, vii, xxii–xxiii). Mancini's dating, I believe, has been the reason for the common dating of 1443–50, but the references from Filelfo suggest that that work may still be in progress, and a likely allusion to the collapse (in late August 1454) of the tower Nicholas V built at the Vatican suggests a date sometime after that event (C. Smith, 2004, 170n25; Grafton, 2000, 309). As for Filelfo's possibly being a model for the figure of Momus, this certainly is plausible for two reasons: first, an incident in which Momus has his beard torn resembles a mishap that befell Filelfo (Alberti, 2003, 37, 384n17; Ponte, 1981, 81–82); second, as arch-polemicist, Filelfo has been rightly associated by Scott Blanchard and Jeroen De Keyser with the tradition of *parrhesia* (Filelfo, 2013, xxii). On Filelfo and Momus as parallel disaffected exiles, see Simoncini, 1998, 454.

[33] Garin, 1975, 133–96.

[34] From Alberti's *Commentarium Philodoxo fabulae*: Latin cited in Santinello, 1962, 28n, my trans.

[35] For instance, on his orphan status, see the *Pupillus* (Alberti, 1987, 16–18).

learned and the good do in fact languish.[36] In a lengthy consolatory dialogue, the *Theogenius*, written to comfort Leonello d'Este upon the death of his father and to console himself for "adverse fortune," he expounds on the vicissitudes of fortune and the evils of mankind.[37] His fullest psychological treatment, the *Profugiorum ab erumna* (or *Della tranquillità dell'animo*), was, like the *Theogenius*, written during his time in Florence (1439–43) following his bitterness over a failed poetry contest he organized in Florence.[38] As the Latin title of this work suggests, Alberti returns to the problem of "*erumna*." But as the vernacular title reveals, this time he will venture to offer Stoic prescriptions in the spirit of similarly entitled treatises by Seneca and Plutarch, both of whom he drew upon. What is most distinctive here is a particularly Albertian remedy for "inborn, obdurate, grave melancholy" in Book 3, where he stresses the benefits of constant activity and creativity: "Nothing so greatly eradicates my mental vexation, nor so greatly sustains me in quiet and mental tranquility as to occupy my thoughts in some worthy task, to endeavor [*adoperarsi*] in some arduous and rare investigation."[39] The interlocutor declaiming this (Agnolo Pandolfini), who is a surrogate for Alberti himself, explains that this activity would entail not only intellectual and literary exercises but also more tangible creations:

[E]specially at night – when my mental stimulations keep me solicitous and wide awake – in order to divert myself from my bitter cares and sad solicitudes, I am accustomed by myself to investigate and to mentally construct some unheard-of machine for moving and carrying, for fastening and establishing very large and inestimable things. And sometimes it happened that not only did I become calmed in my mental agitations but also I added things rare and most memorable.[40]

[36] Alberti, 1987, 82–90.
[37] Alberti, 1960 73, 2:55. Grayson dates the work roughly to 1438–41, December 26, 1441 being the date of the death of Leonello's father Niccolò (2:411).
[38] On this contest, the *Certame Coronario*, alluded to in the *Profugiorum ab erumna* (Alberti, 1960–73, 2:144–45), see Gadol, 1969, 218.
[39] Alberti, 1960–73, 2:159, 181, my trans.
[40] Alberti, 1960–73, 2:181–82, my trans.

46   *Doubting the Divine in Early Modern Europe*

The dual essence of Alberti's regimen is an eradication of melancholy and the creation of something new and "memorable." When this therapy is then extended to architecture and applied mathematics, Alberti reveals that he is truly describing himself:

And sometimes such [scientific] investigations failing, I mentally composed or built some very compound edifice, and arranged there more orders and numbers of columns, with various capitals and unusual bases, and with convenient links and new grace of cornices and planking. And with similar conscriptions I occupied myself until sleep occupied me. And when I still felt myself not suited to regain my serenity with these remedies, *I engaged some reason in knowing and debating causes and the state of things hidden and concealed by nature.* And above all else, as far as I have experienced, nothing so satisfies me in this, nothing so completely contains and employs me, as mathematical investigations and demonstrations, especially when I reduce them to some useful application in life – as does Battista [Alberti] here, who derived his rudiments and also his elements of painting from mathematics and derived those incredible propositions *de motibus ponderis* [on the motions of weight].[41]

Alberti's response to misfortune and despair relied upon restless industry: pursuing an activism fully grounded in the secular world, he embraced worldly work and glory as antidotes to worldly travail. One feature of this dynamic striving included the penetration of nature's hidden secrets – a nearly Faustian ambition that he condemns as one of the evils of mankind in the *Theogenius*. This paradox may go to the heart of Alberti's fully heroic and anti-heroic vision of human nature, a paradox re-figured in the character of Momus.[42]

Garin argues that the scholarly attempt to reconcile the "dynamic" and "dark" sides of Alberti – by, for instance, claiming that he does fully vanquish *fortuna* with *virtù* – is mistaken.[43] For him, as for some others, the contradiction is played out in the joint ventures of *De re aedificatoria* and *Momus*, written around the same time: one an affirmation of the (literally) constructive Alberti;

---

[41] Alberti, 1960–73, 2:182, my trans. and emphasis. Cf. Tafuri, 1992, 54–55. On Alberti's lost treatise *De motibus ponderis*, see Gadol, 1969, 204.

[42] Alberti, 1960–73, 2:92–94; Boschetto, 1993.

[43] Garin, 1975, esp. 152–56.

the other a grim nihilistic epic of the destructive Alberti.[44] The two
works do in subtle ways speak to each other and to Alberti's vision
of the lone individual vying for autonomy vis-à-vis Nature (whose
domain he conquers with his arts), the Pope (whose architectural
hubris he mocks), and God (whose governance he questions).

Was Alberti's secular self-reliance an indication of attenuated
religious beliefs? Ironically, one measure of his secularism is
thrown into relief by an outlier work that epitomizes traditional
spirituality. An undated "Epistola consolatoria" (before 1440) to
an unknown recipient is the only truly religious work in Alberti's
corpus. He invokes all the conventional religious consolations
for adversity: that tribulation tests patience and increases virtue,
that God is infinitely wise, merciful, and just; that the history of
mankind since Adam – including such figures as Abel, Abraham,
Jacob, Moses, Job, and Jesus – has been characterized by misery
and hardships; that the eventual reward is "eternal glory" and
"true beatitude"; that an individual "should never be contumacious, and should endure with patience his discipline."[45] All this
is rather odd advice from a writer who unceasingly bewailed
his unjust victimization by fortune. In any case, Alberti warns
his addressee that if he dares to consider himself "not iniqui-
tous" he will merit even more punishment than he has already
received.[46] He is even reluctant to use the term "fortune," referring at one point to Joseph's enduring "adverse, as they say, fortune."[47] Clearly, human misfortune and misery are in the divine
plan, as Alberti reminds his friend "to recognize yourself a man
born to endure what everyone must endure who is placed in this
life of mortals."[48] In closing, he once again urges his acquaintance not to be "contumacious" in regard to God's discipline –
the reward for which being that God will feel less need to

[44] Garin, 1975, 152–53 (where he dates the completion of the *Momus* and *De
re aedificatoria* to 1450 and 1452, respectively), 178–80.
[45] Alberti, 1960–73, 2:290–91, my trans.; on Cecil Grayson's dating of the
letter, see 2:445.
[46] Alberti, 1960–73, 2:291.
[47] Alberti, 1960–73, 2:293, my trans.
[48] Alberti, 1960–73, 2:294, my trans.

48 *Doubting the Divine in Early Modern Europe*

"punish you under the yoke."[49] This Christian answer to misfortune contrasts dramatically with the secular laments for and solutions to misfortune Alberti voiced in regard to himself and others in the *Intercenales*, *Theogenius*, and *Profugiorum*. And warning about "contumacy" and rebellion against God makes all the more telling his depiction of Momus's epic rebellion against Jupiter's authority and justice.[50]

An early moment in Alberti's career signaled a notable turning point in his (non-)religious interests. Soon after entering the papal court as a secretary, he was asked by the director of the Curia, Biagio Molin, to launch a series of martyrs' lives. Sometime between 1432 and 1434 Alberti turned out only one such biography, that of the Sardinian Saint Potitus, martyred by Antoninus Pius in the second century. Cecil Grayson and others have noted one especially odd feature of this hagiography: namely, the attention given to explicitly secular sentiments in the story that embody some of Alberti's own views as later expressed in other writings.[51] When the devil appears before Potitus to try to shake his belief, Alberti has him rather persuasively argue "how much the civil life differs from the solitary one; indeed how much would it be preferred to be involved in honors and commands than to grow cold in idle solitude; that [civil life] helps many, this one no one; men are born for the sake of men"; the wealth and goods of this world are divine gifts bestowed for mortals' use; and "fame and glory should be eagerly sought."[52] A far lengthier oration by the emperor Antoninus assails the "new religion" and here especially Alberti's imagined version of the speech condemns sloth in repeated terms: the Christians are

[49] Alberti, 1960–73, 2:295, my trans.
[50] The secular tone of the *Profugiorum* is ironically enhanced by a token paragraph on Christian forbearance against adversity at the end of the second book: this, one paragraph in the midst of seventy-six pages of secular psychological theory (Alberti, 1960–73, 2:157). Also, for other evidence of the relative balance between the religious and secular elements in Alberti's corpus, compare the number of citations of the Bible (*c.* forty-five) to, for instance, citations of Lucian (*c.* 130) (Cardini, 2005, 438–39, 496–97).
[51] See Grayson's comments in Alberti, 1954, 33–36; Guarino, 1955; Paoli, 1999, 90–91, 113–14.
[52] Alberti, 1954, 69–70, my trans.

"slothful (*desidiosus*), idle (*ignavus*), supine" types, who "have learned to pursue no labors, no arts, submit to no civil discipline and languish in sloth (*otium*), solitude, and sleep."[53] Alberti's investment in dramatically presenting the pagan argument for the active life is more vigorous than would be warranted in a work affirming Christian withdrawal and the traditional values of the *contemptus mundi*. And, in fact, some of these arguments on the active life can be found in the *Della famiglia*, the first three books of which were written in this same period.[54]

Not surprisingly, Alberti did not continue with this hagiographical project, as his sentiments ranged too much on the wrong side of this culture war. Depicting a historical era when Roman paganism vied with Christianity – he cites Antoninus' decree that "Jove, Phoebus, Minerva, and all the other remaining gods" be worshiped on pain of punishment – Alberti's curiosity may have been piqued (more than that of the typical classicizing humanist) to consider the very possibility of competing beliefs and worldviews. From this point on, with the exception of one consolatory letter, the language of Christianity and the name of Christ are absent in his writings. Instead, in the *Intercenales*, his Aesopic fables, and *Momus*, he inhabits the world of the classical gods.[55] Yes, these gods were everywhere a vehicle for allegory in Renaissance Italy. And no, their presence obviously did not signal a belief in these gods. But this turn in Alberti's writing does suggest that classical gods like "Jove, Phoebus, Minerva and all the other remaining gods" in fact offered him a more comfortable home to discuss various philosophical, psychological, and even theological issues. Thus, the appearance of Apollo, Mercury, Jupiter, Neptune, Minerva, Fortune, Fame, and Envy in the *Intercenales* and the Aesopic *100 Apologues* would culminate in the universe of gods in *Momus*.[56]

---

[53] Alberti, 1954, 78, my trans.
[54] Grayson in Alberti, 1954, 34–35; Guarino, 1955; Paoli, 1999, 113; but also cf. Grafton, 2000, 64–68, who emphasizes somewhat more the traditional religious views of the work.
[55] Cf. Symonds, 1898, 1:179–80.
[56] For an edition and translation of the *100 Apologues*, see *Renaissance Fables*, 2004, 31–83.

50   *Doubting the Divine in Early Modern Europe*

More revealing than the absence of Christian views was the growing presence of attacks on the clergy or the idea of religion itself in the *Intercenales*. "The Coin" (1438–40) depicts priests consulting the oracle of Apollo as to which god should be worshiped above others. When the oracle fails to deliver the promised verdict, the priests conclude that the oracle meant to convey that there is no god – or, when one notices a simple coin on the altar, they realize that it (namely, greed) should be their god.[57] In "The Cynic" a dialogue between Mercury, Phoebus, and a Cynic assails priests as the first target among several professions, mocking their miters and their hypocrisy, and twice accusing them of indolence.[58] Most scathing, however, is the dialogue "Religio" (*c.* 1434–37), which depicts an exchange between Lepidus ("witty," a pseudonym for Alberti) and Libripeta ("book-hunter," a cover for Niccolò Niccoli). When Lepidus reveals that he has just returned from offering sacrifices in the temple for the gods' favor, Libripeta assumes the role of complete disbeliever, mocking him for his assumption that the gods help those in adversity and presenting a completely non-theistic view of the human condition. Mortals make their own trouble. If mortals would cease causing their own woes, then they would never have need of any gods to rescue them. If it is men who harm other men, men must reconcile, in which case the gods are irrelevant. If gods were the cause of human ills, do not imagine that prayers from puny creatures will deter them. If, as philosophers claim, they manage matters in the heavens, they will not have time or inclination to alter course for us. If they did, they would be slaves to mortals. Therefore, the gods are deafened by the entreaties of the wicked, and the good should be content with their lot and accept adversity.[59] Lepidus ends the exchange with a brief insistence that the gods do care about mortals and are merciful to them. This very skeptical encounter anticipates similar themes in *Momus*, as we shall

[57] Alberti, 1987, 50–51.
[58] Alberti, 1987, 74–75.
[59] Alberti, 1987, 20.

see. In according full belief to himself and disbelief to Niccoli, Alberti might well be engaging in a bit of misdirection.[60] Why else would he give the lion's share of the dialogue to the disbeliever, a strategy that recalls his too vigorous challenges of the devil and the emperor Antoninus in the *Vita S. Potiti*? With its serious questions of human agency vs. divine transcendence (and neglect), the "Religio" clearly shows that Alberti's discussion of religion in a polytheistic framework has obvious applicability to monotheistic belief as well.

If, in fact, the "Religio" was written between 1434 and 1437, it may have borne the influence of Lucian's *On Sacrifices* (probably his most anti-religious work), which was translated by Lapo da Castiglionchio and dedicated to Alberti *c.* 1436–38.[61] This likelihood is further suggested by Lepidus' comment that he has just been offering propitiatory sacrifices. Finally, this same period saw the writing (in October 1437) of Alberti's appraisal of clerical life in his *Pontifex*, a dialogue between two members of the Alberti family who were bishops. This work treated not only the ideals of episcopal service but also the snares of hypocrisy, ambition, and simony in contemporary ecclesiastical life.[62] Thus, from the writing of the *Life of Saint Potitus* in the early 1430s to the "Religio" and *Pontifex* later in the decade, Alberti shows himself to be critical of religious institutions and possibly even religion itself.

---

[60] Alternatively, Grafton, 2000, 63–64, argues that Alberti consistently depicted Niccoli as "irreligious and cynical," and thus the "Religio" could been intended only as an attack on him. But if this were the case, why give Libripeta such persuasive arguments, why give Lepidus such a feeble reply, and why defend the providence of the gods when Alberti so often complained of being the victim of undeserved misfortune?

[61] On the dating of the "Religio" see Ponte, 1981, 29; Alberti, 1987, 227n1. On Lapo da Castiglionchio's translation of Lucian's *On Sacrifices* and *Tyrannicide*, see Luiso, 1899, 282–83; Mattioli, 1980, 61–75. In all, between 1434 and 1438 Lapo translated eight of Lucian's works, beginning with the *On Funerals* and *The Dream, or The Cock*, both of which he dedicated to Eugenius IV (Luiso, 1899, 276–85).

[62] Alberti, 2007, 100–14, 227, 248, 280; Grafton, 2000, 194–97; Paoli, 1999, 92–93.

52   *Doubting the Divine in Early Modern Europe*

Alberti returned to Rome in 1443 and likely over the next decade or more wrote *Momus*. Appraisals of the work are usually tentative or negative. Joan Gadol fairly summed it up: "a confused work ... [that] has given rise to confused interpretations."[63] Critics have found the characters inconsistent, the plot convoluted and "délibérement désordonnée," the story lacking a logical order, the ending forced, the larger point elusive.[64] The chaos of the work, however, may be the point. Alberti takes the germ of Aesop's and Lucian's Momuses and creates a figure by whom "the salvation of mankind, the majesty of the gods and the government of the world were brought almost to a final crisis."[65] Beyond mere critic and doubter, Alberti's Momus becomes the modern world's first great antihero replete with deep recesses of self-reflective interiority and insightful challenges to both the divine and human worlds. Eugenio Garin first realized the implications of the pessimistic chaos of the novel, opposing it the confident positive mentality of the *On the Art of Building*, written at around the same time: "the *Momus* [is] the celestial and terrestrial parody of the *On the Art of Building*. Here is fabricated the city of man, by the measure of reason. There it is established that reason and virtue have no place either in heaven or earth; that no architect can help Jove refashion a world useless and absurd."[66] Certainly, one way to find order in the work is to define and decode its calculated disorder – and Momus is the obvious figure in this as he subverts the political, moral, and theological order.

[63] Gadol, 1969, 222; Mattioli, 1980, 92.

[64] Tenenti, 1974, 324; Gadol, 1969, 222–23, Mattioli, 1980, 91–100.

[65] Alberti, 2003, 199. And see the similar comment at the beginning of Book 2 that Momus "using new and hitherto unknown arts of agitation ... nearly drew men, gods, and the whole machinery of the world into utter calamity" (93).

[66] Garin, 1975, 179, my trans. For the celebration of the architect as the virtual savior of mankind and symbol of the activist conquest of nature, see the preface to the *On the Art of Building* (Alberti, 1988, 3–4); on the polarity between the dark currents in the *Theogenius* and *Momus* vs. the dynamic optimism of the *On the Art of Building*, also see Tafuri, 1992, 52–57; Boschetto, 1993. For other treatments of the work, see Simoncini, 1998; Ponte, 1981, 79–90; Marsh, 1998, 114–29; Blanchard, 1995, 67–71; Kircher, 2012, 225–56.

Renaissance Antihero

The story in its broadest lines (omitting the countless subplots) begins and ends in the heavens. Jupiter has decreed that all the gods create something in a larger effort to properly adorn his new creation, the world. Hateful to the other gods and unable to submit to authority, Momus only reluctantly and unworthily obeys this dictum, challenges Jupiter's decisions regarding mankind, and escapes from heaven when he is charged with treason against Jupiter and ordered by all the gods to be chained "to the spot that held Prometheus!"[67] Fleeing to Tuscany, where he finds an obsequiously pious population, he sows atheism via Lucretian arguments with the result that mortals no longer fear the gods and cease to offer sacrifices. When the gods decide to send Virtue down to recall Momus to the heavens, Momus opts to abandon his frank-speaking ways and become the model of dissimulation, which he enacts first in the human world (turning himself into a girl and teaching the arts of cosmetics) and, back in heaven in Jupiter's court, where he ingratiates himself as the ideal, faux courtier.

When girls begin beseeching the gods for beauty, a rash of votive objects and requests from them swamped the gods. And when Momus falsely reports the widespread unbelief he found on earth, Jupiter despairs at the human world and decides that he needs to remake it. At Momus's suggestion he goes down into the world to investigate matters on his own. His interviews (in disguise) with philosophers finally end with the Epicureans, who frighten him back to heaven. Pleased that he has brought Jupiter even closer to despair, Momus further tries to win his goodwill by collecting a notebook of advice for kings, which Jupiter ignores until the end of the novel. When the other gods come to resent Momus's elevation in the eyes of Jupiter, and Juno and Hercules reveal that it was Momus who spread unbelief among the humans, Momus is fully turned into a woman (having earlier been castrated by Juno's female devotees) and chained to a rock in the sea.[68]

---

[67] Alberti, 2003, 31.

[68] Alberti, 2003, 273. The analogy to Prometheus in being chained to a rock is clear, especially as Alberti indicates that "many deities, principally those of the sea, approached Momus to greet him and lighten the wretchedness of

54   *Doubting the Divine in Early Modern Europe*

As the story continues, the mortals are beset with all manner of natural disaster. They attempt to propitiate the gods by staging elaborate games in a lavishly decorated theater with resplendent statues of the gods. When those are toppled by winds, harming the gods themselves, Jupiter (his nose having been broken) orders the statues righted, lest humans laugh to find no images of them in the theater. With divine dignity so compromised, he finally regrets his decision to remake the world and reads Momus's notebooks on proper kingship. At the end, then, the frank-speaking, exiled critic becomes the source of truth for the addled prince.

In his preface Alberti says that his purpose in the work is to offer "ideas which have in view the shaping of the best sort of prince."[69] Although there is no textual evidence Alberti ever titled or subtitled it thus, one of the two editions of his work that first appeared in 1520 gave its title as *De principe*, and the first Italian translation of 1568 entitled the work "*Momus overo del principe.*"[70] And yet of the 394 paragraphs of this Latin text, only two – the last two – expressly convey a "mirror for princes." *Momus* could be classified in this genre only by inversion – or, even, by deconstruction. In illustrating the travails of the frank-speaking courtier and the sorry triumph of dissimulation, the novel does provide ample negative warnings for the worst sort of prince. Certainly courtly life is a target, but Alberti may have had in mind as well another layer of hierarchy and another setting of the lord–subject dynamic. There are perhaps three plausible contexts for the satire. One is the secular court. Alberti's time in Ferrara at Leonello d'Este's court would have given him firsthand experience in this world. And his treatment of the courtier's life in Book 4 of *On the Family* was almost a primer in this.[71] A second, more likely target is the papal court, which obviously was no less a venue for political maneuvering

---

his spirit, in accordance with the custom they had long practiced in the case of Prometheus' calamity" (277).

[69] Alberti, 2003, 9.

[70] And as Sarah Knight and Virginia Brown point out, this subtitle persisted in modern editions of the work (Alberti, 2003, vii, xxiv [note 1], 399).

[71] Grafton, 2000, 197–200, 206–7.

Renaissance Antihero

and careerism. A third, more submerged target may have been theism itself, in which Alberti resurrects and extends Lucian's critique of Late Antique polytheism to late medieval monotheism. These last two categories can, of course, have considerable overlap, as the pope can function simultaneously as a Renaissance prince and as God's vicar.[72] And naturally these three targets are not mutually exclusive: Alberti could have been critiquing all three, if at varying places in the novel. I want to suggest a reading of the text mainly from the third, theological point of view, extending Garin's and, before him, Grayson's arguments concerning the relative absence of God in Alberti's works.[73] And when the "Jupiter" of the text is read variously as

---

[72] Tenenti, 1974, 327.

[73] Grayson, 1998, 139; Garin, 1975, 153, where at note 34 he comments: "Sul silenzio dell'Alberti a proposito di Dio dovrebbe farsi più longo discorso, ma è difficile non rimanerne colpiti." I hope that my reading will provide this "longer discourse." Indeed, Alberti's occasional references to God can seem forced and perfunctory. For instance, in the *Profugiorum ab erumna*, in which Alberti presents wholly classical and secular remedies for misfortune and despair, he ends the second book with a rather unconvincing, token nod to God: "But since we come to this most religious church, let us enter to salute the name and figure of God, who helps above all the writings and warnings of the most prudent writers; let us pray that he does not bring us any harsh condition of living and lends us good health of mind, good will, full strength to our limbs, and concedes to us a virile and steady mind to sustain and endure each blow and burden of adverse things" (Alberti, 1960–73, 2:157, my trans.). This terse paragraph, standing alone among seventy-six pages of secular psychological theory, is hardly persuasive. A similar disconnect between Alberti's thought and traditional Christian spirituality regarding the therapeutic power of music appears in Book 3 of the *Profugiorum*: "Not without benefit was established that most ancient custom – which later the Council of Arles [in 452] prohibited – that funeral mourners keep their vigil singing. I believe that the good ancients did this in order to divert the mind from those sad thought of dying. But to our very religious-minded folks [*nostri religiossimi*] perhaps the remembrance of being mortal, similar to that one who is dead seemed more useful; it seemed a more pious office to recognize oneself as mortal and falling hour by hour, than to give oneself over to any levity or lust. But to dispute of this would not be appropriate here" (2:178, my trans.). But he just did rule on it, dismissing the *memento mori* and *contemptus mundi* of traditional spirituality that was still very much alive in humanist predecessors such as Petrarch (on which see McClure, 1991, 22–24).

56   *Doubting the Divine in Early Modern Europe*

the pope and as God, Alberti's novel becomes a critique of both institutional religion and traditional theology.[74]

The earlier mythography of Momus – for instance, in Aesop's Babrius 59 – alludes to his departure from heaven but does not fully offer an account of his fall. Alberti wants to fill in this gap and assign Momus an even cosmic agency:

> Tradition has it that because of outrageous insolence (*procacitas*) of his tongue, he was, by universal agreement and consent, expelled and barred from the ancient councils and assemblies of the gods above, yet, through the unheard of wickedness of his disposition and the worst kinds of trickery, he was strong enough to drag all the gods, all heaven and finally the whole machinery of the world to the point of ultimate catastrophe.[75]

Alberti provides the narrative in such a way as to simultaneously demonize and heroize Momus as both a Luciferian and Promethean figure. When Jupiter orders all the gods to create something for his newly made world, Momus, "by nature ... an aggressive obstructionist,"[76] refuses at first and only relents to create wasps, hornets, cockroaches, and the like. He then turns

---

[74] Crediting Simoncini for first noting hints of the Apocalypse in the work (on which see, e.g., Simoncini, 1998, 408), Christine Smith offers an intriguing reading of *Momus* as a parody of the Book of Revelation, which ends with God's decision to make a new world. Recognizing the connection between God and Jupiter, and Nicholas V and Jupiter, she sees this work in terms of "biblical black humor" (C. Smith, 2004, 163) and explores its more serious theological content: "*Momus* is not funny. It is, perhaps, Alberti's most desperately serious and deeply religious work as well as a devastating critique of Nicholas V's pontificate" (165). Her central argument is that Alberti was attacking the papacy's (specifically Nicholas V's) "blasphemous" attempt to impinge upon the divine realm and presume to act as God. She sees Alberti as a reform-minded figure who is still very invested in the "divine majesty'" (177). In my reading, I explore the theological parallels to a different end: to show Alberti's doubts about divine majesty. As for another, quite different, theological reading, Rinaldo Rinaldi (1999) implausibly argues that the *Momus* should be read in the vein of Church Fathers such as Tertullian, Lactantius, and Augustine, as a piece of Christian apologetics against paganism: a nonsensical thesis, given that paganism had been vanquished for a millennium (and Alberti would hardly have wasted his satirical wit on a dead issue) and given that features of contemporary Christian devotion (such as images) neatly re-figured pagan worship and were the likely target of Alberti's satire.

[75] Alberti, 2003, 13–15.

[76] Alberti, 2003, 13.

to criticize the other gods' creations and, varying the names of the gods in Babrius 59, derides the cow of Pallas Athena, the house of Minerva, and the humans of Prometheus.[77] Whereas in Aesop Momus was offering criticisms in a contest between gods in making something beautiful, in Alberti this is linked to a more fundamental (and potentially theological) creation story. Moreover, Alberti adds a fourth gift from the goddess Fraus (Fraud), who creates charms for women, including the "arts of insincerity."[78] This addition reveals not only Alberti's misogyny – on display elsewhere in the novel – but also his preoccupation with fraud and dissimulation, as evidenced by Momus's criticism of the creation of man: "For man's mind had been hidden in his chest, among his internal organs, whereas it ought to have been placed upon his lofty brow, in the open space of his face."[79] This theme of dissimulation (vs. frank-speaking) is a major one in the story. When Momus is forced to flee the heavens for his *parrhesia* (or, in Latin, *procacitas*), he assumes the ways of a corrupt court and corrupt world by perfecting the art of dissimulation. In one of his longest soliloquies, Momus even presents what is in effect a primer for "practicing simulation and dissimulation."[80]

[77] In Babrius 59, Pallas made the house, Poseidon the bull, and Zeus the humans.

[78] Alberti, 2003, 17. Oddly, whereas Momus's criticisms of the first creations (of the Aesop tale) are detailed, no explicit criticism of Fraus's creation is presented.

[79] Alberti, 2003, 17: this is a slight variation of Babrius 59, in which Momus complained that there should have been a grill or window over man's chest to reveal his true heart; but the larger point about openness and sincerity is the same.

[80] Alberti, 2003, 100–5. Oddly, in this speech and once before (44–45) Alberti has Momus depicting his earlier persona as a "disagreeable critic" with an "odious keenness to scold and criticize" as a mask as well, to be replaced now with another mask to suit the circumstances (100–1). This would seem to suggest that *all* of Momus's public selves were masks (and perhaps this is how he viewed the human condition, as he has a scene in Book 4 in which Charon reveals that people reach the other side of the Acheron only after their masks have been dissolved by the river's vapor [310–11]), though the thrust of the novel generally suggests that he was one "imbued with a perverse nature" (12–13), that the fawning mask he takes on is out of character, as he wonders how he "cannot not be Momus ... cannot not be who I have always been without sacrificing my freedom and my consistency" (44–45),

58 *Doubting the Divine in Early Modern Europe*

Certainly, these arts of flattery and deceit were ever at work in court life, and Alberti is prescient in anticipating the literature of courtly hypocrisy that will flower in the following centuries, as Torquato Tasso indicted it (in his *Malpiglio overo de la corte* of the 1580s) and Torquato Accetto prescribed it (in his *Della dissimulazione onesta* of 1641).[81] Dissimulation is the perfect antithesis of *parrhesia* and a fitting target for Alberti's satire of the courtier personality. It could even be Alberti's refiguring of original sin, given that insincerity (*ars fingendi*) is the quality shared and dispensed by the female Fraus, an Eve-like figure who helps orchestrate Momus's fall in Book 1.[82]

As this last comment suggests, and as Stefano Simoncini and Christine Smith have proposed, the Olympian allegory of Alberti's novel may well have biblical and theistic undercurrents, with Jupiter as surrogate for God, Hercules for Christ (or his vicar), and Momus as Satan.[83] A clue to his submerged allegory may come in the preface, where Alberti opens by referring to God as "The prince and maker of creation, Best and Greatest God" (*Optimus et Maximus Deus*).[84] This is the same epithet by which he describes Jupiter (*Iuppiter optimus maximus*) on several occasions.[85] Although transpositions between

---

and one who had been "in the habit of matching my beliefs to the truth, my zeal to my true allegiance, my words and my expressions to the innermost, sincerest workings of my heart" (336–37). On the theme of simulation vs. the "fenestrated chest" (open heart, sincerity) in *Momus* and its religious aftermath in the next century, see Simoncini, 1998, 413–27.

[81] Tasso, 1998; on which McClure, 2008, 782; Accetto, 1997. On dissimulation and sincerity, also see Zagorin, 1990; Martin, 1997; Tafuri, 1987, 69.

[82] Alberti, 2003, 16–31. Momus and Fraus clearly have a rather bizarre love–hate relationship: Momus is smitten with her, but they lay traps for each other, her ruse resulting in Momus's planned trial and necessary escape from the heavens. This is but one of the many contradictory features of Alberti's story. Momus, who hates dissimulation, nonetheless is in love with Fraud and even admires her devious ways. Their only logical tie is that they are both troublemakers. Still, as his beloved, as a source of the key sin in Alberti's story (insincerity), and as the cause of his downfall, she could be seen as an Eve figure.

[83] See notes 6 and 74 above and note 105 below. On the classical and biblical roots of the rebel god and Satan, see Forsyth, 2003, 24–76; Revard, 1980.

[84] Alberti, 2003, 2–3.

[85] Alberti, 2003, 14, 20, 26.

pagan and Christian terminology for the chief deity could be found elsewhere in writings of the period, the juxtaposition of the functions and titles phrasing for Jupiter and God (both "princes" and "creators," both "optimus" and "maximus") may be telling here – especially given that Alberti depicts Jupiter in such a consistently bad light and as such an inept creator.[86] In fact, Alberti may be giving a hint at the very start of his novel that his depiction of Jupiter is a hidden commentary on God. The explicit comments in the preface belie this, as he says that he is using the gods as allegories, that his work is simply about the political realm, and that maybe some other time he will "write of sacred matters and gods."[87] But this claim may be a bit of misdirection, as the theological implications of the novel slowly unfold.

Additionally, there is a strange tension presented in the opening two paragraphs of the work that seems to pit Alberti, the creator, against God, the Creator. In the first paragraph *Optimus et Maximus Deus* is described as having given gifts to all the natural elements, creatures, and souls of the world, but he wanted to "be the only one possessed of an undiminished, perfect and concentrated virtue whose equal you will never find. This uniqueness, unless I am mistaken, must be deemed the primary characteristic of divinity. Only God is uniquely one and uniquely set apart from all else."[88] His God is a rather

---

[86] As for other such transpositions in the Renaissance, Boccaccio, for instance, in the *Filocolo* fully conflates the classical and Christian in retelling Satan's rebellion against God, the creation of mankind, and Christ's intervention in terms of Jove (God), Pluto (Satan), and Prometheus (Adam) (Boccaccio, 1985, 6–7, 11–12, 473n4; Symonds, 1898, 1:104), and, more recently, in his *Commentationes Florentinae de exilio*, Francesco Filelfo three times refers to "*Christus optimum maximus*," similarly adapting "*Jupiter Optimus Maximus*" (which was his name in his temple on the Capitoline Hill) though not using both in the same text, as does Alberti (Filelfo, 2013, 184, 214, 362, 456n3). Also, in the early seventeenth century, Giovan Battista Andreini will refer to Jove as "sommo Padre" and to God as "Padre Eterno," though again in different works, respectively the *Dialogo fra Momo e la Verità* and *L'Adamo* (Andreini, 1612, [A2r]; Andreini, 2007, passim).

[87] Alberti, 2003, 9.

[88] Alberti, 2003, 3.

60   *Doubting the Divine in Early Modern Europe*

proud and possessive prince and creator. The second paragraph explains that this is why the ancients thought that anything rare or unusual (in nature or in mankind) was practically divine. Alberti then reveals that in his unusual work that will join humor with real-life truth he aims to be that kind of "man who introduces new, unheard-of, and unorthodox material (*praeter omnium opinionem*)," who strives to be "a member of this rare genus of humankind."[89] There is implied an agon in this preface between a proud God (jealous of His singular virtue) and an almost defiant Alberti seeking to become "*quasi divina*" via his own creation.[90] Wittingly or unwittingly, Alberti sets himself up against God, just as his story sets Momus against Jupiter.

Fittingly, Momus's first criticism of Jupiter concerns his wisdom as creator. Girlfriend "Fraud," recognizing that Momus is "too much of a free spirit," sets him up to be overheard voicing his criticisms of Jupiter's plans in regard to mankind. Having initially created humans with an Edenic bliss, Jupiter incurred the wrath of the other gods, who resented this new race of beings, so he then decided to inflict anxiety, fear, disease, and death upon them so that the gods no longer envied mortals.[91] His tongue unleashed, Momus criticizes Jupiter's creation and mistreatment of mortals. His critique suggests a triangulation of Jupiter, the gods, and mortals that anticipates (or informs) Milton's triangulation of God, angels, and mortals:

At first, of course, Best and Greatest Jupiter was overjoyed that he had created men: if he became angry, rightly or wrongly, with us gods, he

---

[89] Alberti, 2003, 4–5. As for his quest for rarity, just as his work will be a type of anti-"mirror for princes," so too his preface is an anti-preface, in which he claims that there will be no praises of the dedicatee. Alberti wants to create a new genre that rejects even the traditions of literary patronage. He is Momus the literary modernist.

[90] For the statement that the ancients thought that "all things rare and unique" were "quasi divina," see Alberti, 2003, 2–3. Alberti in the *Profugiorum ab erumna* similarly has one of his interlocutors praise the psychological theory in the work as "quasi divina" (Alberti, 1960–73, 2:162); also in the *De commodis litterarum atque incommodis* he refers to the "ingenium pene divinum" required for learned pursuits (Alberti, 1971, 96).

[91] Alberti, 2003, 20–21.

could push them forward as our rivals to excite our envy. But when he realized it would be better for heavenly homes to be occupied by their old inhabitants rather than by an upstart crowd of mortal gods, he decided to keep men down there, to pour out his raging floods of anger on their heads, and to run riot against them with his bestial savagery. Hence he heaped up lightning, thunder, pestilence and everything wretched human souls find harsh and unbearable, also anxiety and fear and every evil that can be devised and fashioned, and inflicted them all upon mankind at once.[92]

This portrait of divine malice seems to have ventured rather far from the purely political allegory Alberti claims to be writing. In fact, the Fall of man has been re-written without the agency of human sin or transgression. Instead, it revolves around an act of divine regret or afterthought. And while this remotely *could* reflect the power politics of a prince at court, it more plausibly ponders the theological purposes of a heavenly creator. As Garin first suggested, Alberti is drawing here on the *Hermetica*, the Neoplatonic writings of the second and third centuries CE, available to Alberti in Latin excerpts from Stobaeus (*c.* 500 CE). In excerpt 23, the *Kore Kosmou*, Momus warns Hermes Trismegistus that this new creature, man, will be ceaseless in his investigations and exploitation of nature and in probing the heavens, and thus advises that this creature needs to be restrained by hardships.[93] In this account, Momus is the originator of man's woes, but in Alberti's it is Jupiter who has imposed these miseries as an afterthought and Momus who rightly criticizes him for it. Alberti thus has given this story a twist of divine malevolence, and any responsibility of human hubris evident in the *Kore Kosmou* is missing here.[94]

[92] Alberti, 2003, 27.
[93] *Hermetica* 484–85; Garin, 1975, 149–50; Yates, 1969, 215–17. Momus also has a destructive role in the human world in the Homeric *Cypria*, fragment 1, in which he advises Zeus to solve the overpopulation of mortals on earth by orchestrating the Trojan War (*Greek Epic Fragments* 80–83).
[94] The notion that humans were beginning to challenge the gods was found earlier in the *Kore Kosmou*, where Isis reveals that they "began to array themselves in presumptuous audacity, and transgress God's commands; for they sought to vie with the gods in heaven, claiming nobility equal to theirs" (*Hermetica* 471). In *Momus*, Alberti does not mention this role of human

62   *Doubting the Divine in Early Modern Europe*

Alberti even takes divine malice one step further. He has Momus complain that Jupiter, after visiting misery upon humans, gives them two options: death or the rather futile hope to vie against him. This second option seems to define an agon between a malicious god and striving man: "If ... it avails them [mortals] to fight, O heedless Jupiter, you have not refused these little men the patience to beat you, *the angry and heavily armed prince of the gods!*"[95] For Alberti, I think, the human battle against such a god – and against melancholy and death – would be the activist striving to be "quasi divina" through creative endeavor, an agon implied in his preface. Finally, resurrecting Lucian's theme in *Zeus Refuted*, Momus mocks Jupiter for having empowered Fate to rule over the stars and even potentially over himself.[96] This theme of Fate or Destiny over the gods and their providence is an Epicurean staple in Cicero's *De natura deorum* and in Lucian. In numerous ways, then, Alberti depicts a god with clay feet: one who might have foolishly outsourced his power to higher forces, and one who maliciously uses humans as a potential counterweight to other gods and later (under pressure) subjects them to divine punishment. Alberti may be drawing upon the zero-sum power politics of the Renaissance court – if one faction rises, another falls – but these themes of human manipulation by a fickle god suggest that he might be brooding as well about a flawed theodicy in regard to the combative relationship between humans and God. Finally,

hubris in provoking divine punishment, though he did make use of this Hermetic theme of human hubris in other contexts, such as in the earlier *Theogenius* (on which see below). Alberti may also be blending some of the Lucifer story into this scene from the *Hermetica*, in that the motive for Jupiter's persecution of mankind was owing to the envy of the other gods of the paradisiacal situation of newly created mankind. Satan's envy of mankind would be a part of the Lucifer myth (Revard, 1980, 67–85; and Chapter 4 below). In any case, Alberti invests the Momus "Fall" story with consequential elements involving the relationship between humans and gods. He also takes the theme of divine malice one step further.

[95] Alberti, 2003, 29, my emphasis. As we shall see in Chapter 5, Milton uses this same in *Paradise Lost* in regard to God's allowing the rebel angels to fight him in vain.

[96] Alberti, 2003, 20–22, 28–29.

Renaissance Antihero   63

when Momus reveals to Fraud that Fate could well allow some other god to unseat Jupiter, that seals his doom. The rebel god is convicted as a traitor, at which point he flees. Alberti has thus written the story of Momus's Fall from the heavens, endowing it with serious political and theological heft. The victim status of this (heroic) god is revealed when the others gods clamor that Momus be chained to Prometheus' rock.

When Momus decamps from the heavens, he goes to Italy, where he finds a "race wholly devoted to religion."[97] In the guise of a philosopher he proceeds to preach atheism,

> arguing that the gods' power was nothing other than a vain, useless, and trifling fabrication of superstitious minds. He said that the gods were not to be found, especially gods who took any interest in human affairs. Or maybe, in the end, there was only one deity common to all living things, Nature, whose calling and labor it was not only to govern mankind, but also flocks, birds, fish and similar creatures.[98]

Alberti has taken Momus's role in Lucian's *Zeus Rants*, where he *reports* of human doubts about the gods, and made him an *agent* of unbelief in a very religious Italian world.[99] These Epicurean themes, found in the *Zeus Rants*, are similar to those Alberti's interlocutor Libripeta voiced in his "Religio." The replacement of the gods with Nature (capitalized) would seem to be a particularly Albertian addition, perhaps inspired by his reading of Lucretius' *De rerum natura*, which had recently been rediscovered (in 1417) by Alberti's friend, Poggio Bracciolini, who lent it to Niccolò Niccoli (the alter ego of Libripeta in the

---

[97] Alberti, 2003, 31.

[98] Alberti, 2003, 33.

[99] How Alberti gained access to the *Zeus Rants* is an intriguing and as yet unanswered question. When teaching in Florence in 1397 to 1400, Manuel Chrysoloras apparently included some of Lucian's works: an anonymous student transcribed a set of Lucian's pieces (*Charon, Slander, The Dead Come to Life, or the Fisherman, Icaromenippus, Timon*, and a partial *Zeus Rants*). The first five were complete and contained Latin glosses; the last was transcribed only up to *Zeus Rants* 17 (before Momus makes his appearance at 19) and did not contain any Latin glosses (E. Berti, 1987, 3–5; Marsh, 1998, 117n34). Perhaps Alberti gained knowledge of the piece via Lapo da Castiglionchio.

64   *Doubting the Divine in Early Modern Europe*

"Religio").[100] Garin noted the prominence of nature and the "machina orbis" in both *Momus* and *On the Art of Building* in conjunction with the notable absence of God.[101] We are perhaps at the beginning of the early modern progression toward Spinoza's "Deus sive Natura."

The discourse on atheism mushrooms in Book 2, where Momus, newly recalled to heaven, falsely reports an epidemic of unbelief he found among mortals during his exile. In one of the longest speeches (fifteen paragraphs) in the novel, Alberti lays out the many arguments against a benevolent or providential theism. Some of these repeat Lucretian arguments – that the world is a product of atoms randomly colliding – but he adds political and ecclesiastical arguments not found in Lucian's similar speeches by Momus or Damis in *Zeus Rants*. Namely, that some secret unbelievers simply feign belief "so that they could use the fear of the gods to fortify and render impregnable their arms, their camps and their empires" – a stronger version of an argument Machiavelli later made in his *Discourses on Livy* 1.11–15. Or, that some "preten[d] to be interpreters of the god" – presumably a swipe at the clergy.[102] Momus's longest account concerns the opinion of intellectuals who argue that the gods show no concerns for mortals' woes, that they claim death to be a relief from woes but do not partake of it themselves, and that they allow the wicked to prosper and the good to languish. In regard to this last point, Alberti goes far beyond Lucian's (and others') complaints about a flawed theodicy concerning just and unjust deserts for individuals to portray a *universal* human misery, made all the more relevant by the frivolous reason given earlier for Jupiter's dispensing human woe (i.e., to appease envious gods):

O, how the human race is loathed by the gods! As well as those dreadful evils I've listed, they also give us grief, fever, disease, bitter woes in our

---

[100] Brown, 2010, 1; on Alberti's direct and indirect citation of Lucretius in the *Theogenius*, *De re aedificatoria*, *Della famiglia*, and *Momus*, see ibid., 7–8.

[101] Alberti, 2003, 92; and for Alberti's assertion regarding the world that "totam hanc machinam deum esse" (214); Garin, 1975, 153–54; on Alberti's view of nature, see Paoli, 1999, esp. 139–42.

[102] Alberti, 2003, 155; Machiavelli, 1979, 207–18.

hearts, stormy emotional outbursts, and brutal psychological torment! Alas for us mortals, plunged into extreme wretchedness under the heaviest of burdens [*erumnae*]. Alas for us, whom the gods so torture, so afflict with daily evils, that we are never free from calamity. Even in the midst of continual, bitter misfortunes some new form of suffering is always rising up to threaten us. To that extent mankind always has to live in sorrow and lamentation.[103]

Alberti's own bouts with despair and *erumna* surely animate this diatribe, which is a particularly secular type of *contemptus mundi*: that is, not a "contempt of world" in anticipation of other-worldly salvation, but a "misery of the human condition" maliciously imposed by gods who not only do not exercise protective providence over humans but actually torture them. The closing of the speech clinches the autobiographical dimension: "Will it not be allowable for us to get angry at so much wretchedness? For us to believe the gods above have no concern for mortals, or hate us? ... Let's stop being so foolish and bothering them with pointless rites. The gods are taken up with their own pleasures; *they hate ingenious and active people*."[104]

This, I think, is Alberti's clearest profession of anger at the divine in this work. The gods hate his ilk: the ever-active, ever-working, ever-creative mortal. All of his earlier psychological writings that profess his ethic and remedy of work converge in this statement of humans' alienation from the divine. In all, this lengthy speech by Momus goes far beyond the doubts posed in Lucian's *Zeus Rants*: it is very likely a testament to Alberti's own agnosticism or unbelief. Why else replay this scene in such detail? Lucian took aim at the last gasp of polytheism in Late Antiquity; Alberti renewed the motif with such vigor for a new target. The inescapable woes and sufferings of mankind enumerated in this speech might be Alberti's "contumacious" – and thereby impious – objection to the miseries of

---

[103] Alberti, 2003, 162–63.

[104] Alberti, 2003, 167, my emphasis. In one of his references to God in the *Della famiglia*, he condemns the Epicurean idea that "the highest happiness of God consists in doing nothing" (Alberti, 2004, 133), but this would seem to be the desire of Jupiter in *Momus*, who wanted *otium* above all else (Alberti, 2003, 22–23).

66 *Doubting the Divine in Early Modern Europe*

mortals depicted in his religious "Epistola consolatoria," which proper believers should recognize to be a part of the purifying and testing justice of God. Perhaps Alberti thinks this divine plan for mortals is a flawed one. If Jupiter and God are interchangeable, this might explain why Alberti had Jupiter thoughtlessly and maliciously visit hardship and woes upon mankind merely to appease other gods' envy.

A second, and not incompatible, meaning of Momus's speech here is that Alberti is targeting the institutional Church. The figure who rises up to challenge Momus's report on worldly unbelief is Hercules, a figure who might represent Christ – as a mortal son of a god – but almost certainly represents the voice of Christian theology in rebutting Momus.[105] He protests that humans recognize the "greatness and majesty" of the gods and appreciate the divine gifts of human intelligence, reason, and memory; that "learned men" (clergy) are right to convey these truths and have rightly "been responsible for the honor paid to the gods, for the performance of religious ceremonies and for the cultivation of piety, holiness, and virtue."[106] Finally, in a moment of powerful irony, Hercules defends the philosophers whom Momus has misrepresented as agnostics and atheists, and claims that it is philosophers (in this case meaning theologians) who "have succeeded in bringing it about that no one may not perceive and confess the power and divinity of the gods, and conform himself to good morals and a right standard of living."[107] He argues that in fact "the gods *love* this clan of scholars."[108] Alberti has clearly moved the argument to the world of contemporary theology. And in having Hercules defend these intellectuals, Alberti virtually declares that the divine realm itself

---

[105] For the suggestion that Hercules could represent Christ in *Momus*, see Simoncini, 1998, 408, who views the work as a duel between Hercules ("antropocentrica … improntata a un conformistico umanesimo civile e cristiano") and Momus as Antichrist ("naturalistica, pessimistica, vagamente lucreziana e avveroistica"). In my reading, I want to explore more fully than Simoncini or C. Smith the possible analogy that Jupiter is God.

[106] Alberti, 2003, 173.

[107] Alberti, 2003, 175.

[108] Alberti, 2003, 175.

is a creation of theologians, a radical assertion of unbelief. It is surely no accident that immediately after Hercules presents this solid defense of the institutional Church, a triumphal arch that Juno ordered to be made from the endless votive offerings of mortals collapses. Grafton suggests that this incident may have referred to the collapse of the tower (Torrione) that Nicholas V had built adjacent to the papal palace.[109] In any case, the allegory suggests the irony of a collapse of an institution buoyed up by the weak claims of the clergy and theologians.

The institutional allegory becomes even more pronounced in Books 3 and 4. When the humans are besieged with disasters (Heat, Hunger, Fever) they decide to propitiate the gods with games and a "grand theatrical spectacle," and lavishly decorated statues were put in a theater.[110] This elaborate project and especially Jupiter's plans to rebuild the world, it has been suggested, likely allude to the plans of Nicholas V to rebuild Rome and St. Peter's.[111] Though some have argued that Alberti may have been the pope's advisor in his building plans, Manfredo Tafuri cites one document suggesting that he discouraged Nicholas's plan to rebuilt St. Peter's. In that case, *Momus* might have been intended in part to mock this project, which, when revived in the following century by Julius II, of course eventually led to the indulgence controversy and the start of the Reformation.[112] In any case, the plan for a lavish spectacle to appease the gods certainly is meant to satirize modern devotion: staging games for the gods alluding to celebration of saints' days; statues of the gods to statues of the saints in churches; and votive offerings to the gods to prayers to the saints.[113]

---

[109] Grafton, 2000, 309; if this association is true, it would mean that the *Momus* was not completed until at least 1454, the date of the Torrione collapse.

[110] Alberti, 2003, 263.

[111] Alberti, 2003, xxii; Grafton, 2000, 306; C. Smith, 2004, 171–75. As for the architectural allegory and the connection to Alberti's *De re aedificatoria*, note the language when Jupiter announces his rebuilding plan: "alius erit nobis adeo coaedificandus mundus. Aedificabitur, parebitur!" (Alberti, 2003, 186).

[112] Grafton, 2000, 313; Tafuri, 1992, 63.

[113] As Sarah Knight and Virginia Brown point out, there are precedents for criticism of votive prayers and offerings in Seneca's *Ad Lucilium* 10. 5 (but this only a brief allusion) and Lucian's *On Sacrifices* (Seneca, 1917, 1:58;

68   *Doubting the Divine in Early Modern Europe*

Also, it is possible that Hercules, aside from his role as a Christ figure or as a priest/theologian, may also represent a saint figure. In presenting the philosophers' unbelief in Book 2, Momus refers to those mortals who "have risen to augment the number of gods."[114] Though this passage could refer to the ancient theory of Euhemerism (the idea that all gods are simply former mortal heroes) or to Lucian's criticism of demigods like Hercules who have entered the pantheon, it could also refer to Christian sainthood or the sacral status of the clergy. Momus suggests that "the wickedness and folly of mankind have added still more occasions for some to be lifted up to the height of the highest gods," and in the novel Fortune teaches Hercules how to get to heaven (unworthily) without the fire of Virtue.[115] In all, Alberti seems to have fully moved Lucian's critique of polytheism to an attack on the contemporary Church with its surfeit of offerings, ceremonies, spectacles, dubious gods (saints), images, "theaters" of superficial belief, and institutional grandeur.

In Book 4 Alberti offers his most scathing mockery of mindless belief and likely professes his own religious stance. Wanting to witness the theatrical spectacle about to be staged for them, the gods decide to turn themselves into their own statues and hide the statues elsewhere. The conflation of the gods with images is a rather clear commentary on the materializing of piety that reformers from Erasmus to iconoclasts such as Andreas Karlstadt and Ulrich Zwingli would assail in the next century. And while this has some precedent in the statues of gods that Lucian depicts in the convening of *The Parliament of the Gods*, Alberti develops the theme with a radical twist that goes to the heart of religious belief.[116] An unbelieving philosopher and actor named Oenops, who had been converted

Alberti, 2003, 387nn1 and 5), but the practice of intercessory prayers to the saints and votive offerings certainly was at such a level in Alberti's time to provoke Erasmus's criticism in the *Praise of Folly* in the next century (Erasmus, 1989b, 41–43, 48).

[114] Alberti, 2003, 165.

[115] Alberti, 2003, 79–80, 165.

[116] On materialism and such statues, see Branham, 1989, 169–71; Marsh, 1998, 119.

Renaissance Antihero 69

by Momus's atheistic proselytizing, is captured by robbers and taken to the cave where the god Stupor has hidden his statue. When the robbers see this statue as a divine presence, they are frightened and flee. As a result, Oenops becomes a believer and soon threatens a drunken slave who is urinating on the statue of Jupiter. This slave is astonished that "You [Oenops], a man who has always denied the existence of the gods – are you now going to worship a lifeless statue and imaginary likenesses?"[117] When Oenops' friends ask why he has had this sudden conversion, he names Stupor and says he wants to thank him, at which point his colleagues take him to view the statues (but really gods) in the theater. When Oenops sees Stupor and begins praying to him, while his friends mock the disguised god, Stupor – the present god, not the image back in the cave – remarks on the folly of human belief: "What can I say about this evil among mortals? They mock a god who's right in front of them, while they [the earlier robbers] fear and dread the likeness of an absent deity!"[118] Humans cannot distinguish between the image of the divine and the divine itself. Even worse:

This one fellow [Oenops], on the mere suspicion of a divine blessing, blotted out his longstanding disbelief in the gods and the obstinacy of his disbelief. These other men, though reminded by the sun, the moon, and similar manifest signs of divinity which they profess they can and ought to believe in, refuse to acknowledge them.[119]

This last comment is rather oblique, but Alberti seems to be saying that human belief is misdirected: Oenops naïvely becomes a believer in a "Stupid" god, whereas others surrounded by the signs of divinity *in nature* fail to worship that true source of the divine. That Alberti would seem to be mocking institutional

---

[117] Alberti, 2003, 187. This burlesque goes further. When the drunk breaks wind before the statue of Stupor, claiming he is offering his sacred rites, his "burnt offerings," Oenops beats him up. The drunk marvels that the former atheist – now deluded believer – mistreated him for imitating his unbelief.

[118] Alberti, 2003, 291; on this incident, cf. Di Stefano, 2002, 523–24.

[119] Alberti, 2003, 293. It is worth noting that Alberti's language of unbelief here is "contra deos opinio" (292).

70   *Doubting the Divine in Early Modern Europe*

religion in favor of Nature is buttressed by a section in Book 3 that depicts first Jupiter and then Apollo surveying philosophers on earth. Here the greatest amount of time is spent with the materialist Democritus, who closes the interview with a question that Apollo cannot answer: namely, "where are the gods going to put the raw material the world is made of, if they decide to destroy it?"[120] That Democritus and Lucretius are two of the key influences in *Momus* reflects the materialist, naturalist alternative that Alberti turns to in opposition to the religion manufactured by theologians and enforced by the clergy.

In a second incident in Book 4, Alberti joins this instance of *deluded* belief with an example of *feigned* belief – an example in which, I believe, he reveals himself. Curious to see human affairs before Jupiter scraps the current world, Charon, ferryman of souls, comes up for a visit. He enlists the shade of a philosopher named Gelastus to be his guide. As Garin noted, Gelastus ("laughable") is, like Lepidus in the earlier works, an alter ego of Alberti himself. This role is made clear later when Gelastus recounts his life story to Charon: he was "battered by perennial poverty and by continual injuries both my enemies and my own family inflicted upon me"; he suffered the envy of rivals and deserved better for his cultivation of letters; and he "employed every effort and all my devotion and zeal so that I would never regret the expenditure of my time."[121] This most unlucky, yet ever diligent striver perfectly matches Alberti's self-perception. This identification makes all the more important two exchanges with Charon. In one, Charon, admiring the beauty of the natural world, asks Gelastus about the origins of such wonders. Gelastus proceeds to explain the "rerum natura" (recalling Lucretius' title), and when he finishes Charon essentially labels him a Lucretian Epicurean: "So, what you're telling me is, everything is generated by means of reciprocal and harmonious struggle,

---

[120] Alberti, 2003, 253. Democritus even explains the origins of anger in a materialist sense (249). On Democritus in Alberti see Garin, 1975, 135; Boschetto, 1993, 4–34.

[121] Alberti, 2003, 339; Garin, 1975, 154, 162.

Renaissance Antihero

and under normal circumstances things change because of the aggregation and disaggregation of minute particles."[122] Once again, then, Epicurean thought is evident in this as in all three of the previous books of the novel.

Gelastus' Epicurean views take on theological significance when he and Charon reach the "massive structure" [St. Peter's basilica?] of the "theater ... used for acting out stories" that contained the statues of the gods.[123] The analogy of the theater as church, actors as clergy, stories as theology, and statues as icons of saints seems undeniable. Then, there is a key exchange. Viewing the theater and its decorations, Charon asks Gelastus how all "these man-made constructions" can possibly compare to the beauty of a flower, that is, to nature? How can the performances in this theater (or church) – "since you claim that in this place they perform publicly many things which contribute to the good life" – really profit anyone? Gelastus explains that when a crowd fills the seats of the theater, "*as they say*, only a divinity makes this many people gather together," and though the individual gods may seem worthless, the aggregate of the gods inevitably inspires respect.[124] "As they say (*uti aiunt*)," Gelastus explains, as if this is merely conventional wisdom. Is he creating a separation from his own belief? Charon homes in: "Then, Charon, turning first to one then to another of the gods' statues, said, 'Tell me, Gelastus, do you think *these* are individually worthless; won't you respect them when they're gathered together?' *Gelastus smiling, said, 'If I was alone perhaps I would laugh, but if there were many others present I would revere them.'*"[125] Gelastus confesses that his belief is feigned, coerced by the pressures of the crowd. This might be the key theological statement in *Momus* in regard to Alberti's

---

[122] Alberti, 2003, 302–5. Brown and Knight observe that some of Gelastus' preceding statements on the "structure of nature" and "matter" drew on Aristotelian and Platonic terminology and views (Alberti, 2003, 396nn14–16), but this characterization of position by Charon is clearly Lucretian.

[123] Alberti, 2003, 311.

[124] Alberti, 2003, 313, my emphasis.

[125] Alberti, 2003, 313, last line my emphasis; cf. Ponte, 1981, 87.

72   *Doubting the Divine in Early Modern Europe*

own religious views. He thus pairs incidents of feigned belief in Gelastus with a senseless, "stupid" belief in the case of the newly converted Oenops. In both cases, Alberti is casting doubt on the logic or authenticity of religious belief.

Appropriately, shortly after this exchange, winds rushed in to topple parts of the theater including some of the statues of gods stored on top of the walls, which fell and injured some of the gods below. Whether polytheism, monotheism, or both, religion has literally collapsed upon itself. Later, when Charon and Gelastus come upon Momus chained to a rock in the "Greater Ocean," Momus and Gelastus recognize each other from their former contacts during Momus's exile on earth. There they had "often held disputations ... about important and weighty matters," including the advice Momus assembled in his notebook for Jupiter.[126] Yet again Alberti creates a nexus between Momus, the doubting god, Gelastus, the doubting mortal, and himself. The atheism that Momus so convincingly sows and reports earlier in the story is tied to the concealed doubts of the Epicurean Gelastus. Alberti uses both figures to voice his own *parrhesia* about religion. The constraints of the day – namely, the social pressure and coercive force of orthodoxy – necessitate his use of a complex allegory to make his own confession of agnosticism.

In the end, Momus is a tragic victim of a flawed divine justice and/or corrupt court. Chained to a rock in the sea, he offers a summation of his tale to Charon and Gelastus:

Consider the fairness of great Jupiter and the gods. They proscribed me, whose only offense was acting well and providing good counsel! When I ravished the virgin goddess [Praise] in the temple, they all laughed! I returned to the gods the same old Momus I had always been, though imbued with a new resolution. Up to that day, I was in the habit of matching my beliefs to the truth, my zeal to my true allegiance, my words and expressions to the innermost, sincerest workings of my heart. After I returned, though, I learned to adapt my opinions to prejudice, my zeal to lust, and my expression, words, and heart to devising tricks. [A]s long as I used these perverted arts in that college

---

[126] Alberti, 2003, 335, 337.

of the blessed, I was dear to my prince, universally approved, individually trusted, and, I daresay, liked even by my enemies.[127]

He then goes on to say he finally regained his "former freedom of spirit" (*pristina animi libertas*) and, in talks with Gelastus, compiled his notebooks to guide Jupiter in his rule. For his troubles he was driven out again and chained. This speech shows Alberti's vision of a world of unjust deserts. When honest, frank-speaking, free, and earnest in advice-giving, he was punished. When a scoundrel – even a rapist – he went unpunished; and when a dissimulator, he was praised. Alberti's moral world is the very opposite of Dante's in the *Divine Comedy*, where at every station of Hell, Purgatory, and Paradise there is a fitting fate for souls. Alberti has written the epic of the alienated hero/villain, who finds the world of the princely/papal/divine court out of sync with any coherent moral scheme.

Alberti not only has written the first Latin novel of the Renaissance, but also he constructed the prototype of the anti-hero. Certainly, as malefactor, dissimulator, and sower of discord, Momus is no orthodox hero, but as truth-teller, who would fully reveal his heart and mind in frank speech and who offers powerful criticism of the heavenly and earthly world, he is no conventional villain. Whereas Aesop made Momus an insightful critic, and Lucian rendered him an ironic skeptic, Alberti has fully fleshed him out as a figure of cosmic agency and rich introspection. The novel offers groundbreaking soliloquies in which Momus debates his moral choices or schemes. For instance, when pondering whether to change his stripes as truth-teller, he muses: "I cannot *not* be Momus, and I cannot *not* be who I have always been without sacrificing my freedom and consistency."[128] Or, in another lengthy rumination, as he plans his mischief: "But I have not yet decided whether I should first congratulate myself because I've been restored from exile and am about to recover my former dignity, or because I've thought of a way of avenging myself. Nothing could be more

[127] Alberti, 2003, 337.
[128] Alberti, 2003, 45.

74   *Doubting the Divine in Early Modern Europe*

entertaining than that."[129] Or, ruing some decision: "You're finished, Momus, finished!"[130] Or, later, when deciding to forsake his "keenness to scold and criticize" for dissimulation: "Can you do something so completely against your own nature, Momus? Yes, I can, as long as I want to. And will you want to? Why not?"[131] In these soliloquies of a tragic antihero, Alberti has certainly anticipated the interiority of Milton's own divine rebel.[132]

But the most striking feature of Momus's tragic quality comes in his comparison with Prometheus. And this theme alerts us to the meaning this novel has not merely as a political statement about princes but also as a theological statement about divine justice. When Momus is suspected of being a usurper and traitor in Book 1, the gods clamor for his being chained to the spot that held Prometheus, who earlier is described as the god who stole a spark from the fire on the altar of Fate that can confer immortality.[133] Later, in Book 3, after his rehabilitation and even elevation in Jupiter's court, when he again runs afoul of everyone, Jupiter decrees that Momus, "the wickedest disturber of the universe," be chained to Prometheus' rock.[134] Juno, angry

[129] Alberti, 2003, 61.
[130] Alberti, 2003, 81.
[131] Alberti, 2003, 101.
[132] There are other interior speeches in the novel (such as Pallas debating an issue with herself at 98–99) – which in turn speaks to Alberti's innovator as a polyphonic voice in the novel – but the speeches of Momus are certainly the prominent ones. And particularly these soliloquies of Momus are ironic projections of subjectivity from a writer who elsewhere depicts himself under other identities as Lepidus in the *Intercenales* and as Gelastus in *Momus*, and even likely wrote his autobiography in the third person (see note 8 above). This reluctance to openly voice thoughts in the first person might indicate both the necessity of Nicodemism (hidden belief or feigned conformity) in Alberti's world and the psychological function of the novel to vicariously express the struggles of the self.
[133] Alberti, 2003, 23, 31.
[134] Alberti, 2003, 271–73. Although the site is not named here as Prometheus' rock, at the start of Book 4 (274–77) he is said to be visited by consolers as in the case of Prometheus' calamity, and when the gods initially call for his punishment in Book 1 they name Prometheus' rock as the site for his confinement.

at Momus's criticism of women, increased the punishment. Earlier castrated by Juno's female devotees, Momus is now fully turned into a woman and "the gods always called the banished and mutilated Momus 'humus' [a feminine noun], mutilating even his name."[135] Although guilty of other trespasses as well, Prometheus' main crime was stealing fire and skill in the arts to rescue mankind. He is, in a word, the great champion of mortals vis-à-vis the gods – and, consequently, a tragic victim of Zeus's wrath. To equate Momus with Prometheus is to make Momus a symbol of the human agon with the divine, a martyr for the human cause. As Virginia Brown and Sarah Knight suggest, the mangling of Momus's name to "humus" – thought by many at the time to be the derivation for "homo" or human – might suggest that Alberti's Momus was a symbol for mankind itself.

There were two possible sources for Alberti's views of Prometheus: Lucian's dialogue, *Prometheus*, is a sympathetic defense of Prometheus' "undeserved misfortune," owing in part to Zeus's insecurity that the newly created mortals threaten the status of the gods.[136] Even more likely, however, is the influence of Aeschylus' tragedy, *Prometheus Bound*, which Alberti cites in the *Theogenius* and *Profugiorum ab erumna*.[137] There is some doubt as to Alberti's facility in Greek and whether he knew Aeschylus directly or through the mediation of Carlo Marsuppini, but the impact of the work is unmistakable.[138] In

[135] Alberti, 2003, 273. Alberti's misogyny, castration fears, and transgender fantasy might be worth a thoroughgoing feminist analysis at another time.

[136] *Prometheus* 2 and 13; Lucian, 1913–67, 2:245, 257. The dialogue depicts Prometheus defending himself (to Hermes and Hephaestus, who are crucifying him on the Caucasus) for having tricked Zeus by serving him bones rather than meat, for having created humans (as he was reputed to have done in some myths, such as in Ovid's *Metamorphoses* 1), and for stealing fire. For an excellent treatment of the parallels between Momus and Prometheus, see Boschetto, 1993, 34–52.

[137] Boschetto, 1993, 41, 45–46.

[138] Boschetto, 1993; Bertolini, 1998, 77–104, argues that Alberti likely drew all of the allusions to Aeschylus from Marsuppini's consolatory letter of 1433 to Cosimo and Lorenzo de' Medici on the death of their mother, a work that in turn drew heavily on the Ps.-Plutarch's *Consolatio ad Apollonium* (though as Bertolini shows, at least a couple of lines in Marsuppini's letter

76   *Doubting the Divine in Early Modern Europe*

defending himself, Prometheus shows that he gave to a defenseless mankind all the powers and arts and sciences that have allowed mortals to understand nature, exploit its bounties, conquer illness, create letters, and preserve memory (*Prometheus Bound*, lines 437–506). It is the same vibrant portrait of man the activist and creator that Alberti depicts in so many of his writings. Second, when Prometheus claims that he will not tell Zeus the secret as to how he will be unseated until after he is released, the Chorus condemns his "outspokenness," a feature he shares with Momus.[139] The price for standing up to Zeus (or Jupiter) – being chained to a rock – was the same for Prometheus and Alberti's Momus. Clearly, Alberti wanted to assign Momus the tragic victimhood of Prometheus, whose punishment was depicted by Aeschylus and Lucian as an example of divine injustice.

But the Promethean motif in Alberti might also offer a clue to a major paradox scholars have found in Alberti's writings: namely, that man's triumph over nature (and the gods) is simultaneously a boon and a curse. Thus, for instance, the motif of *homo faber* is celebrated in the preface to *On the Art of Building*, but in *Theogenius* it appears as one of the sources of human misery:

The other animals are content with what guides them; only man, always investigating, infests himself … Oh animal, restless and impatient with his own state and condition! Man is such that I believe that sometimes nature, when our arrogance troubles her – through our wishing to know her every secret, to amend her, and to act against her – finds new calamities in order to play games with us and in order to train us to acknowledge her. What stupidity of mortals that they wish to know when, how and for what reason, and to what end would be every establishment and work of God? … Nature hides metals, god, and other minerals under great mountains and in very remote places; we murderous imps bring them to light and make optimal use of them. Nature disperses the brightest gems and in a form that seemed most

> reveal that he knew Aeschylus' text directly). On Alberti's possibly reading some Greek sources himself or with the help of others, see Grafton, 2000, 391–92n54.
>
> [139] The term here at *Prometheus Bound*, line 182, is not *parrhesia*, but *agan d'eleutherostomeis*; and later, Oceanus accuses him of "too vaunting speech" (*agan upshegoron glōsshes*) (lines 320–21) Aeschylus, 1922, 232–33, 244–45; cf. Boschetto, 1993, 46.

appropriate to her, the most apt mistress; we gather them even from the utmost and most distant regions and hacking them we give them new file and form.[140]

As Garin and, following him, Luca Boschetto have shown, Alberti is turning the argument of human grandeur and power on its head.[141] This constant striving and activism – soon to be cited as a source of consolation in the *Profugiorum ab erumna* – is here cast as a part of man's restless overreaching and cursed destiny. The paradox of this positive and negative vision of human destiny is perhaps encapsulated in the Promethean story, which offers a Faustian view of the human condition: an irresistible drive for conquest that is both destructive to mankind and threatening to the gods or nature.

Other than the *Prometheus Bound*, another source for Alberti's view of dynamic human striving was to be found in the earlier mentioned Hermetic fragment, *Kore Kosmou*, involving Momus. It was from this source that Alberti likely drew his story of Jupiter's afterthought to visit hardships on mortals once the other gods began to resent the blissful world he initially bestowed upon them. According to this fragment, it was Momus who chided Hermes for creating a mankind who will "look with audacious gaze upon the beauteous mysteries of nature," who "will send forth his designing thoughts to the very end of the earth," who will cut the forests, "dig mines, and search into the uttermost of the depths of the earth."[142] Alberti did not attribute to Momus the source of this warning about mankind and the recommendation to inflict misery upon mortals – instead he made Momus the critic of Jupiter's fickle decisions. But the portrait of overreaching man and threatened

---

[140] Alberti, 1960–73, 2:92–93, my trans.

[141] Garin, 1975, 147–183; Boschetto, 1993, 8. Garin discusses the classical loci for this theme in Cicero's *De natura deorum* 2, 60–61, and the humanist flowering in, for instance, Giannozzo Manetti's *De dignitate et excellentia hominis*; on which see Trinkaus, 1970.

[142] *Hermetica* 483; Garin, 1975, 149–50. And Momus urges that mortals' "presumptuous eagerness be disappointed of its expectations" and they be led on by hope to even more frustration and misery. Hermes agrees to bring mankind under subjection via Fate and the stars (*Hermetica* 484–85).

78   *Doubting the Divine in Early Modern Europe*

deities may well have joined with the dynamic portrait in *Prometheus Bound* to inspire Alberti's notion of a tragic agon between man and the gods.[143] This agon was in play in Alberti's preface, where he depicts God as claiming perfect virtue exclusive to Himself and announces his own effort to create something truly rare that will make him, by implication, "almost divine." This agon was apparent in Jupiter's cruel treatment of mortals, leaving them only the respite of death or the "patience" to try to fight against him, the "angry and heavily armed prince of the gods."[144] This agon was, I believe, at the heart of Alberti's life-long struggle to create, to invent, to work in order to vanquish a malevolent Fortune, the true surrogate for God in most of Alberti's writings, in which there is virtually no presence of a God of salvation.

Momus is Prometheus, a tragic figure who defies the gods. Prometheus is the champion of human struggle against the gods. He is the herald of human dynamism that the gods fear – and hate. And if Momus as "humus" is indeed meant to be mankind, Alberti has created several equivalencies – Momus as Prometheus, Prometheus as mankind – that pit mortals against the gods (or God). Finally, of course, Momus is also Alberti, a frank-speaker and critic disenchanted not only with court life but also with divine authority and divine justice. Yes, much of the novel can be read as a critique of politics of the court. Jupiter at one point gives a long lament on the miseries of being a prince, refereeing quarrels among the gods (courtiers) and dealing with ingrate mortals (subjects).[145] As an independent-minded courtier Momus is ignored when he tells the truth and embraced when he dissimulates. His prince is an indecisive bungler who realizes only late the wisdom of his candid advisor. Alberti may be the first to infuse court politics into the Lucifer

---

[143] Another source for this topic of human overreach was likely the apocryphal *Epistola ad Damagetum*, which influenced the portrait of the scientific materialist Democritus in Book 3 of *Momus* (Alberti, 2003, 246–52; Boschetto, 1993, 6–34).

[144] Alberti, 2003, 29.

[145] Alberti, 2003, 178–87.

tale as he subtly begins to join the two myths. Certainly one of the chief ills of any court, envy, is a recurrent them at several levels of hierarchy: Momus envies Jupiter's unwarranted authority; the gods envy the newly created mortals; and, at one point in the story, when Jupiter elevates Momus in Apollo's absence, the other gods envy him.

Status and envy may be the twin companions of any court, but equally linked in Alberti's mind are *creativity* and envy, and that nexus goes beyond the court – or social realm generally – to possibly embrace the relationship between humans and gods as creators. The gods hate "ingenious and active people," Momus claims at the close of his longest atheistic speech.[146] Time and again the novel offers themes that have little or no bearing on political life. The extended and repeated arguments for Epicurean atheism and against flawed theodicy, the prominence of scientific materialism and naturalism, the critique of institutional religion, the mockery of gullible belief, and the confession of feigned belief all suggest that Alberti's novel has a theological subtext. The incorporation of the recent revival of Lucretius and of Lucian's long-condemned *Zeus Rants* suggests that Alberti was flirting with controversial new (old) ideas.

The two levels of the text are in evidence in the last two paragraphs of the novel. In the penultimate one, when Jupiter finally opens the political notebooks that Momus has prepared for him, he reads some general maxims of good rule: for instance, the proper distribution of goods and power, the recognition of the hidden qualities of people, generosity in the public domain, frugality in the private, and so on. Having given such advice to Jupiter *qua* prince, Momus's notebooks in the closing paragraph seem to advise Jupiter *qua* god. Alberti in a sense fashions his own new theology in which Jupiter will have new gods dispense what mortals want. The gods Industry, Vigilance, Zeal, Diligence, and Constancy (in effect Alberti's own self-perceived virtues) will hand their gifts to mortals who want them. The gods Envy, Ambition, Pleasure, Laziness, and Cowardice will

---

[146] Alberti, 2003, 167.

80   *Doubting the Divine in Early Modern Europe*

likewise freely give out their bounty. This is Alberti's correction of a flawed theodicy not only with a "religion" of just deserts, but also with a privileging of human choice over divine personalities or arbitrary divine dispensations. Not surprisingly, Alberti's chief personal ideal, Industry, is the lead virtue; his life-long *bête noire*, Envy, the leading vice.[147] Humans choose their fate, much as Alberti's doubter, Libripeta, affirmed long before in the *Intercenales* dialogue "Religio."

Alberti's remaking of religion in the *Momus* is much more consequential than his manual for political rule. This is not the first time Alberti has pursued an agenda that belies his stated purpose: about two decades earlier in his *Life of Saint Potitus* the devil and pagan emperor gave speeches far too persuasive for their setting. The brief list of "mirror-for-princes" bromides at the end of *Momus* seems incidental and tacked on to a story more fully about the hollowness of divine authority, the flaws of theodicy, the logic of atheism, and the trials of a truth-teller and Promethean rebel who runs afoul of the gods (or God).

Indeed, at one crucial point in the novel, Alberti seems aware that he has possibly stepped over the line in regard to religious matters. In a rare first-person address to the reader – aside from those in the preface and openings of each book – he offers something of an apology. Tellingly, this comment follows the scene in which Oenops, newly and absurdly converted to theism, prays to the god Stupor (standing in for his own statue in the theater) and tries to scrape off the rust that shows his decay. At the close of this scene – a harsh satire of deluded belief, religious icons, and discredited gods – Alberti remarks:

All this took place in the theater [*read*: St. Peter's basilica?]. I know that, to those who enjoy reading our little books, this circumstance

---

[147] The tyranny of Fortune is minimized in this scheme. She will control generally superficial things that are neither good nor bad in themselves but only in how they are used, such as "riches, honor, and such things as mortals sought" (Alberti, 2003, 355), which she will mete out according to her whim. She seems to have far less sway and destructive force than she did in the "Erumna" in the *Intercenales* or in the *Theogenius* and Book 1 of the *Profugiorum ab erumna*.

may seem alien to my literary principles, if not positively scurrilous, and *I have always avoided in word and deed tackling subjects that were less grave and sacred than my literary conscience and piety (litterarum religio et religionis cultus) would allow.* But if you think again of what I'm trying to express in all these books and in this passage specifically, you'll surely realize that princes who are devoted to pleasure commit far more disgraceful acts than any we've recounted. For that reason, I would have you judge me as someone who is following the logic of a given plot rather than some antique standard of life and learning.[148]

This is once again, I believe, Alberti's attempt to protect himself with misdirection, assuring the reader that the novel is simply about a hedonistic prince; that the plot must go where it must, even if against all conventional values; that he has never before so entered a realm that would violate the *"litterarum religio et religionis cultus."* Indeed, this scene in the theater did take Alberti to a dangerously heterodox ledge, as his twin usages of the term "religio" bear witness. The claim of political allegory, which he also offers up in the preface to the novel, seems especially forced here.[149] As a cleric in the employ of the Papal Curia, Alberti had to encrypt his attacks on religion. And like Gelastus, he may have been forced to express belief in conventional religion when in the presence of others. Momus's challenge to *Jupiter Optimus Maximus* may have in fact been Alberti's necessarily veiled challenge to *Optimus Maximus Deus.*

[148] Alberti, 2003, 293–95, with slight alteration. On this passage, see Paoli, 1999, 120–21; Kircher, 2012, 253.

[149] Michel Paoli similarly implies that Alberti was defensively (or even deceptively) packaging his message: "Dans ce passage, Alberti gêné par le caractère irrévérencieux de son récit, tente de se justifier en réinsérant l'épisode dans le context plus large du livre et de son propos – rappelons que le subject est theoriquement l'éducation du prince" (Paoli, 1999, 121, my emphasis).

3

Momus and the Reformation

In Alberti, Momus could be deployed as a coded message for religious doubt in the fifteenth century, but this tack became increasingly impractical once the Reformation was underway. Momus became ever more radioactive in the course of the sixteenth century, as authors variously avoided him, carefully channeled him, used his name as an epithet, and defiantly embraced him. As we shall see in this and the following chapter, his history in the sixteenth century takes us from Erasmus, bitterly accused by Luther of being a new Momus, to Giordano Bruno, executed after radically flaunting him. The Protestant challenge raised the temperature on all religious writings: allusions that may have been merely playful or gently satirical before could become shibboleths for heresy. In this climate Momus and his chief spokesmen, Lucian and Alberti, certainly became more pointed targets (and weapons).

Erasmus and Luther

Erasmus was a perfect epitome of this phenomenon. He could be a jocular critic of the Church before 1517, but afterwards became increasingly a symbol of reform who was claimed by both Protestants and Catholics – and, ironically, eventually attacked by both. Moreover, as the heir to Alberti as a Lucianic writer, he confronted both the temptations and the

Momus and the Reformation 83

dangers of embracing a figure who flirted with unbelief. His reception of Lucian between 1500 and 1517 reflects a cautious interest in reviving a religious satirist who spoke to Erasmus's *institutional* doubts, though not perhaps to his *theological* ones. Even so, in his *Table Talk* comments recorded by his associates Luther condemned Erasmus as a "true Momus."[1] A fair charge? What, in fact, was Erasmus's relations to the controversial god?

Erasmus's first substantive notice of Momus and Lucian came in his *Adages* of 1500. Here he devoted an entire satire to Momus, invoking his persona as arch-critic. In this entry "To Satisfy Momus and the Like" (1.5.74), Erasmus takes a somewhat ambivalent attitude toward the god. On the one hand, he criticizes him for the "habit of producing nothing of his own, but staring at the work of the other gods with inquisitive eyes, and if anything is lacking or wrongly done he criticizes it with the utmost freedom": in short, a non-productive, envious malcontent.[2] On the other hand, he praises Momus's understanding of human nature. After relating Lucian's account in *Hermotimus* of the Aesopic fable (Babrius 59) regarding Momus's criticisms of the gods' creations, like Lucian he focuses on the complaint that "in the making of man the craftsman [Vulcan] had not added some windows or openings in the heart" and he praises Momus as the gods' vital non-flatterer and truth-teller: "This god is not as popular as the others, because few people freely accept true criticism, yet I do not know if any of the crowd of gods is more useful. Nowadays, however, our Joves shut out Momus and only listen to Euterpe, preferring flattery to wholesome truth."[3] Like Alberti, Erasmus seems to appreciate especially Momus's insight that dissimulation is humankind's greatest flaw. In another adage, "Open-Heartedly" (3.5.34), he deals directly

---

[1] Luther, 1912, 390.
[2] Erasmus, 1982, 448.
[3] Erasmus, 1982, 449.

84   *Doubting the Divine in Early Modern Europe*

with this theme of the open heart and again cites Momus's criticism of the flawed design of man.[4]

While Erasmus embraced Momus's attack on the inauthentic character of mortals, he would avoid his assault on the inauthentic stature of the gods. Between 1505/6 and 1514 Erasmus translated thirty-six of Lucian's works.[5] Although two of these – *Alexander* and *On Sacrifices* – were serious indictments of priestly fraud and religious practices, Erasmus omitted the dialogues in which Momus played a key role in challenging the integrity of the Greek pantheon and belief itself: namely, *The Parliament of the Gods* and *Zeus Rants*. This omission was likely not coincidental. Nor perhaps was his ceasing to translate and publish Lucian. In a lengthy letter – virtually an autobiography of his literary career – to Johann von Botzheim in 1523, Erasmus suggests that he took up the Lucian translations to help him learn Greek and that he quit because Greek was becoming more widely known and his Latin translations increasingly neglected.[6] Was this completely the case? Not only did his translations, contrary to his claims, continue to be printed – over forty times from 1506 to 1550 – but Erasmus returned to Lucian after his early stint, working on new translations that appeared in 1514.[7] His last publication of Lucian came in 1517, when the Froben press published an edition of his and Thomas More's Lucian translations – and in that year Erasmus wrote a dedicatory letter to his translation of the *Banquet* to a friend (probably Johann Huttich).[8] While it may be only coincidental that 1517, the year Luther launched his indulgence controversy, marked the end of Erasmus's role as Lucian's publisher, we must consider the possibility that Erasmus pulled away from Lucian in part because of the deepening religious crisis. As early as 1506, in a dedicatory preface to his translation

---

[4] "The phrase is an allusion to the words of Momus, who is said to have wanted to make openings in men's breasts so that what was hidden in those cavities could be examined" (Erasmus, 2005a, 86).

[5] Thompson, 1940, 11–13.

[6] See his list of Lucian translations in the letter at Erasmus, 1989a, 301–2, 353.

[7] Thompson, 1940, 17–18, 22; Erasmus, 1989a, 302n49.

[8] Erasmus, 1977, 281–82.

Momus and the Reformation 85

of *Gallus*, he felt the need to defend Lucian against the charge of atheism: "He likewise laughs and rails at the gods and with no less freedom [than he mocks the philosophers]; for which he has been given the nickname of atheist, which naturally acquires positive credit because those who seek to attach it to him are irreligious and superstitious men."[9] And he would likewise have to defend his own Lucianic *Colloquies*, some of which were seized upon by enemies as heretical.[10] To translate and defend a reputed atheistic writer after 1517 may have been inviting suspicion.

Why were the Momus dialogues excluded in the Lucian pieces he translated? Craig Thompson has observed that "Erasmus not only translated more of Lucian's writings than anyone before had done (eighteen short dialogues and eighteen longer pieces), but he also translated many for the first time."[11] Yet, *Zeus Rants* and *The Parliament of the Gods* were not among them. Certainly, he saw Momus as a particularly dark figure. In the 1506 dedicatory letter of his translation of *Alexander* to René d'Illiers, the Bishop of Chartres, Erasmus comments, "You will, besides, be able to find in Lucian, in fullest measure combined, both that 'black wit' with which Momus is credited and the 'fair wit' which is associated with Mercury's name."[12] In fact, Momus as a trope may have been too harsh for Erasmus. When Erasmus undertook his own most comprehensive satire on the world of mortals and gods in his *Praise of Folly* (1509–10), he created a gentler god, Moria ("Folly") – a tribute to his friend Thomas More – as his critic and relegated Momus to a minor role. When Folly catalogues the misbehavior of the pagan gods, including the "scandalous escapades of Jove

---

[9] Erasmus, 1975, 116; Thompson, 1940, 21.

[10] In the 1523 letter to Botzheim, Erasmus claimed that his *Colloquies*, which began to appear in unauthorized editions in 1518 and his own edition in 1522, were attacked for comments about "monks, vows, pilgrimages, indulgences," even prompting a Spanish writer, Diego López Zúñiga, to devote a pamphlet in 1522 to the *Blasphemies and Impieties of Erasmus* (Erasmus, 1989a, 305, 328–32).

[11] Thompson, 1940, 20.

[12] Erasmus, 1975, 122.

86   *Doubting the Divine in Early Modern Europe*

himself, the thunderer," she introduces Momus as the truth-teller regarding these foibles:

Stories like these they ought to be hearing from Momus, and in fact they used to hear them regularly from him until they got angry and threw him along with Ate [Discord] down to earth because he interrupted the bliss of the gods with his ill-timed truth-telling. Nor did any mortal offer shelter to this exile, least of all anyone in the court of princes, where my follower Kolakia [Flattery] reigns supreme; she and Momus would get along together about as well as a wolf and a lamb. And so, in the absence of Momus, the gods revel much more freely and carelessly, "taking all things lightly," as Homer says, now that they have no censor.[13]

At this point, Folly says she will not go into any more details of the gods, "lest some snoopy god overhear me telling about matters that weren't safe even for Momus to mention."[14] Erasmus, thus, like Alberti, adds a bit to the classical lore of Momus, by saying that he was not even harbored on earth; this addition, plus the allusion to his being "overheard" by the gods – an incident that brought about Momus's expulsion in Alberti's novel – suggests the possibility that Erasmus could have known Alberti's novel.[15] Although Alberti's *Momus* was not published until 1520, a manuscript compilation of his writings that included *Momus* was, according to Eugenio Garin, circulating between Bologna, Florence, and Ferrara around the time Erasmus was translating Lucian's dialogues and decamping from Bologna to Florence in anticipation of Julius II's siege of the city.[16] If indeed Erasmus

[13] Erasmus, 1989b, 17.
[14] Erasmus, 1989b, 17.
[15] Another possible influence of Alberti's *Momus* could be found in Erasmus's criticism of the elaborate church decorations, including "gold statues," for instance in the colloquies "A Pilgrimage for Religion's Sake" and the "Godly Feast" (Erasmus, 1965, 307, 70). On which, cf. Alberti's account of the humans' attempt to propitiate the gods' anger with elaborate temples, theaters, sacrifices, games, and "statues of the great gods, all shining with gold and jewels" (Alberti, 2003, 263); also see Erasmus's response to Alberto Pio in Erasmus, 2005b, 223–29. Lucian devotes a brief section to religious statues in *On Sacrifices* 11, but Alberti and Erasmus emphasize more the lavish nature of religious spectacle and decoration.
[16] Garin, 1971, 11; for the contents of this manuscript collection, Canon. Misc. 172 in the Bodleian Library, see www.mirabileweb.it/manuscript/oxford-bodleian-library-canon-misc-172-(S-C-19648)-manoscript/12965; Erasmus, 1975, 127–28.

read *Momus*, he might have realized its theological implications. If so, his concerns could have influenced his decision at the time not to translate Lucian's Momus dialogues and his decision a few years later to deploy Folly rather than Momus as arch-critic. In any case, Erasmus's Folly unlike Lucian's or Alberti's Momus never wades into the waters of disbelief and even, as readers know, seriously celebrated Platonic divine frenzy as a feature of true spiritual experience.[17]

Given that Erasmus thus steered clear of the more dangerous theological legacy of Momus, why then did Luther tar him with that brush? It is worth noting that, although Luther generally rejected the use of the Momus persona for religious criticism, one of his early supporters did deploy it for attacks on the Catholic Church in defense of Luther. Late in the year 1520 an anonymous Latin dialogue, *Momus* – long dubiously thought to be by Ulrich von Hutten but possibly written by Crotus Rubeanus – depicted Momus, Menippus, and Pasquillus discussing, among other matters, the hypocrisy and corruption of the clergy. Momus, identified as "Momus Asianus," had been dispatched along with Menippus by Jove to survey matters in Europe. Momus, who has been in the East, reports on matters in Germany: he finds that the Muslims are far more devout than the Christians; castigates European theologians who are "supercilious and exalted with magnificent titles"; mocks the logic-chopping of scholasticism; and learns from Pasquillus of the Papal decree against Luther's writings.[18] These were, however, matters more of institutional corruption than of theological substance.

---

[17] Erasmus, 1989b, 83–87. For another view of Erasmus's attitude toward Momus, see Cast, 1974, who, I think, exaggerates Erasmus's embrace of Momus. While I agree that Erasmus acknowledges his salutary role as a truth-telling critic of the misbehavior of the classical gods, I do not see his embrace of Momus to be as positive and unalloyed: else, Erasmus would have made his role larger in the *Praise of Folly*, he would have translated Lucian's Momus dialogues, and he would not have made the unfavorable comparison of the "black wit" of Momus to the "fair wit" of Mercury (see above) to the Bishop of Chartres.

[18] Von Hutten, 1860, 555–60, esp. at 555–56; Relihan, 1996, 268n9, 276–77.

88   *Doubting the Divine in Early Modern Europe*

Clearly, Luther saw the theological dangers of the Momus persona, and like Erasmus he chose the Folly guise in assailing the Catholic hierarchy. No doubt under the influence of Erasmus's *Praise of Folly*, Luther defines his role in the 1521 *Address to the German Nobility* as that of the court fool.[19] He sought Erasmus's support as a like-minded reformer in the early days of his challenge to the Church, but all of this changed after the mid 1520s, when Erasmus came out against him in the *Freedom of the Will*, which provoked Luther's *On the Bondage of the Will* and an ensuing stream of invectives against Erasmus. In the latter work, Luther accuses Erasmus of being a Skeptic and even worse, "showing that you foster in your heart a Lucian, or some other pig from Epicurus' sty who, having no belief in God himself, secretly ridicules all who have a belief and confess it."[20] In a lengthy letter to Nicholas von Amsdorf in March of 1534, he repeats all of these charges and adds that of Arianism.[21] This letter makes clear how the boundaries between the Christian and classical worlds could still be seen as dangerously porous in some theologians' eyes. Luther seizes upon a comment Erasmus makes about the "intercourse" (*coitum*) between the Virgin and God in which Erasmus expressly clarified that he did not mean the carnal sense of intercourse.[22] Luther, dismissing that disclaimer, charges that Erasmus knew exactly what he was doing by using such language, "by which God could be said to unite with the Virgin, so that it would be made into a fable similar to that in which Mars couples with Rhea and Jupiter with Semele and the sect of Christians would almost be like one drawn from

[19] See his dedicatory letter to Nicholas von Amsdorf in Luther, 1962, 404.

[20] Luther, 1972, 24. On Erasmus's response in the *Hyperaspistes* to Luther's charge that he is a "secret Epicurus or an atheist Lucian, saying in his heart, 'There is no God, or if there is, he does not care about the affairs of mortals'" see Erasmus, 1999, 105, 112, 296–97.

[21] For this lengthy attack on Erasmus, see Luther, 1937, 28–40, esp. 34–35.

[22] Luther, 1937, 35, 37; Erasmus responded to Luther's published letter to Amsdorf (published in 1534) in a lengthy *Against a Most Slanderous Letter of Martin Luther*, in which he defended his use of "*coitum*" in his Paraphrase of Luke 1:35 and addressed the many other charges Luther laid against him; Erasmus, 2011, 412–82, esp. 439–44. On Luther's charges and Erasmus's response, see Gordon, 1990, 241–45.

Momus and the Reformation 89

the fables of the pagans."[23] He claims that Erasmus did thus try to plant doubt and subvert belief. Whatever Erasmus intended, Luther exposed a primal fear of Christian theology with his defensive exegesis.

Aside from serious threats to religion Luther perceived in Erasmus, comic ones also offended him. At the end of his letter to Amsdorf, he counsels that Erasmus's writings should be kept out of the schools, "for he teaches to speak or reflect gravely concerning nothing serious, but only how, in the way of a crow ... to laugh at everyone else ... In this true levity and vanity he gradually becomes unaccustomed to religion, until he would abhor or deeply profane it."[24] And here perhaps is where Erasmus's Lucianic temperament rankled theologians for whom there should be no commerce between humor and religion. Although Erasmus stopped translating Lucian in 1514, he continued to imitate him in the *Colloquies*.[25] And some readers

---

[23] Luther, 1937, 37, my trans.

[24] Luther, 1937, 38–39, my trans. Erasmus defends his humorous tone in three ways: that he is "by natural inclination rather given to jesting, both in my writings and in my conversations with friends"; that, as in in some of the *Colloquies*, when he does jest, "I do not jest to no purpose"; and that he "prefer[s] to seem slightly foolish to some than a kind of harsh, πληκτς 'violent,' Procrustian character, constantly puffing tragic words"(Erasmus, 2011, 458–59). Clearly, he is defending his satirical approach to reform in contrast to Luther's overly harsh, "forceful" approach; on the application of the archetypes "*homo rhetoricus*" and "*homo seriosus*" (from Richard Lanham) to Erasmus and Luther respectively, see Gordon, 1990, 12–13. For Erasmus's defense of the moral messages in many of his *Colloquies*, see the "Usefulness of the Colloquies" in Erasmus, 1965, 623–37. As mentioned earlier, however, it should be noted that Luther also referred to himself as playing the fool in the dedicatory letter of the *Address to the German Nobility*.

[25] There are only passing explicit allusions to Lucian, but several of the colloquies draw on Lucianic tropes. For direct allusions, see Erasmus, 1965, 49, 439, 582, on Lucian themes see, for instance, the "Charon" (1529) (388–94); also, on Lucian's influence on earlier works of Erasmus, of course, see the *Praise of Folly* (Marsh, 1998, 7–8, 146–47; Robinson, 1979, 165–97; Gordon, 1990, 63–67). In fact, in his *Against the Slanderous Letter of Luther*, Erasmus suggests that Luther – saying that "I have a horror of all religions, especially Christianity" – is in effect calling him a modern-day Lucian: "For what else is the reader to understand but that Erasmus,

90   *Doubting the Divine in Early Modern Europe*

saw these works as dangerously Lucianic – even Momic. In his 23 *Books* (of criticism of Erasmus) Alberto Pio in one section assails Erasmus's criticism of church decorations: "But you would still not have played the role of a very Momus among priests and ceremonies if you did not covertly criticize this devout and praiseworthy embellishment as well."[26] In the early 1530s it was Luther's turn to brand him as Momus. In the *Table Talk*, Luther labels him a foe of religion and a rhetorical trickster who could find a sympathetic audience even among the Turks:

Erasmus is a true Momus. He mocks and trifles with everything: all religion and Christ, and in order to do this better day and night he invents double meanings and ambiguous terms, so that his books can be read even by the Turks. And although he is thought to have said many things, he says nothing at all. In whatever way all of his writings can be interpreted, nothing can be grasped either by us [Protestants] or the papists, unless you first remove the ambiguity from them.[27]

Luther could also deploy Momus in his simple role of critic, as he attacked scholastic theologians for being Momuses shortly after he issued the *Ninety-Five Theses*.[28] But here, in this jab at Erasmus, he fully invokes Momus as the archetype of a scoffer of "all religion and Christ." Moreover, Luther's attendant charge that Erasmus's writings are filled with ambiguous meaning may allude in part to the comic frame of many of his works. Once estranged from Erasmus over the free-will issue, Luther no longer finds the satirical writings humorous: what may have been welcome attacks on Catholic abuse prior to the mid 1520s now become destructive assaults on Christianity itself.

following Lucian's example, condemns the religions of the Spartans, the Scythians, the Thracians, the Athenians, and so on, and that the Christian religion is one of them?" (Erasmus, 2011, 446–47; cf. Luther, 1937, 30).

[26] Cited in Erasmus, 2005b, 223n691. Erasmus defends his comments in "For the Sake of the Pilgrimage" and the "Godly Feast" on this matter, ibid., 223–29.

[27] Luther, 1912, 390, my trans.; Cast, 1974, 29.

[28] In a letter of November 11, 1517, twelve days after he posted the *Ninety-Five Theses*, he labels both Aristotle and the scholastic theologians as Momuses; the former, oddly, he even calls the "Momus of Momuses" (Luther, 1913, 64–65).

In another *Table Talk* entry from the same period, Luther condemns Erasmus as a type worse even than Lucian:

Erasmus stands by the fence. He does nothing openly; therefore his books are very poisonous. On my deathbed I will forbid my sons from reading his *Colloquies*, where under fictitious and other personas he speaks the most impious things and teaches how the given works are invented for opposing the Church and Christian faith. Let him then laugh at me and all the other men! ... I praise Lucian over Erasmus. That one [Lucian] openly derides everything; this one [Erasmus] under the highest pretense of sanctity and piety attacks all things sacred and all piety. Therefore, he is far more harmful than Lucian himself.[29]

Luther's charges against Erasmus reveal the impact of religious conflict on the reception of Momus and Lucian. At least at this stage of the crisis, religious scoffing is suspect.

What then of Luther's charges against Erasmus? No one should presume to plumb Erasmus's personal belief, but we can speculate about matters regarding his intellectual temperament. Luther is probably correct to charge him with skepticism, because Erasmus was in fact reluctant to pronounce dogmatically on certain issues of theological uncertainty.[30] He was, however, probably wrong to call him a Momus, because Erasmus avoided the virulent legacy of this religious agnostic. Later, in the Enlightenment, some would see Erasmus's restraint as a function of fear. In 1765 Voltaire published a *Conversation de Lucien, Érasme, et Rabelais dans les Champs Élysées*, in which Erasmus tells Lucian that religious satire has become a more perilous affair in the interval between their respective eras: "There was an enormous difference between the ridiculous people of your time and those of mine: you had only to deal with gods that you depicted on the stage and with philosophers who had even less credibility than the gods. But I am surrounded by fanatics, and I need great circumspection in order not to be burned by the one or assassinated by the other."[31] The truth of this attribution of fear to Erasmus is questionable. He certainly shied away

[29] Luther, 1912, 397, my trans.
[30] Popkin, 1979, 5–8.
[31] Voltaire, 1939, 146–47, 497n131, my trans.; Mansfield, 1992, 21–22.

92   *Doubting the Divine in Early Modern Europe*

from placing his name on *Julius Excluded from Heaven*, which libeled the recently departed Julius II in every conceivable way, but he did put his name on the *Praise of Folly*, which forcefully took aim at the ecclesiastical hierarchy, monks, popular piety, and theologians.[32] He did so, however, in the more playful name of Folly rather than Momus, never named names, and addressed belief in positive terms. Erasmus's cautious use of Momus may have been a function of intellectual and literary predisposition. Peter Bietenholz suggests that Erasmus sympathized with the tactic of dissimulation, or prudential restraint, as a necessary compromise in controversial matters.[33] He was, in a word, no true Momus by nature, a truth-teller who defied authority regardless of the consequences. Whether his distancing himself from the agnostic Momus was more a matter of personal pragmatism or theological conviction is impossible to know, but he seems to have known that Momus was a dangerous doppelganger for any sixteenth-century religious writer. As it turned out, it was not only Lucian's Momus who took on greater theological baggage in this century, but also Alberti's.

Expurgating and Emulating Alberti's *Momus*

In 1553 a Spanish translation of Alberti's novel appeared that purged the text of its potentially dangerous elements while preserving its safer reform message. Eugenio Garin has argued that the eventual publication of Alberti's Latin text in 1520 may in fact have been inspired by the recent appearance of Erasmus's *Praise of Folly* (1510) and More's *Utopia* (1516), as well as by the emergence of the reform movement. That is, features of the text – the satire on images and votive prayers – readily spoke to the reform sensibilities of figures such as Erasmus and Luther. And yet, this same heightened religious climate would have made even more evident or suspect those features of the text that flirted with agnosticism or even atheism.[34] As Mario

[32] Erasmus, 1989b, 3–87, 142–73.
[33] Bietenholz, 2009, 141–48.
[34] Garin, 1975, 140; Damonte, 1974, 259–60.

Momus and the Reformation

Damonte has shown, when Agustín de Almazán, thought to be an Erasmian *converso*, composed his Spanish translation at mid-century, he seems to have tried to walk the line between promoting salutary reform (in Erasmian style) and sanitizing the text (in Counter-Reformation style). In some cases, he excised or recontextualized materialist and pantheistic passages from the text: for instance, in the scene in which Jupiter comes down to earth and overhears a mortal say that no architect could have created the world, Almazán removes the speaker's additional line that the "whole edifice [*machina*] is a god."[35] Almazán, or the censor, was also troubled by the notion that everything is full of gods," excised in one place in the text and in another explained it to mean that the various parts of the world are governed by "spiritual administrators" assigned their task by the "great God," an interpolation meant to transform a dangerous pantheism into a divine scheme conforming to conventional monotheism (and monarchy).[36]

Almazán's major alteration of the text, however, was to fully convert any theological framework for the novel into a fully political one. In the "Prologue of the Translator" Almazán clarifies that the "invention of introducing the mythical and false gods that the pagans worshiped" was a strictly political metaphor:

Seeking to represent in Jupiter, whom those help as the prince of the other gods, the prince; and for the other gods, the courtiers of the prince and grandees of the realm; and for the men who worship them and make sacrifices, the vassals and people who obey and serve them; for the sky, the lofty palaces and distinguished buildings; for the Earth, the lowliness of the subjects.[37]

Almazán, of course, takes his cue from Alberti, who claimed that his story is a political analogy: once in his preface and again in Book 4, following the scandalous account in the theater. In the latter case, after a burlesque scene in which a drunken atheist urinates and defecates before Jupiter (disguised as a statue of

---

[35] Alberti, 2003, 214–15; Alberti, 1553, fol. 42v; Damonte, 1974, 264–65.
[36] Alberti, 1553, fol. 57r, fol. 42v; Damonte, 1974, 265.
[37] Alberti, 1553, sig. a3v, my trans.; Vega, 1998, 16–17.

94   *Doubting the Divine in Early Modern Europe*

himself) and a former atheist finds religion "at the feet of the god Stupor [Stupidity]," Alberti felt the need to insist – perhaps too defensively – that his story was really political in nature. This, the vilest depiction of religion in the novel, which Alberti admitted would seem to violate his normal regard for piety and "antique standard[s] of life and learning," prompted his reminder that the story dealt with the misbehavior of princes.[38] This apology, placed where it is, only reinforces the likelihood that Alberti knew that his tale had scandalous religious implications: all the more important to proclaim here again that it did not. Almazán seizes upon this apologia and at the start of his translation, after his own "Prologue of the Translator," he includes a "Protestation of the Author," repeating Alberti's statement in Book 4. Moreover, as María José Vega has argued, Almazán took the liberty to intensify the piety of Alberti's statement: Alberti's reference to his possibly being seen to diverge from the "literarum religio et religionis cultus" is amplified into "la buenay santa religion Christiana" and "el culto santo y pio de la religion."[39] He also alters lines to have Alberti state that no one should turn his "wholesome intention to bad ends" and adds a comment stating his assumption (or hope?) that men "of evil intentions" will not read him.[40] Clearly, Almazán realizes how the book could be misread (or, rather, *correctly* read), and he helps Alberti make his case with added caveats.

Almazán's concerns also extended to the section prologues where time and again he emphasizes the political allegory.[41] For

---

[38] Alberti, 2003, 293–95.

[39] Alberti, 2003, 294; Alberti, 1553, sig. a4r; Vega, 1998, 17–19.

[40] In this section Almazán converts Alberti's passage that he not be judged "secutos ... pristinam studiorum et vitae rationem" (implying, perhaps, traditional religious standards) to his wish that "no en que juzgassedes mi sana intencion a mala parte" (Alberti, 2003, 294; Alberti, 1553, sig. a4r.). Also, to Alberti's comment here that he has said more than he wants and less than he should, Almazán tacks on "pues no pienso me leen hombres de damnados higados y malas intenciones," which seems to indicate that he does not expect or hope to be read by those with bad temperaments and evil intentions. My thanks to Miguel Herranz Cano for help with this passage.

[41] Vega, 1998, 17, 19–20.

instance, in Momus's "report" of the lengthy atheistic speech in Book 2, Almazán suggests this key for decoding this controversial section: "By Momus is meant a rebellious courtier ... who tries to cause trouble between the people and their lord. And by the men who complain of the gods, [are meant] vassals who always complain of their princes, although with unjust complaints."[42] The censor, Alejo de Venegas, who includes a lengthy statement on the nature of classical mythology and fables, ends by saying Alberti, in the "vituperation and life and customs of such gods [in the *Momus*], elevates good judgment in the knowledge of the prince, who deals with the true religion, which is Christian."[43] Like Almazán, he defines the work as only a political allegory.[44] But this view distorts or conceals the heterodox features of the novel. I entirely agree with Vega's conclusion that the political reading simply ignores too many of the prominent currents in the work: "[T]he moralization of Almazán not only deactivates the Lucianism [of *Momus*], the Epicurean points, the dispute on the naturalness of the gods or the parody of Stoic theology, but also, in order to fully convert *Momus* into a treatise 'On the Prince,' it also 'sanitizes' the ridicule of the very genre to which he claims it to belong."[45] Almazán, thus, with a template from Alberti and with the aid of the censor, wants to redirect – or erase – the radical features of Alberti's text to guarantee a safe reading. Why, then, did Almazán translate a work that he had to manipulate so much? Perhaps it was to rescue the less controversial "Erasmian" critiques of religious vows, imagery, and excess from the novel's agnostic currents. In any case, as Vega suggests, Almazán apparently feared that the unembellished text could indict Alberti of impiety.[46] Almazán thus must have seen the thinly disguised subtext of the story, recognizing dangers that Erasmus may have seen in Lucian's Momus – and, possibly, in Alberti's *Momus* as well.

[42] Alberti, 1553, fol. 31r, my trans.
[43] Alberti, 1553, sig. b1v–b2r, my trans.; Vega, 1998, 23–24.
[44] Vega, 1998, 25.
[45] Vega, 1998, 38, my trans.
[46] Vega, 1998, 19.

96   *Doubting the Divine in Early Modern Europe*

Whereas Alberti's *Momus* required a literary defense in Spain, it may have inspired emulation in France. Probably in early 1538 (New Style), there appeared from the press of Jean Morin in Paris an anonymous French work under the Latin title *Cymbalum mundi*. Widely condemned by both Catholics and Protestants, the book was assailed as an atheistic attack on all religion.[47] In this charge, the author resembled Lucian, whose dialogues he clearly was imitating. Textual evidence suggests, however, that he also drew on Alberti's novel, published twice in Rome eighteen years earlier. Like Alberti, the author features as his main character a feckless god who descends to earth and stirs up trouble and doubts. This time, however, the nettlesome god is not Momus but his sometime companion, Mercury. The two were often paired: for instance, in Lucian, and more recently in Erasmus, who characterized them as two sides of the same coin – Momus the champion of black wit, Mercury of fair.[48] In the *Cymbalum*, however, Mercury's role takes on the more subversive tone of Momus. More specifically, as Olivier Millet argues, some of the themes and incidents reveal striking parallels to those in Alberti. I would go further and argue lines of influence.[49]

The authorship of the *Cymbalum* is not a settled matter, although tradition has privileged Bonaventure Des Périers

---

[47] Des Périers, 1723, xv–xli; Des Périers, 1958, x–xi. There is some debate about the date of the first edition (whether late 1537 or early 1538), largely owing to the colophon of Morin's edition, which lists 1537, but which might indicate Old-Style dating. I follow the speculation that the work was likely published in early 1538 around the same time as an edition in Lyons, which similarly lists itself as the first edition; Giraud, 2003, 25.

[48] Erasmus, 1975, 122; Millet, 2003, 329.

[49] In an analysis of Lucianism in the *Cymbalum*, Millet argues: "mon hypothèse, c'est que le Mercure du *Cymbalum* joue en partie un rôle parallèle à celui de Momus dans le roman d'Alberti" (Millet, 2003, 329). He does not argue for direct influence, but rather suggests that the two works offer "certains traits communs révélateurs d'une certaine manière de lire et de recevoir Lucien" (329). I thinks that one reason Millet does not pursue further the issue of direct influence is that he assumes that Alberti's *Momus* is "une allégorie morale, philosophique et politique" (332), when in fact I think that it is also a religious allegory.

Momus and the Reformation 97

(1500?–44?), a figure whose circle included the proto-Protestant Marguerite of Navarre, in whose court he served, and Étienne Dolet, executed for atheism in 1546.[50] Scholars agree that the author devised an anagram in his dedicatory letter titled "Thomas du Clevier a son amy Pierre Tryocan," which decoded reads "Thomas Incrédule à son amy Pierre Croyant" (changing the "v" in "Clevier" to "n"). Thus: "Doubting Thomas to Believing Peter." Other names in the dialogue have similarly been recognized as anagrams: namely, in Book 2 Rhetulus and Cubercus represent Luther and Martin Bucer respectively.[51] The chief character in the first three books is Mercury, sent down to earth by Jove to have bound his Book of Destiny, which is stolen by two characters in a tavern who replace it with a book detailing Jove's philandering with mortal women. When these two indulgence sellers and a hostess challenge Mercury's piety or status, he vengefully threatens to remove all of them from the Book of Destiny, which guarantees mortals eternal life with Jove.[52] In Book 2 a skeptical interlocutor Trigabus ("triple-scoffer") engages a fairly agreeable Mercury in a discussion of mortals' misguided attribution of natural phenomena to the power of miracles that could be worked from the powder resulting from Mercury's pulverizing of the Philosopher's Stone (faith) that he had spread in the sand of theaters (churches).[53] Trigabus also surveys the deluded faith in relics, fasts, and vestments, and mocks scholastic theologians. Invited to witness this himself in a theater, Mercury, disguised as an old man, mocks Bucer's and Luther's belief in the dust of the Philosopher's Stone, and even scorns the god Mercury *himself* as an impostor and trickster. Mercury thus mimics Alberti's Momus, who similarly spread doubt among mortals.

[50] Cooper, 2003, 3–4.
[51] Des Périers, 1958, xxxix, 3; Febvre, 1942, 9.
[52] These figures accuse Mercury of blasphemy when he proclaims the wine in the tavern to be as good as Jove's nectar (Des Périers, 1958, 8–9); later, in Book 3, Cupid reveals that these two men who stole the Book of Destiny, are selling admission to the "livre d'immortalité" (27–28); Spitzer, 1951, 798.
[53] On the derivation of "Trigabus," see Gauna, 1992, 165.

98   *Doubting the Divine in Early Modern Europe*

The historiographical debate on the meaning of the *Cymbalum* is spirited and as yet inconclusive.[54] Some scholars see the author as an Erasmian spiritualist wary of complex theological systems and ceremony.[55] Others view the work as fully anti-religious – including, oddly, Lucien Febvre, who in 1942 took pains to argue that atheism could not truly exist in the sixteenth century in his famous but flawed *The Problem of Unbelief in the Sixteenth Century*.[56] That same year in a lengthy analysis of the *Cymbalum*, Febvre argued that the work represented a "radical ... attack" on Christianity and in effect constituted a blueprint for the "Libertine Life."[57] And before him Abel Lefranc declared that the *Cymbalum* "without doubt ought to be considered from one end to the other as the least disguised and most violent attack that had been directed against Christianity in the course of the sixteenth century."[58] He suggests that Des Périers based his book on a reading of Celsus' atheism as recorded in Origen's *Contra Celsum*, which had recently appeared in Latin translations beginning in 1512.[59] Especially critical to unravelling the book's meaning is, of course, the allegorical identity of Mercury. Recognized expressly as the son of Jove, sent down to earth to spread faith (the dust from the Philosopher's Stone), and given authority to include or exclude mortals from eternal life, he is plausibly viewed by some as a Christ figure. Others suggest that he is simply a rather arch version of Mercury the trickster.[60] Yes, Mercury traditionally was the god of deception, but that might itself make more blasphemous the Christ-like

[54] Febvre, 1942; Spitzer, 1951; Gauna, 1992, 108–204; M. Smith, 1991; Giacone, 2003.
[55] Des Périers, 1958, xxxix.
[56] Febvre, 1982; Gauna, 1992, 113.
[57] Febvre, 1942, 130–31.
[58] From Lefranc's "La pensée de Rabelais" in the introduction to his 1922 edition of *Pantagruel* (Rabelais, 1922, lxi, my trans.).
[59] Febvre, 1942. He concludes by arguing that the *Cymbalum* represents the "première et complete transfusion de l'esprit celsique dans notre littérature" (131); Origen, 1965; on Latin editions of the *Contra Celsum* beginning in 1512, see Febvre, 1942, 76–77.
[60] Spitzer, 1951, 796–801, refutes Febvre's contention that Mercury is Celsus' Christ; also see Gauna, 1992, 184–86.

Momus and the Reformation 99

qualities the *Cymbalum* grafts onto him. The strains of Momus are adjoined as well. The tenor of his brash comment that the tavern's Burgundy is as good as Jove's nectar, and his mocking of relics and deluded belief argue for the influence of Lucian generally and Momus specifically. The theft of the Book of Destiny and its replacement with a book of Jove's debauchery recalls themes in Lucian's *Zeus Refuted* (where Zeus cowers at his vulnerability to Destiny) and *Zeus Rants* (where his unseemly reputation is rehearsed). Themes of the dubious stature of the gods and the dubious state of mortal belief suggest the blasphemies reported or imputed by the Momuses of Lucian and Alberti.[61] More specifically, common themes and incidents in the *Cymbalum* and Alberti's novel suggest the strong likelihood of textual influence: the descent to earth of a god who stirs up unbelief; the theft of Jove's Book of Destiny recalls the stealing of Apollo's purse bag of fortunes in Book 3 of *Momus*; the equating of theaters with churches, and especially the mocking of belief in these settings; the reference to a scar on the forehead of a character (who refuses to talk about it) recalls Momus's misfortune of suffering a torn beard and bloody face after being accosted because of his profession of atheism in Book 1.[62]

In this last incident the character is a dog, one of two who are the principals in the final book of the *Cymbalum*. Though rather enigmatic as to its true meaning, the dialogue between these two has likely grounding both in atheism and in the legacy of Lucian. The two dogs, Hylactor and Pamphagus, are identified as two of the hunting dogs of Acteon, who suffered a tragic end due to his offense to Diana. When he saw her bathing in the forest, she turned him into a stag so that he could not speak

[61] As for Mercury's status as a deceiver or impostor, at the beginning of Book 2 Trigabus calls him "ung abuseur, et fusses-tu filz di Jupiter troys foys" (a deceiver, even if you would be three times the son of Jupiter) (Des Périers, 1958, 12) and later the disguised Mercury indicts "Mercure, le grand aucteur de tous abuz et tromperie" (Mercury, the great author of all deceit and trickery) (18).

[62] For this last instance, compare Alberti, 2003, 36–37; Des Périers, 1958, 37. For an alternative theory, M. Smith, 1991, 602, proposes that the scar refers to a violent encounter Dolet had in late December of 1536.

100   *Doubting the Divine in Early Modern Europe*

of the incident; when his hunting dogs came upon him as a stag, they tore him apart (Ovid, *Metamorphoses* 3.138–252).[63] This story may be important to the author of the *Cymbalum* for three reasons. One is the theme of *silence* (not announcing one's heterodoxy) and *speaking* (controversial speech and, possibly, *parrhesia*).[64] Another is the tradition, dating from the *Suda*, that Lucian was torn apart by dogs, a just punishment for his atheism. In this sense, then, as Malcolm Smith has persuasively argued, Acteon becomes Lucian, and the dogs in the *Cymbalum*, hitherto silent, gained Lucianic speech by eating Acteon's tongue. In this reading, the dog Hylactor may have been Étienne Dolet – a figure reported to have acknowledged his atheism at least orally – and Pamphagus may have been Rabelais.[65] Third, the eponymous Cynics were "dogs," which further reinforces the Lucianic link, particularly evident in Lucian's character Cyniscus – little dog – who voiced Zeus's vulnerability to Destiny in *Zeus Refuted*.[66]

Such a reading of the two dogs as representing the growing voice of atheism in the sixteenth century would contextualize certain comments in the *Cymbalum*. At the beginning of Book 4, Hylactor professes his frustration at having to remain silent until finding a fellow dog (atheist) to speak with: "What a great sorrow is it to remain silent, especially to those who have so much to say, like me!"[67] Hylactor also relishes the opportunity to be among fellow dogs, where he could "speak freely" (*parle librement*), and he embraces his role as vocal troublemaker, citing Aulus Gellius' *Attic Nights* 1.15 on "Vain and Troublesome Speakers," a diatribe against loquacity that quotes, if only tangentially, the choral condemnation of Pentheus' blasphemous

---

[63] Ovid, 1921, 1:134–43.
[64] On silence and speech in the *Cymbalum*, see Spitzer, 1951, 806–15.
[65] See M. Smith, 1991, 599–608, whose superb analysis of Book 4 I largely follow. On Pamphagus as Rabelais, also see Lefranc's discussion in Rabelais, 1922, lxv–lxvi.
[66] M. Smith, 1991, 600–2, 605–8. Smith also observes that figures such as Agrippa and Calvin referred to heterodox thinkers or atheists as dogs.
[67] Des Périers, 1958, 34–35, my trans.; Des Périers, 1723, 62.

Momus and the Reformation

"unbridled" insolence regarding Dionysus (*Bacchae* 386).[68] This theme of constrained silence and dangerous speech echoes Momus's acts of *parrhesia*. Finally, when Hylactor recounts various acts of troublemaking – several of which have been identified as transgressive acts tied to biblical references – he mentions "pissing on the pots of the potter [God, in Rom. 9:20–21] and dumping on his beautiful vases."[69] Possibly, this scene draws upon that of the drunken atheist who urinates and defecates on the statue of Jupiter in Alberti's *Momus*.

If the religious position of the author of the *Cymbalum* remains a question, his use of the Momus trope – both in the depiction of the explicitly blasphemous Mercury and the implicitly blasphemous dog Hylactor – is reasonably certain. So too is the author's likely familiarity with Alberti's *Momus*, which provided the general theme of a god sowing religious doubt on earth and several specific incidents: pilfering a divine book, mocking belief in the setting of a theater, desecrating divine objects, scarring a blasphemer.[70] The *Cymbalum's* response to Alberti's work thus would represent an antipodal one to Almazán's: using it as a template for religious doubt, rather than trying to rescue it from that fate. In the early eighteenth century Prosper Marchand wrote a lengthy appraisal of the work, largely aimed at defending it against numerous writers who judged the work anti-Catholic, anti-Christian, or overtly atheistic. His defense in fact reveals what might have been the strategy of writers like Alberti and the author of the *Cymbalum*: "I can see but one pretext to be made use of for the hideous out-cry against the Book I am speaking of [the *Cymbalum*], namely, to demonstrate, that under the Mask of Pagan Deities, the Author endeavours absolutely to

---

[68] Des Périers, 1958, 35–36; Aulus Gellius, 1927, 1:79; Euripides, 1912, 3:32.

[69] Des Périers, 1958, 36; M. Smith, 1991, 598; interestingly, in the 1723 English translation of the *Cymbalum*, this passage is eliminated; Des Périers, 1723, 64.

[70] It might also be worth noting that Alberti introduces the image of a dog in the scene involving Momus's attack for his atheistic proclamations: ironically, it is a Cynic philosopher who bites off his beard and who is identified as a "Cynic biter" (Alberti, 2003, 37).

102   *Doubting the Divine in Early Modern Europe*

deny the Existence of the Supreme Being, and to turn whatsoever is believ'd in Religion, into Ridicule."[71] Marchand defends the author with the same argument extended to Fathers of the Church, who mocked the pagan deities: namely, that he and they were simply mocking *false* religion.[72] Or maybe the critics were correct: sixteenth-century figures needed a mask to voice the Lucianic doubts about *all* religion.

Two Sixteenth-Century Italian Satirists: Niccolò Franco and Anton Francesco Doni

Back in Italy, Momus also made an appearance in the vernacular. Two figures in the emerging popular press, Niccolò Franco (1515–70) and Anton Francesco Doni (1513–74), made use of him in satirical writings that reflected both reform currents and Counter-Reformation constraints. Both of these figures were among the group of writers that historians such as Paul Grendler have classified as *poligrafi* (polygraphs), professionals of the press world who served variously as writers, copyeditors, publishers, plagiarists, and gadflies.[73] Franco and Doni were sometime associates – until bitter ex-associates – of the famous bad boy, Pietro Aretino, the pornographer and "scourge of princes" whose motto (via Terence) was *Veritas odium parit* (Truth begets hatred).[74] Ironically, even though Aretino himself was the embodiment of a sixteenth-century Momus – an identification Thomas Carew would later make – I find no use of Momus by this king of the caustic pasquinade.[75] His lesser-known colleagues, however, did find the god to be a handy vehicle for cultural and religious criticism.

---

[71] See the "Letter to Mr. B, P; and G. Concerning the Book Entitled, *Cymbalum mundi*," in Des Périers, 1723, xvii.

[72] Des Périers, 1723, xvii.

[73] Grendler, 1969, 3–69.

[74] Waddington, 2004, 6, 15, 96–103.

[75] Waddington, 2004; for Carew's identification of Aretino with Momus in the *Coelum Britannicum* of 1634, see Carew, 1634, 5–6.

Momus and the Reformation

No doubt largely owing to the presence of the papacy, Italy did not become a major center for Protestantism, but some reform currents were in play in the sixteenth century. There emerged a like-minded group of *spirituali* (or Evangelists), who promoted moderate, Erasmian-like reforms: a rejection of ceremony and complex theology, a criticism of clerical abuses, an emphasis on Scripture, and a preference for faith over works.[76] As Emily Michelson argues, scholars have recently resisted the historiographical polarity between these reform-minded *spirituali* and reactionary *intransigenti*, and instead favor viewing the religious climate in Italy along the lines of a continuum between Protestant left and Catholic right. Indeed, the wide range of *spirituali* included high-ranking ecclesiastical figures such as Cardinal Pole (papal legate in Viterbo) and Cardinals Sadoleto and Contarini; literary women such as Vittoria Colonna and Giulia Gonzaga, associates of the Spanish reformer and exile Juan de Valdés; the Capuchin leader and reformer Bernardino Ochino; and Pietro Carnesecchi, a close friend of Giulia Gonzaga with similar Valdesian sympathies. With the launching of the Roman Inquisition in 1542, the somewhat latitudinarian climate tightened, leading to the defection to the Protestant camp of some reformers, such as Ochino and Bishop Pier Paolo Vergerio; the exile of others, such as the Sienese Anti-Trinitarians Lelio, Camillo, and Fausto Sozzini; and the execution of yet others, such as Carnesecchi, convicted of heresy in 1567.[77] This constriction also led to the increased scrutiny of censors which flowered into the publication of the papal *Index of Forbidden Books* beginning in 1559. It was in this setting that Franco and Doni wrote. As Grendler has revealed, both of these figures

---

[76] Grendler, 1969, 104–35; Robin, 2007, 28–33.

[77] Michelson, 2013, 7–8; Grendler, 1969, 105–6; Grendler, 1977, 146; Caponetto, 1999; on Colonna and Gonzaga, see Robin, 2007, here, esp. 1–40, 160–62; on Ochini, the Sozzini, and Siena, see Marchetti, 1975; on Carnesecchi, convicted in part because of the discovery of 228 letters he wrote to Giulia Gonzaga (found in her effects at her death), see Black, 2009, 123–30.

104   *Doubting the Divine in Early Modern Europe*

shared some of the views of the *spirituali*.[78] Both figures found
Momus a useful voice.

In his *Dialogi piacevoli* (Amusing Dialogues) of 1539, Franco
featured Momus in two dialogues in his role as Olympian bureaucrat at Jove's court, where he reads complaints from the
mortals and announces decrees from the gods. In Dialogue
1, when a poet, Sannio (Franco's alter ego), unsuccessfully
attempts to enter the heavens under the guidance of Virtue,
Momus intervenes to gain him an audience with Jove.[79]
In Dialogue 6, Momus reads all manner of complaints and
petitions put to the gods with the eventual decision to convene
a council.[80] Thus, Franco's Momus is not so much Alberti's
ornery mischief-maker but closer to the figure in Lucian who
reads decrees and is, alongside Mercury, a principal court
administrator. Still, in both dialogues Franco raises issues of theodicy and particularly of the institutional Church. In Dialogue
1, Sannio is a satirical version of a Job-like figure appealing for
a hearing with the chief deity to gain relief from his hard life.
In his cheeky appeal to Jove – whom he characterizes in rather
biblical terms as "the consoler, who comforts the afflicted and
[is] guide for the lost" – his plea is all the more insulting: "Stir
yourself at least to pity; not the pity for my words but for the
misery of this poor and unhappy Virtue that you have given
me. I care for it [my Virtue] more than for myself. On account
of it I ask not for states, kingdoms, or subjects who might
worship me, nor servants who might bow to me, or Ganymedes
who might serve me wine."[81] Momus is both scandalized and
impressed by this snarky appeal that castigates the deity's envi-
able life. In fact, he proclaims that he is happy to see "that
I am not alone the evil tongue, the pestiferous and ill-speaking

[78] Grendler, 1969, 104–35. In 1547 Doni published a confession by an
anonymous weaver, which stressed salvation by faith and divine election,
which may have (but not necessarily) reflected some of his own religious
interests (Grendler, 1969, 127–33 and, for an edition of the confession
dated 1546, 250–52; Caponetto, 1999, 300).

[79] Franco, 2003, 18, 91–167.

[80] Franco, 2003, 253–71.

[81] Franco, 2003, 96–97, my trans.

Momus and the Reformation 105

mouth."[82] Franco thus channels Momus's spirit of *lèse-majesté* in his alter ego. After confronting various other gods, Sannio makes his last stand, grimly telling Jove that he had "always believed that Justice was in the heavens, for not having seen it on earth."[83] When Jove insists that divine Justice prevails, Sannio presents a lengthy rebuttal:

What justice made at night is it that in the world only the perfidious, scoundrels, the wicked, the sacrilegious, the homicidal, and the irreligious wallow [in good fortune], and that the good, the virtuous, and those who merit the blessing, grace, and favor of heaven are seen abandoned with no way to sustain themselves in that dog's life that you have given them? I do not hear anything but "Whose superb palace is that?" "Some scoundrel's"; "Whose that other one?" " Some usurer's"; "Whose is that great kingdom?" "Some unjust man's"; "Whose great dominion?" "Some dog's"; "Whose great wealth?" "Some traitor's, some pimp's, and some gigolo's."[84]

Sannio's indictment, however, goes further and seems to charge Jove with perverse irony (or malice): "O Jove, to how many do you give biscuits who do not have teeth, who for not being able to chew, must eat worms? To how many who can chew and taste do you give only the *panem doloris*?"[85] In citing the last two words in Latin, Franco is presumably recalling Psalms 127 (6):2, reinforcing the association of Jove with God.[86] In this psalm it is clear that without God's help, in vain "manducatis panem doloris" (do you eat the bread of toil), so Franco turns this to opposite effect with a god who maliciously consigns humans to ironic miseries. The result of this injustice will lead humans not only to doubt Jove, as Lucian's Momus warned, but also to mock him – and now the language bespeaks sixteenth-century heresy and sectarianism in regard to God:

O Jove, if for this reason there are more miserable people than happy ones, do not marvel why there are more of those who hold you in

[82] Franco, 2003, 98.
[83] Franco, 2003, 157.
[84] Franco, 2003, 157, my trans. On the theme of justice, cf. Simoncini, 1998, 435–49, esp. at 446–47.
[85] Franco, 2003, 157, my trans.
[86] Franco, 2003, 157n230.

106   *Doubting the Divine in Early Modern Europe*

contempt and your name in ridicule, than there are those who adore you and bow in praise. *O Jove, do you not see that, because of this, sprout forth the buds of heresies, because of this the sects and the confusions that whisper with strange grumbling of our being?*[87]

This diatribe ends on a particularly secular note that essentially mocks any notion of a blessed afterlife, as Sannio tells Jove "that I would prefer to enjoy [life] in the world and, when I am dead throw me in the ditch and shit on my head. Is there not less evil, O Jove, in suffering punishments *after* death than in life and death?"[88] This is a purely worldly view of human happiness and destiny in which Purgatory or Inferno or the Elysian Fields are of less concern to Sannio than a tolerable earthly existence. To Franco the fears or rewards of the afterlife would appear to hold little power.

Franco's Sannio, whom Momus has identified as his mortal counterpart, thus laments Jove's enabling of social injustice in the world and challenges his malicious mistreatment of his mortal charges. With his talk of heresies and sectarianism, Franco has surely grafted the sixteenth-century Christian God onto Lucian's Jove. Jove tells Sannio that he will entrust his case to "the will of Momus, he being your good friend."[89] When Momus reads the decree of the "curia celeste," Sannio's plight is remedied in many ways, although the proclamation suggests that more would be done if Jove "did not have a thousand troubles that impeded him": namely, repairs to temples and sacristies of the thirty-four cults of Jove and support of the priests of these cults.[90] Franco clearly is parodying the massive size of the Church, its buildings,

---

[87] Franco, 2003, 157, my trans., emphasis added.

[88] Franco, 2003, 158, my trans. This burlesque of the afterlife continues: "Se Megera m'ha da dare de le staffilate su 'l culo, poi che son morto, vuoi tu che il freddo e la fame me ne debbiano dare mentre son vivo? Vuoi ch'io mi muoia di sete vivendo, perché morendo me ne vada a bere ne l'isole fortunate e stare ne i campi Elisii con l'anime de' beati?" (158) Cf. the almost identical speech of Cyniscus – little Cynic – in Lucian's *Zeus Refuted* 17 (Lucian, 1913–67, 2:83).

[89] Franco, 2003, 158, my trans.

[90] Franco, 2003, 160–61.

Momus and the Reformation

and clergy. As for Sannio's brashness in making his appeal, the divine tribunal grants a *"plenaria indulgenza."* The institutional dimension of the satire becomes evident as now Jove appears not so much God as pope, whose Curia issues a plenary indulgence and must attend to the many economic demands of a massive bureaucracy.

The institutional metaphor of Olympus as the papal court fully flowers in Dialogue 6, in which grievances from mortals prompt the convening of a divine council. Here, because Mercury has been dispatched to deal with "heretical sophists who have wished to make new laws in our religion," Momus is deputed as convener. Franco Pignatti persuasively suggests that this divine deliberation is meant to simulate Gasparo Contarini's convening of a council of cardinals in 1536–37 to recommend reforms in advance of a planned papal council, which would eventually materialize as the Council of Trent.[91] Despite this ecclesiastical framework, many of the complaints Momus reads out to the tribunal are either pedestrian or satirical gravamina: the poor appeal for more grain from Ceres, the "good and wealthy" complain about the insolence of poets, the tavernkeepers lament the invasion of querulous philosophers who eat like wolves and drink wine straight from the jug; protests are lodged against moral injustices, as are complaints about the professional shortcomings of physicians, lawyers, artisans, and others. There are even objections about moral failings that might be not merely ironic but a commentary on the corrupting nature of current society: "Protests of the good that, if they become bad, it is not their fault. Protests of the religious that, if they become heretics, it is not their fault. Protests of the poets that, if they slander Jove, it is not their fault."[92]

---

[91] Franco, 2003, 253n1. In this scenario, Pignatti argues, Mercury might have symbolized the dispatch of the papal nuncio Pietro Paolo Vergerio to Germany to make known Pope Paul III's plans for a council (ibid.) (though also compare the incident in Alberti's *Momus* in which Momus is elevated at court in the absence of Apollo [Alberti, 2003, 230–31]). Momus, then, as convener of the council of gods, would be Contarini, whose commission recommended reforms that leaked to the Lutherans.

[92] Franco, 2003, 266, my trans.

108   *Doubting the Divine in Early Modern Europe*

There is also one possibly serious theological grievance, which seems to conflate themes from Lucian's *Zeus Refuted* (in which Zeus's power vis-à-vis Destiny is challenged) and *The Parliament of the Gods* (in which the admission of counterfeit gods to the Pantheon is challenged). Momus records the request of the "devout" that the goddess Fortuna be removed from the "college of the gods" because she has come to be worshipped with such devotion, incense, and vows that many believe her to govern the world. Jove should eliminate her power lest she dispossess him of his. If, on the other hand, she does have power over the gods, the mortals will submit to her – a comment that sends Jove "into a fever" (much like the panic he experiences in Lucian's *Zeus Rants* 45).[93] In reviving this Lucianic theme, Franco moves the argument from pure social satire to the edge of theological doubt. And while Franco's Momus is himself more the recorder than the originator of such secular suspicions, he nonetheless is the literary vehicle for these sentiments. And the challenge to divine justice and the embrace of mortalism by Franco's alter ego Sannio in Dialogue 1 squarely puts Franco in the tradition of both Lucian and Alberti in his cynical (better, Cynic) use of Momus.

Around the same time as Almazán published his Spanish translation of Alberti's Momus in 1553, Anton Francesco Doni published his own rendering of Momus that made cautious use of Alberti's novel. After leaving the Annunziati monastery of Servites in Florence in 1540, Doni, son of a scissorsmaker, led an itinerant life, often searching for a secular or ecclesiastical patron. For a brief period he established his own press in Florence with the aid of Duke Cosimo, but this venture was short-lived, possibly in part owing to Cosimo's doubts about Doni's religious views.[94] Doni's anti-monastic and anti-scholastic views were apparent in his *Letters* (1544–45), which were placed on the *Index of Forbidden Books* in 1559

[93] Franco, 2003, 264.
[94] Grendler, 1969, 49–56; Del Fante, 1976, 179. On Doni's life and works also see Longo, 1992; Cordíe, 1976; Biow, 2010, 157–85. On editions and assessments of his works see Ricottini Marsili-Libelli, 1960.

Momus and the Reformation 109

and remained there until 1930.[95] His contacts and publishing suggest the likelihood of heterodox influence: In 1546 he was named secretary of the Florentine Academy, which included figures who would subsequently be persecuted as heretics, and his letter collection reveals contacts with Francesco Linguardo (tried for heresy in 1548) and the Anti-Trinitarian Lelio Sozzini, whom, he writes in 1547, he anticipates meeting "per l'odor delle virtù vostre."[96] In 1546 he published Giambattista Gelli's *I capricci del bottaio* (Caprices of the Cooper), which ended up on the *Index*.[97] Scholars have generally appraised Doni's own religious views in the general category of Italian evangelism and the moderate Erasmian rejection of ceremony and embrace of religious simplicity.[98]

In fact, however, a darker side to Doni's religious views is apparent in a pseudonymous work he published in 1546. This brief dialogue, *Gli spiriti folletti* (The Impish Spirits), was published under the name "Celio Sanese" (Celio the Sienese), possibly revealing his interest in the heretical currents in Siena and the exile the previous year of Lelio and Camillo Sozzini from the city.[99] The dialogue features Dathan and Abiram, two of the apostates in Numbers 16:1–35 who, for challenging the authority of Moses and Aaron, were swallowed up by the earth and dispatched to the underworld. In their misery and eternal service to Lucifer, they describe their mission to ensnare mortals in evil ways: Abiram to tempt them to necromancy and Dathan to lure them into idolatry. As one who bristled at the ecclesiastical

---

[95] Del Fante, 1976, 179–85; on the censorship and expurgation of both Franco's and Doni's writings, also see Grendler, 1969, 180–82; Grendler, 1977, 258, 262.

[96] Doni, 1972, 28, 45; Del Fante, 1976, 189–92.

[97] Del Fante, 1976, 193; on the offending passages, see Ugolini, 1898, 9–10n3.

[98] Grendler, 1969, 127–35; Del Fante, 1976, 188; Del Fante, 1980, 117–19. A good encapsulation perhaps of his religious views comes in the "Mondo Savio e Pazzo," where the speaker Savio characterizes his religious teaching: "Insegnavo a conoscere Dio e ringraziarlo di tanto dono, e che s'amassino l'uno l'altro" (Doni, 1994, 172 and note 55 therein).

[99] On *Gli spiriti folletti*, see Longo, 1992, 160. On the inroads of reform in Siena starting in the later 1530s and 1540s, see McClure, 2010, esp. at 1156–57.

110 *Doubting the Divine in Early Modern Europe*

establishment, Doni might be suspected of being sympathetic to these Ur-rebels against priestly authority. Although this may be why he chose them, the story is less about their disobedience to God's priests than their perverse obedience to Lucifer: Doni creates a demonic religious world that ironically throws into relief features of the Christian one. The mischief of Dathan is especially revealing: in describing his efforts to lead mortals to "adore beasts as gods," his tactics have a familiar (Christian) ring in regard to deceiving believers into sacrificing their lives for an otherworldly figure. In their idolatrous worship, he reports, "they have a priest pray before an idol, saying that for the gods one wishes willingly to die in order to serve them, and so great is the force of persuasion that I [Dathan] give [the priest] that men insanely are induced to die willingly with this contrivance."[100] Thus, Doni's veiled implication is that it is a demonic force that empowers the Christian ministry to persuade people to die for God. In one image playing upon the deadly stricture of the priestly collar, the clerical analogy is unmistakable:

[The people] chose an iron ring, made like a collar, cutting in like a sharpened razor and placing it at the neck. They have a chain hanging down to the feet, fully binding the person together and when they hear these words inspired with cleverness and force, in one flash they distend themselves, such that the great tug of the feel pulls the chain and cuts the neck. Thus, they believe themselves to sacrifice and die for God.[101]

In another case, Dathan inspires people to throw themselves under carts in a religious festival, so that "thus dying they think to go to God."[102] The biblical Dathan and Abiram's rebellion and subsequent punishment would appear to be recast in "Dathan's" perverse perpetuation of torture and martyrdom in the service of religious idols – a demonic mission inspired by Lucifer.

If there is any question as to which side – Heaven or Hell – Doni is on in this scenario of rebellious believers, he offers a

---

[100] Del Fante, 1976, 202, my trans.
[101] Del Fante, 1976, 202, my trans.
[102] Del Fante, 1976, 202, my trans.

clue in the paean by Abiram to the "Prince of Darkness." When he praises the power and reach of the devil's kingdom as dwarfing that of the Athenians, Spartans, Carthaginians, and Romans, the reader at first supposes that Doni is simply parodying praises of secular states, but at one point he appears to praise the moral calculus of the underworld as the corrective of the upper world: "Here honors are not given to wealth, but to integrity which is declared by knowledge. In this kingdom comes no offense to the timid by the fierce, nor are the noble subject to the most vile, nor the poor disdained by the rich, but the bridle pulls all equally and the bit is placed equally hard, soft, and fierce to all."[103] Infernal though it might be, there is a social equality in this kingdom – themes Doni will revisit a few years later with the aid not of biblical rebels but with the help of the pagan god Momus.

In his *I mondi e gli inferni* (1552–53) Doni uses Momus at great length, offering up his second-most extensive portrayal (after Alberti) in the Italian Renaissance. As in the case of Almazán, however, Doni – who has also been characterized as having Erasmian sentiments – was careful to imbed Momus in more orthodox terms than had Lucian or Alberti. Even so, later editions of the work in 1597 and 1606 eliminated many passages deemed unacceptable to religious censors.[104] Doni apparently conceived the idea of the worlds in part from Thomas More's *Utopia*, a translation of which by Ortensio Lando he edited in 1548.[105] Certainly, the most famous of the worlds in the *Mondi* is one in which, like More, Doni promotes common property.[106] If it was the recent exploration of the New World that inspired More's new world in Book 2 of the *Utopia*, in Doni's

[103] Del Fante, 1976, 206, my trans. He celebrates Lucifer in terms that parody praises of God in Christian literature, confessing the limitations of his rhetorical powers to adequately match the task: "Se a la mia lingua da voi fosse concessa la potenza del dire, per che da sè non è potente, mai satia se ne vedrebbe, ne' secoli de' secoli, del dire et del lodar voi" (206) Cf. the tone in Augustine's *Confessions*, Book 1.1–6 (Augustine, 1991, 3–6).

[104] Doni, 1994, lii–liii.

[105] Doni, 1994, viii.

[106] Doni, 1994, 162n1; Grendler, 1969, 17–77; Cordié, 1976, 572–74, 588–89.

112 *Doubting the Divine in Early Modern Europe*

case the framework was not new discoveries in worldly geography but the invention of a cosmic geography oddly blending Christian theology and pagan mythology. Doni presents seven worlds. In the initial plan there were to be three orthodox worlds: a Small World (man as microcosm), a Large World (the actual world), and the Greatest World (God). These were to be followed by four fanciful worlds: a Mixed World, an Imagined World, a Laughable World, and a Wise and Mad World – all worlds in which Momus is a prime character.[107]

Doni changed his mind, however, about the actual order of the worlds as the text unfolded or as it was published. He imbedded the four capricious and unorthodox worlds within the three orthodox ones, so that they followed the Small World and Large World and preceded the Greatest World (of God).[108] Why the re-ordering? At the beginning of the treatise, Doni advises that all of the fantasies found in his worlds should be superseded in readers' minds by the foundations of Scripture and Christ.[109] At the end of the work, as he introduces the "Greatest World" of God – an exegesis on the description of the Ark of the Tabernacle in Exodus and a plagiarism of Giovanni Nesi's theological treatise *On Charity* – he roundly dismisses the failings, sins, fictions of all six preceding worlds, which can be remedied only by the "lesson of the true greatest world, Omnipotent God" and "his son Jesus Christ, true wisdom and true perfection."[110]

---

[107] Doni, 1994, 10 and note 33 therein. The discussions of these worlds often took place between characters identified as members of the Accademia dei Pellegrini, the existence of which scholars have questioned but is thought to have been at least an unofficial circle of intellectuals in Venice and its environs; Del Fante, 1980, 112–14; Cordié, 1976, 583.

[108] For a discussion of the work and its structure, see Marziano Guglielminetti's discussion of "I mondi di Momo" in Doni, 1994, xix–xxvii.

[109] Doni, 1994, 6.

[110] Doni, 1994, 189. Despite this proclamation of the spiritual precedence of the Greatest World, Doni clearly groups with it the Small World and the Large World as a benign trinity. One of Doni's speakers at the close of the Small World affirms God's benevolent plan regarding these worlds: "Dio, per sua bontà, ci conserve il picciol mondo sano e in pace il mondo grande, e all'estremo della vita ci doni (per sua pietà) e cif facci godere il suo regno, che non ha né termine né fine" (56).

Momus and the Reformation

In melding the Christian and the mythological, Doni thus takes a different tack from Alberti. Whereas Alberti wholly framed his novel in a pagan setting (except for the opening paragraph, which hints at an analogy between Jupiter and God), Doni creates parallel universes that allow him to lay out certain theological criticisms in mythic settings and then putatively disclaim them in an overtly pious closing. Why did he ultimately structure the work this way? The most obvious explanation – and one, of course, that may well be true – is that he wanted to reaffirm belief. Alternatively, however, he may have wanted to guard against criticism of any controversial discussions in the fanciful and darker mythological worlds. In that reading he, like Alberti, may have deployed Momus in order to disguise or license theological doubts.

Like Alberti, in his mythological worlds Doni depicts Jupiter's plan to re-make the flawed world.[111] Picking up the story of the re-creation of mankind via the tale of Deucalion and Pyrrha (in Ovid's *Metamorphoses* 1), Doni depicts Jupiter's eventual decision to restore the world by re-installing souls into mortal bodies and worldly professions. After finding so much dishonesty in numerous vocations (whether astrologers, princes, historians, or doctors), Jupiter is too disgusted to proceed with this, so he eventually decides that he should send Momus down to reverse the outward appearance of things: such that pleasures appear miserable, honor shameful, good bad, and so on.[112] Momus adds to this topsy-turvy solution by recommending that souls be assigned to bodies and social stations by lot. Doni's "theology" is very confused. On the one hand, this reversal of appearance and social leveling almost conjures Christian notions of the Sermon on the Mount (Matt. 5:3–10). On the other, these reversals lead not to otherworldly rewards, but to worldly despair and disbelief. Momus reports to Jupiter that mortals find

---

[111] Doni, 1994, 79n1.

[112] This decision is made after Momus suggests that Jupiter let mortals choose what they will of the good and the bad, and Jupiter says that he tried that and no one has chosen shame, poverty, or bitterness but only honor, riches, and delight (Doni, 1994, 92).

114   *Doubting the Divine in Early Modern Europe*

these reversals maddening and will seek relief. If they do not find it, he warns, they will turn elsewhere and worship the sun, fire, the moon, or a bull. Momus here echoes the strains of unbelief voiced by Lucian's Momus and human counterpart Damis in *Zeus Rants* 19–22 and 42.[113] A critique of the divine governance of the world that Lucian's Momus and Alberti's Momus both expressed is taken up by Doni in his mythic (and thus safer) parallel universe. The chaos of reversals and the random dispersal of souls into sometimes undeserving bodies has led to unjust lords, shameless women, dishonest youth, corrupt artisans, and so on. Momus and Jupiter realize that the world is in disarray.[114] At this point, although having helped create disorder (as Alberti's Momus did), Momus now recommends that Jupiter put all aright. When Jupiter asks, "since the world is broken, what will we do?" Momus counsels that he should see to it that the "great should esteem the lowly and the rich the poor, the learned should teach the ignorant, the good should be placed in high station and the evil abased."[115] Illness and lust should be eliminated, and all wealth redistributed. Momus thus calls for a correction of a flawed world, the full realization of which comes later in the utopian World of the Wise and Mad.[116]

Before that, however, Doni presents a Mixed World, one of varied conditions that in effect represents a parallel version of the Great World of earthly reality that Doni presented earlier in largely spiritual terms in the strains of a *contemptus mundi*. Most significantly, in this Mixed World, depicted as ordained by Jove, Doni ends with another critique of divine justice that is his most elaborate. When Momus invokes the "ancient shepherds and pure farmers" as the epitome of a simple, good life, the soul of one such figure protests at their exploitation by the world. Upon hearing this, Momus confronts Jove with a diatribe against divine injustice in the world, which in effect rehearses the attack

[113] Doni, 1994, 105nn17–18.
[114] Doni, 1994, 105–7.
[115] Doni, 1994, 107, my trans.
[116] Doni, 1994, xxii.

Momus and the Reformation   115

Franco presented in the voice of Sannio in his Dialogue 1 – only now the critique comes in the voice of Momus. Thus, Doni's Momus now fully becomes heir to Lucian's and Alberti's:

O Jove, the mixed world does not have any remedy to repair itself. What will you do, Jove? Purity flees that world, goodness does not wish to hear about it, and virtue prefers to be buried than to enter there. Dispel with thunderbolts, Jove, confound, I say, O Jove, naughty Fortune, who is made queen of the greater part [of this world]. *If you are the greatest monarch, you are able to do this.* If peace contents you, if goodness pleases you, and if virtue comforts you, why do you support so much war, malice, and ignorance? All the food, which ought to go to the poor, goes to dogs, falcons, and pimps. The plebs are raised into the seats of the virtuous, and the ignorant occupy almost all the places worthy of deserving, honored personages. O Jove, do you not hear the plaints of the good, the laments of the just, the sighs of the simple, the afflictions of the poor, the cries of the unjustly assassinated ...? Do you hear the voices of those who are tyrannized; do you hear the violence done to them by the most dissolute types, those who are placed in servitude, who are oppressed, who are deprived of their own home, deprived of their clothes, goods, and life? Vices prevail ... and conquer virtue. Alas, Jove, superstition contaminates faith, iniquity presses and tramples upon truth, usury devours poverty – when do you want to stir? O Jove, O Jove, wake up [and realize] that justice will soon cede to force, and infamy and shame will be able to remain, and in a short while little by little corrupt honesty, honor, and loyalty [which] by falling into a precipice will never again be able to rise up. [Momus enumerates a string of family betrayals and then closes.] Alas, Jove, everything is broken, everything mixed, confused, and turned upside down![117]

Although inspired by Franco's Dialogue 1, Doni moves the complaint from the human plane (of Sannio) to the divine plane (of Momus). The charges of his Momus are more direct than those of Lucian (who has Momus speculate as to mortal doubts) or those of Alberti (who has Momus fabricate atheistic beliefs among mortals). No, this is now an unmediated confrontation of a lesser god questioning the justice or power of the highest god. Momus's taunts have theological heft: If your power, Jove, is total, then your justice is flawed. If your justice is lacking, then

---

[117] Doni, 1994, 128, my trans., emphasis added; Grendler, 1969, 90–91.

116   *Doubting the Divine in Early Modern Europe*

your power is lacking. Invoking an invidious comparison to the power of the goddess Fortuna, Momus dares Jove: "If you are the greatest monarch, you are able to do this." Thus, Jove, prompted here to be omnipotent, is the counterpart to God, identified by Doni in the later Greatest World as "God omnipotent."[118] Although Doni, like Franco, may be truly following in the theological footsteps of Job (though in far greater acts of *lèse-majesté*), still he protects himself, as these complaints about the divine are tucked into a mythological interlude.

What was Doni's intention in the work? Certainly, such a thoroughgoing mixing of the Christian and pagan worlds in one work is unusual. The ex-monk and satirist was thus able to have his cake and eat it too: or proclaim his piety and question it too. The censors did not approve of this inapposite blending of the sacred and the profane. They excised religious language and biblical references in the mythological Worlds, and removed comments in the Imagined World on religious hypocrisy and the distinction between a mortal "soul" and immortal "spirito."[119] Also excised were various sections in the utopian World of the Wise and Mad.[120] In most cases, the task of the Counter-Reformation censors was straightforward, but in one instance at least Doni's mischief may have been a subtle challenge. When Jove and Momus plan to go to earth disguised as pilgrims to talk to the interlocutors of the Wise and Mad World, Momus ponders, "Who would believe that Jove would ever come to earth and take the form of a Pilgrim?"[121] The hint of the Incarnation looms here, and Doni seems to mock the Pauline distinction that true faith is the evidence of things not seen (Heb. 11:1), as he has Momus ponder: "It will never be believed, if it will be

---

[118] Doni, 1994, 189.

[119] See, for instance, Momus's implicit citation of Scripture in the Imagined World at Doni, 1994, 108n31, and lvii–lx; on the excisions in Laughable World see ibid., 134, 140; also an exchange between Jove and Momus on the futile quest for eternity via epitaphs (expurgated in the 1597 edition and completely eliminated in the 1606 edition; ibid., 152–57, and 152n1.

[120] Doni, 1994, 166n15, 172n54. On the expurgation of a story regarding an archbishop originally in Doni's *Dialogo della musica*, see Cordié, 1976.

[121] Doni, 1994, 150–51, 174, my trans.

Momus and the Reformation 117

known and indeed is true; [this following passage is excised] and if it would be believed, being known, it will be necessary to believe it in a certain way that seems impossible to believe, knowing to know it as certain."[122] In Momus's comment here, Doni seems to mock the passage perhaps not as a sublime mystery so much as a perverse paradox.[123]

If this passage hints at a resistance to matters of unquestioned or non-rational belief, Doni's *Mondi* reveals skepticism or cynicism in various contexts. In the Great World (the actual world mortals inhabit), Doni hews to a traditional *contemptus mundi* in his introduction to this section, affirming "the unhappiness of this brief life, transitory, uncertain, miserable, and mortal."[124] There is, however, something other than the conventional acceptance of mortal misery awaiting otherworldly deliverance. Doni presents a discourse on the "laws of God and Nature" ("Mosaic, evangelical, human, civil"), which concludes with a story that challenges the justice of the world and God.[125] One of Doni's interlocutors presents a lengthy story of a virtuous woman, widowed at age 26, who is gradually seduced by a ruthless drifter who marries her, brutally murders her, and steals her estate's wealth. When one of the interlocutors bewails this tragedy as illustrative of "the dreadfulness of the perverse events of the world" which the law often cannot prevent or adequately punish, his respondent urges that they put their reasoning to an end and invokes the example and suffering of Christ, "the sweetest and kindest law."[126] To this conventional religious entreaty, the doubting speaker replies: "Why do I not have a spirit elevated enough to

[122] Doni, 1994, 174 and note 2 therein, my trans. In the accompanying work, the *Infernos*, Doni in fact expressly cites the Pauline passage, which is excised by censors (ibid., 246). Also, cf. Jesus's chastising of doubting Thomas in John 20:29 for believing only after seeing him, following the Resurrection.

[123] Doni had considerable interest in the trope of the paradox, as he had praised Ortensio Lando's recent *Paradossi* of 1543; Grendler, 1969, 29–31.

[124] Doni, 1994, 57, my trans.

[125] Doni, 1994, 68, my trans.

[126] Doni, 1994, 72, 75, my trans.

comprehend [Christ's] mysteries?"[127] This statement may not be so much an admission of spiritual weakness as an indictment of divine justice.[128]

The strains of religious doubt are joined by those of cynicism and materialism in other sections of the *Mondi*. One of Doni's worlds, the Laughable World, in fact mocks the folly of the world in the spirit of Democritus, the "laughing" philosopher depicted in Lucian's *On Sacrifices*, Alberti's *Momus*, and elsewhere.[129] Especially noteworthy in the *Mondo Risibile* is a materialist metaphor of the mill that continually turns to churn out hours, to fill and empty the body, to produce generation and corruption, pleasures and woes, riches and poverty.[130] This fluctuation is akin to the relentless random swerve of atoms in Lucretius' thought and in Democritus' survey of human variability in the Pseudo-Hippocratic "Letter to Damagetus" (which both Alberti and Doni knew).[131] The particularly pessimistic vein in this metaphor comes at the end, where Doni, having pronounced the alphabet subject to the mill, churns out a list of eighty-four examples of the language of "*biasimo*" (blame) from "*arrigante*" to "*volubile*."[132] Pessimism and materialism also may underlie the ridicule of human epitaphs that Jove and Momus undertake in the

[127] Doni, 1994, 75, my trans.

[128] Patrizia Pellizzari (Doni, 1994, 68n9) suggests that some of this indictment of the law likely is inspired by More's attack on the law in *Utopia*, but More's treatment wholly dealt with secular law, whereas Doni's discussion incorporates divine law and ends on a note of religious doubt.

[129] Doni briefly cites the traditional pairing of (laughing) Democritus and (weeping) Heraclitus at Doni, 1994, 129–30; cf. Lucian, 1913–67, 3:171; Alberti, 2003, 249 and 392n18 (for the classical loci of this pairing; on which also Wind, 1958, 53–54, esp. 54n1); Doni was likely inspired as well by Antonio Filareno's *Riso di Democrito e pianto di Heraclito*, to which he referred in his *Libraria* (Doni, 1972, 79; Doni, 1994, 129–30n5). Momus would at times be associated with Democritus, as evident in the 1854 *Laughing Philosopher: Being the Entire Works of Momus, Jester of Olympus; Democritus, the Merry Philosopher of Greece, and Their Illustrious Disciples.*

[130] Doni, 1994, 135–37.

[131] Hippocrates, 1990, esp. at 85 and note 2 therein; Greenblatt, 2011; Doni, 1994, xxiv–xxv; Alberti, 2003, 392n19.

[132] Doni, 1994, 137.

Momus and the Reformation 119

Laughable World, a conversation excised in the 1606 edition of the work.[133] Also censored was part of an earlier section on the quest for immortality via medals in which a distinction between a mortal "*anima*" and an immortal "*spirito*" is proposed and declared by one of the interlocutors as dangerous territory.[134] Such notions of mortalism in man are, furthermore, matched with materialist references in the work to the earth as a "*machina*."[135]

Whether it be Momus's report of the chaos unleashed by Jove's instructions to reverse the appearance of things (in the "Imagined World") or Momus's criticism of Jove's injustice (in the Mixed World), Doni uses him as a figure to air his pessimism regarding the disorder of the world. All of his criticisms and his vision of a communist utopia contained within his four mythological worlds are tucked within a Christian framework that ends with an affirmation of God and Christ – an affirmation that purports to dispel all such earlier fantastical ruminations. He thus takes a cue from Alberti that Momus is a vehicle for theological doubt, but in the Counter-Reformation climate of the mid sixteenth century – when, for instance, Doni's acquaintance Francesco Linguardo had been tried for heresy in 1548 – discretion may have been the better part of valor.[136] Certainly, Momus served Doni as an archetype for criticism and justice in both worldly and otherworldly settings. The year following the publication of *I mondi*, he issued his companion piece, *Gli Inferni*. Here Momus turns from being a critic of a divine judgment to being an admirer of its just display. In a Dantesque journey to Hell, Momus stands in for Dante's Virgil as a constant, but as one implicated as among the fallen. Doni casts him as the exiled figure of Aesop and Alberti (and analogous to Lucifer). In a solo speech Momus reveals: "See what wretched fate is

[133] Doni, 1994, 152–57.
[134] One of Doni's interlocutors ascribes this view to a person (characterized as "stolto") and his respondent reacts to it saying, "Deh, vedete in che discorso voi sete entrato!" (Doni, 1994, 140; if nothing else, this reaction probably helped the censor in his task).
[135] Doni, 1994, 6, 58, 67.
[136] Del Fante, 1976, 191–92.

120   *Doubting the Divine in Early Modern Europe*

mine. I was accustomed to stand among the gods and I have become the intimate of devils. I attended to things high, now to the low; I smiled at happiness and it is necessary [now] to weep at griefs."[137] Whereas Dante's Hell was strictly moral, however, Doni's is populated by professional types, including scholars, doctors, lawyers, poets, artisans, prostitutes, and others.[138] In this, he reflects the growing professional preoccupation in cultural criticism launched by Agrippa von Nettesheim's *De incertitudine et vanitate scientiarum* (1526) and culminating in Tomaso Garzoni's massive 1585 *Piazza universale di tutte le professioni del mondo*.[139] The development of the popular press in the sixteenth century particularly elevated the professional writers, and in my final chapter I shall revisit Momus's role in Doni's Hell of the Poets and Writers.[140]

As for Doni's use of the pagan gods – and especially Momus – for theological and social criticism, the blending of the Christian and the mythological is more thorough in the *Inferni*, presumably because these Hells all deal with just deserts. In the *Mondi*, however, the worlds were generally discrete, and when theological comments and biblical citations intruded in the four pagan sections the censor wielded his pen. Can the caustic and satirical sections of the Imaginary, Mixed, Laughable, and Wise/Mad Worlds be reconciled with the orthodoxy of the Small, Great, and Greatest Worlds? Certainly, Doni seems to offer highly contrasting theological visions. And yet, the pagan interlude is not merely idle, as Momus's lengthy appeal to Jove at the end of the Mixed World suggests. Furthermore, in one instance the two realms overlap when, at the end of the Great World, one speaker confesses that the sacrifice of Christ seems to be a mystery too sublime to account for the tragedy of the virtuous widow horribly murdered by a rogue. Here a believer's implicit objection to Christian theodicy parallels Momus's objections to Jove. Further, the inversions of rich and poor, high and low,

---

[137] Doni, 1994, 233 and note 1 therein, my trans.
[138] Of seven Hells, four are professional; Doni, 1994, 219.
[139] Agrippa, 1542; Garzoni, 1996; Doni, 1994, xvii; McClure, 2004, 70–140.
[140] Doni, 1994, 343–58.

that Jove orders Momus to wreak upon the world creates a pessimism and despair that threatens belief – despite the resonance of such inversions in the Sermon on the Mount. Finally, accompanying the chaos of such inversions is a Democritean materialism and pessimism that resonates with Alberti's theme in the *Momus* and anticipates the dangerous views of Giordano Bruno.

The onset of the Reformation certainly sharpened suspicions about the reappearance of Momus in the sixteenth century, while at the same time it piqued new interest in him. As the religious crisis intensified, mythological gods no longer simply instructed or diverted from the safe distance of an ancient world but potentially roiled the religious climate of the contemporary world. The reform-minded Catholic Erasmus perhaps realized this early in the century with his careful avoidance of Lucian's Momus treatises and his own rather limited and benign use of Momus. This caution did not stop Luther from hurling "Momus" as an epithet against him, when their paths diverged. In this more charged atmosphere, Alberti's *Momus* found new relevance: a mid-century Spanish translator taking great pains to exonerate it of any dangerous theological meaning, an anonymous French writer likely recasting it as controversial religious (or anti-religious) fable. The Italian satirists Niccolò Franco and Anton Francesco Doni deployed Momus as a transgressive act: Franco did so in a critique of divine governance (in regard to social justice) and in a satire of the institutional Church on the eve of the Council of Trent. Doni cut much closer to the bone. The censor's edits were not merely the product of a heightened paranoia due to the confessional struggles: while framing his worlds with three orthodox ones, he nonetheless overwhelmed the Christian vision with pagan worlds that implicitly challenged and destabilized the orthodoxy mandated by the Counter-Reformation. By mixing the Christian and mythological worlds so thoroughly in one work, he made the analogies inescapable. What Alberti lightly hinted at in this regard Doni made unmistakable.

In more guarded terms, religious currents may also have inspired the artistic presence of Momus in the sixteenth century.

FIGURE 1 *Momus Criticizing the Gods' Creations*. Maarten van Heemskerck, 1561. Courtesy of bpk Bildagentur/Gemäldegalerie, Berlin.

A depiction of him appeared in Holland in Maarten van Heemskerck's *Momus Criticizing the Gods' Creations* (1561) (Fig. 1). Erasmus may have been inspirational here as well. David Cast argues that Heemskerck was influenced by the theologian and fellow artist Dirck Coornhert, who wrote against ceremonies and ritual in 1560.[141] The result was a sympathetic Erasmian portrait of Momus as Socrates-like truth-teller engaged in the "unmasking of false gods," or, in this case, flawed religious practices.[142] Possibly, then, in the artistic setting and certainly in the literary one, Momus's antics in the sixteenth century constituted not simply a Renaissance moral metaphor but also a Reformation religious one. By the end of the century, Giordano Bruno took this metaphor to its most radical extreme.

[141] Cast, 1974.
[142] Cast, 1974, 32. Cast's essay is superb on some of the details of the history of Momus, but I disagree with his view of Erasmus's wholly positive attitude toward the god. His interpretation does offer an interesting theory as to why Heemskerck transformed the male creation of Hephaestus into a female: namely, she is meant to be a symbol of Truth (32).

4

The Execution of Giordano Bruno

When the Roman Inquisition condemned Giordano Bruno in February of 1600, the indictment cited his reputation as an atheist when he was in England, specifying a book he wrote while there: the *Spaccio della bestia trionfante* (Expulsion of the Triumphant Beast).[1] This work, published in 1584, featured Momus as one of its principal characters: most notably, it depicted him making a string of comments that could be (and were) seen in only the most blasphemous terms. Like Alberti, Bruno presumes to identify his mythological metaphor in perhaps diversionary terms: whereas Alberti rather unpersuasively states that his work is only about a prince and his court, Bruno suggests that his subject is vice. As he states in his "Explanatory Epistle" to Philip Sidney: "Then is expelled the triumphant beast, that is, the vices which predominate and are wont to tread upon the divine side; the mind is repurged of errors and become adorned with virtues."[2] In fact, however, the "beast" is more likely – or, at least, also – Christianity, as some of Bruno's Catholic readers apparently recognized. As we shall see, his vision in the *Expulsion* draws together literary models from Lucian (and possibly his successors) with Hermetic views

---

[1] See Arthur Imerti's "Editor's Introduction" in Bruno, 1964, 63–64; Stampanato, 1933, 191.
[2] Bruno, 1964, 80.

124   *Doubting the Divine in Early Modern Europe*

that promoted a materialist, naturalist worldview providing an intellectual link between Lucretius and Spinoza.[3]

Like Doni, Bruno was an ex-monk, although one who left his order perhaps more by necessity than simple restlessness. Initially a Dominican in Naples in 1563, by 1576 he left the order owing largely to suspicions of Arianism and began a peripatetic life, which took him to Calvin's Geneva, to France, and then to England, where he wrote the *Expulsion*.[4] After stints in Germany and Bohemia, in 1591 he was invited to Venice to instruct Zuan Mocenigo on the "art of memory."[5] Sadly, it was Mocenigo who denounced Bruno to the Inquisition, leading to eight years of imprisonment and finally execution. Aside from his lifelong interest in the art of memory, predicated largely on the writings of Raymond Lull, Bruno is largely associated with Hermetism, a mystical tradition from the second and third centuries CE. Purported to be the wisdom of the ancient Egyptian god Thoth, who was linked to the Greek god Hermes, these teachings were recorded by the legendary Hermes Trismegistus. This Hermetic tradition readily blended with Neoplatonism and offered an occult lore by which to access the divine world through its physical manifestations – a lore that led to magical views of channeling the divine through statues, amulets, and images. As we saw in Chapter 2, Alberti knew parts of the Hermetic corpus, the *Kore Kosmou*, via the translation of Stobaeus. Subsequently, Marsilio Ficino translated the entire corpus and further popularized the tradition, always careful to try to reconcile it with Christian thought.[6] Bruno drew both on Ficino's Hermetic thought and the study of the occult in Agrippa von Nettesheim's *De occulta*

[3] In fact, the link between Bruno and Spinoza might even have been textual; on the possibility that Spinoza read Bruno, see Imerti in Bruno, 1964, 45.

[4] On Bruno's life, see Yates, 1969, 190ff.; Imerti in Bruno, 1964, 3–65; Rowland, 2008, esp. 71–73. In his Venetian interrogation of January 2, 1592, he admits to citing and somewhat defending the position of Arius and suggests that this was an issue in his troubles in Naples (Stampanato, 1933, 97; Mercati, 1942, 65).

[5] On the "art of memory" see Yates, 1966, esp. 199–230.

[6] Walker, 1975.

philosophia (1510).[7] Agrippa's and Bruno's occult interests flowered in the turbulent religious climate of the Reformation and Counter-Reformation, which offered a natural breeding ground for skepticism of traditional religion(s) and interest in alternative truths.[8] Bruno himself ran afoul of both Catholics (in Naples, Venice, and Rome) and Calvinists (in Geneva), so he could not be called a strong partisan of either party. Some scholars have argued that Bruno at times sought to reconcile the warring sides via a Hermetic compromise.[9] Some of his contemporaries apparently thought otherwise: at the inquest in Venice in 1592, one book dealer reported rumors "that he is thought to be a man without religion" and another a conversation in which a Carmelite prior remarked "that he had no religion so far as he could tell."[10]

Certainly, Bruno was a freethinker in terms of challenging conventional views, even identifying himself on the title-page of one work as "the Academic of no Academy."[11] He wrote the *Expulsion* the same year in which he produced his (now) more famous work, the *Ash Wednesday Supper*, in which he defends the Copernican system, and his Lucretian *On the Infinite Universe and Worlds*.[12] The *Expulsion* reveals his use of Lucian's dialogues for a satirical frame and the use of the Hermetic corpus for a philosophical view. The character of Momus is central in both of these contexts. The treatise generally depicts Jove's recognition that he needs to call a divine council to reform Olympian matters (the format of Lucian's *Parliament of the Gods*), owing largely to his increasing insecurity about the gods' standing on earth and their decrepitude vis-à-vis Fate and Justice (themes in Lucian's *Zeus Rants* and *Zeus Refuted*). The

---

[7] Agrippa, 1992.
[8] On the seemingly anomalous compatibility of skepticism and belief in the occult, see Nauert, 1965, 141.
[9] Edward Gosselin and Lawrence Lerner argue that this is his goal in the *Ash Wednesday Supper* ("Introduction," in Bruno, 1977, 34–53).
[10] Rowland, 2008, 238–39.
[11] Rowland, 2008, 132.
[12] Yates, 1969, 245–46.

126   *Doubting the Divine in Early Modern Europe*

occasion of Jove's resolution to reform the heavens is the feast of Gigantomachy commemorating the Olympian gods' epic defeat of the Giants. Why, he asks, should we dare celebrate the victory "at a time when we are despised and contemned by the rats of the earth?"[13] Bruno depicts a failed divine hierarchy in which "the great reputation of our majesty, providence, and justice has been destroyed."[14] The gods' vices must be expelled and replaced with virtues; the record of their behavior in myths and the subsequent embodiment in the constellations of the heavens must be reformed. Thus, the bulk of the treatise explains how to drive out the "Bear [Ursa Major] of Deformity," the "Orion of Pride," the "Capricorn of Deceptions," and so on, replacing these with virtues.[15]

One could read the treatise simply as a piece of moral philosophy, but given the role of the gods in creating vice – the constellation Ursa Major, for instance, results from Jove's illicit union with Callisto, whom Juno turned into a she-bear – this work is also one of theology.[16] In this theology, Jove is a figure of impotence, who declares his weakness in the face of Chance and Fortune.[17] His admission resembles Zeus's exchange with Cyniscus in Lucian's *Zeus Refuted*, where the "little Cynic" tweaks Zeus regarding his vulnerability vis-à-vis the higher powers of the Fates, Fortune, and Destiny. Bruno, however, adds a further philosophical (or cosmological) dimension to Jove's weakness. In the "Explanatory Letter" to Philip Sidney, he labels Jove as just one force in a Lucretian infinity of entities, forces, and vicissitudes: as "something variable, subject to the Fate of Mutation."[18] He not only reduces Jove to a former mortal raised high – a Euhemerist slight that Lucian broached – but he also dissolves him into the materialist soup that encompasses all entities divine and otherwise. Furthermore, of all the

[13] Bruno, 1964, 106.
[14] Bruno, 1964, 106.
[15] Bruno, 1964, 115.
[16] Bruno, 1964, 113.
[17] Bruno, 1964, 99.
[18] Bruno, 1964, 75.

The Execution of Giordano Bruno

variabilities and conditions that Bruno discusses in the treatise, such as Goodness, Wisdom, Wealth, Poverty, and Fortune, he gives the most power to Fortune. Acknowledging Fortune's universality, Jove grants her no *one* seat in heaven but he sanctions her presence everywhere – in heaven, on earth, even in other worlds – such "that you open for yourself those places that are closed to Jove himself as well as to all the other gods."[19] This elevation of Fortune's powers reads like a cynical version of Pico della Mirandola's "Oration on the Dignity of Man," in which God refuses to assign Adam any one place in the universe given the protean potential of his free will.[20] From Petrarch's massive *On the Remedies of Both Kinds of Fortune* to Machiavelli's famous chapter 25 of *The Prince*, Fortune commanded a prominent place in Italian Renaissance thought.[21] Now she seems to be accorded full cosmic power. As we saw earlier, in his *Pleasant Dialogues 6*, Franco has Momus report the mortals' request to Jove that Fortune be removed from the pantheon. Now, in Bruno, Jove throws in the towel and concedes the day to her, as she proclaims that in her presence all the gods are fear-struck, with teeth "chattering and clicking from fear."[22]

Momus serves as Jove's chief minister in the *Expulsion*, executing the reform of the heavens. Like Alberti's Momus, Bruno's god is one who is alternately both critic and advisor. Bruno alludes to Momus's prior misadventures, even locating his exile – as Alberti's gods proposed to do at one point – in relation to the Caucasus Mountains:

Momus, who had spoken against the gods, and had argued, as it seemed to them, too severely against their errors, therefore had been banished from their consistory and from conversation with them, and relegated to the star which is at the tip of Callisto's tail, without the privilege of passing the limit of that parallel under which Mount Caucasus lies. There the poor god was weakened by the rigors of cold and hunger, but now is recalled, vindicated, restored to his pristine state, and made

[19] Bruno, 1964, 176.
[20] Cassirer, Kristeller, and Randall, 1948, 224–25.
[21] Petrarca, 1991; McClure, 1991, 46–72; Machiavelli, 1979, 159–62.
[22] Bruno, 1964, 168; cf. Lucian, 1913–67, 2:159.

128   *Doubting the Divine in Early Modern Europe*

ordinary and extraordinary herald, with the most ample privilege of being able to reprehend vices without any regard to the title or dignity of any person.[23]

This version of Momus's back story almost certainly confirms Bruno's knowledge of Alberti's novel. In his rehabilitation he now has once again a privileged status in the heavenly court and plays the central role in reconstituting the divine order – much as did the Momus figure in the Hermetic *Kore Kosmou*. His symbolic importance, however, goes further, as Bruno identifies him as an embodiment of moral truth. In the "Explanatory Epistle" to Sidney where he decodes the treatise, he reveals that Jove's intention to reform the heavens is like a human's aim to reform his soul "by a certain light that resides in the crow's nest, topsail, or stern of our soul, which light is called synderesis [conscience] by some, and here, perhaps, is almost always signified by Momus."[24] Momus thus represents human conscience and is identified by Bruno to be the highest moral arbiter. This elevation makes all the more telling the heretical and blasphemous exchanges that Bruno later puts in his mouth.

The treatise depicts the convening of the divine council, at which Momus is the spokesman of the gods in recommending to Jove the reform of the constellations. As in Lucian's *Parliament of the Gods*, the issue here is the legitimacy of those inhabiting the heavens (such as demigods). In Bruno's treatise, however, the point of contention is not so much the divine lineage of figures in the pantheon as the immoral mythology behind the constellations in the sky. Thus, the constellations Hercules and Perseus are expelled because of their derivation from Jove's illicit affairs with mortals.[25] The discussions of two of the constellations clearly reveal Bruno's intention to challenge Christian ortho-doxy. In the first of these, Momus asks Jove what is to be done with Capricorn, the constellation honoring Pan, who in one version of the myth rescued the gods from Typhon in Egypt by

[23] Bruno, 1964, 95.
[24] Bruno, 1964, 79.
[25] Bruno, 1964, 127–28, 187.

The Execution of Giordano Bruno

teaching them to magically turn themselves into beasts.[26] As the god of nature, Pan, or Capricorn, is the ideal god for Bruno to seize upon to develop simultaneously his notions of natural religion and magic. This question provokes Momus and Jove to discuss the immanence of the gods (or God) in nature. One of the dialogue's interlocutors reports Jove's comment here "that animals and plants are living effects of Nature [and that] this Nature (as you must know) is none other than God in things."[27] To this, the other discussant replies in Latin: "natura est deus in rebus."[28] This affirmation of a religion of nature obviously anticipates – and likely shapes – Spinoza's famous formulation of *Deus sive natura*. In any case, Bruno proceeds with a case for naturalism and materialism that implicitly links themes in Lucretius, the Hermetic corpus, and Alberti's *Momus*, to the full flowering of a naturalist religion in Spinoza.

Bruno develops this theme in especially occult, Hermetic terms. When Jove explains to Momus how "one ascends to Divinity through Nature," Momus agrees that these Egyptian

wise men through these means had the power to make intimate, affable, and friendly toward themselves, the gods, who, by means of cries they sent forth through statues, gave these wise men advice, doctrines, divinations, and superhuman institutions; when with magic and divine rites they rose to the height of Divinity by means of the same ladder of Nature by which Divinity descends even to the lowest things in order to communicate herself.[29]

Bruno then brings in the Egyptian goddess Isis herself to explain in great detail to Momus the workings of the divine in animals, showing how the Egyptians worshipped Jove variously in libations to the eagle, the serpent, the crocodile, and other animals. As for how the Egyptians could do this when the Greek cult of Jove came *later*, Bruno essentially dissolves the specific divinities, saying that Jove and Venus were simply humans invested with divinity

---

[26] Bruno, 1964, 235; see the account in the *Mythical Tales* attributed to Gaius Julius Hyginus (d. 17 CE) in Eratosthenes and Hyginus, 2015, 80.

[27] Bruno, 1964, 235.

[28] Bruno, 1964, 235; Bruno, 1927, 186.

[29] Bruno, 1964, 236.

130   *Doubting the Divine in Early Modern Europe*

by human custom. As gods are diminished, so are earthly things elevated as vehicles for the divine. Bruno cites at length from the *Asclepius* the lament of Hermes Trismegistus regarding the decline of Egyptian religion:

From this you can infer how the wisdom of the Egyptians, which is lost, worshipped not only the earth, the moon, the sun, and other stars of heaven but also crocodiles, lizards, serpents, onions. This magic and divine rite (through which Divinity so easily imparted herself to men) is mourned by Trismegistus, who said when reasoning with Asclepius: "Do you see, oh Asclepius, these animated statues full of feeling and spirit that are the cause of such and so many worthy works, these statues, I say, prognosticators of future things ...?"[30]

In assessing Bruno's religious position in the *Expulsion*, scholars generally judge him to be more critical of Calvinism than Catholicism, owing to his attack on the Protestant denigration of good works.[31] His call, however, for the revival of Egyptian magic and pantheism certainly suggests, as Frances Yates argues, that "Bruno takes a radical step, which puts him outside the pale of normal Christian Hermetism, by abandoning the Christian interpretation, and above all, by going wholeheartedly for the magic as the chief thing, the core of Hermetism."[32]

This non-Christian – or even anti-Christian – position will be made more polemical in Momus's treatment of the second constellation, Orion. Here, the full force of the Lucianic dimension of the treatise, which Yates underemphasizes, comes to the fore in blasphemous terms correctly recognized by an anonymous Neapolitan annotator of a copy of the 1584 edition of the work. When Neptune asks what should become of his son Orion, who by legend could walk on water, Momus's reply is that Orion, clearly depicted as an analogue to Christ, be sent to earth to deceive mortals, mislead them regarding the truth, and dissuade them from pursuing magic that could enable them to approach the divine. Momus's advice:

He [Orion] knows how to perform miracles, and, as Neptune knows, can walk over the waves of the sea without sinking, without wetting

[30] Bruno, 1964, 241; Bruno, 1927, 192; Yates, 1969, 214.
[31] Bruno, 1964, 146–47; Yates, 1969, 225–26.
[32] Yates, 1969, 230.

The Execution of Giordano Bruno

his feet [cf. Matt. 14:25–26], and with this, consequently, will be able to perform many other fine acts of kindness. Let us send him among men, and let us see to it that he give them to understand all that I want and like them to understand: that white is black, that the human intellect, through which they seem to see best, is blindness, and that that which according to reason seems excellent, good, and very good, is vile, criminal, and extremely bad. I want them to understand that Nature is a whorish prostitute, that natural law is ribaldry, that Nature and Divinity cannot concur in one and the same good end … that they [Nature and Divinity] are contraries, as are shadows and light.[33]

Thus, having been instructed earlier by Jove that Nature and Divinity are virtually synonymous, Momus now cynically suggests that the gods protect their status by sending down an emissary to deceive them. Orion as Christ is not a figure of light and truth, but all darkness and deception. Not surprisingly, at the start of this section, the anonymous annotator wrote: "De Orione; sed, o Christe, mutate nomine de te fabula narratur" (Concerning Orion: but, O Christ, with the name changed this fable is narrated concerning you).[34]

Why does Momus recommend this? In part, because he re-enacts the role of Lucian's Momus, who purports to protect the status of the pantheon by calling for higher standards for divine behavior and admission to Olympus. But for Bruno's Momus the point is to create benighted devotion to traditional Greek gods through manipulation of the truth, through a false narrative that "no one can be pleasing to the gods except by Hellenizing, that is, by making himself a Greek."[35] All this can be translated into the notion no one can be pleasing to God, except by Christianity, that is, by making himself a Christian, even though it is clear – even to Bruno's Jove – that religious truth is grounded instead in nature. What Momus's ploy would do is protect Olympus not from, say, the dubious demigods

---

[33] Bruno, 1964, 255.
[34] Bruno, 1927, 207n2; on the anonymous commentator see 6n3; Bruno, 1964, 294n3.
[35] Bruno, 1964, 255.

132   *Doubting the Divine in Early Modern Europe*

of Lucian's *Parliament of the Gods*, but from the hubris and ambition of mortals: "With this he [Orion] will persuade them [mortals] that philosophy, all contemplation, and all magic that could make them similar to us, are nothing but follies, that every heroic act is only cowardice, and that ignorance is the best science in the world."[36] In this perverse suggestion on behalf of an insecure divine hierarchy, Bruno's Momus plays the role – probably borrowed – that Momus plays in the Hermetic *Kore Kosmou*, in which Momus, fearing the great power and success of humans, recommends that the gods visit hardships upon mortals.[37] Bruno has adapted this idea, with particular venom, into a ruse in which a Christ figure, Orion, will deceive mortals into a false, subservient belief. If other readers, like the anonymous commentator, saw Momus's Orion as Christ, the blasphemous inference is clear.

Subsequently, however, Momus starts to regret this advice, given that Orion may be overweening and may persuade mortals that "great Jove is not Jove, but that Orion is Jove," a comment that provokes the anonymous annotator to plausibly speculate, "Against Christ, perhaps."[38] Regarding the worship of such a false god, Minerva speaks up and equates Orion, "who is a Greek and a man of some merit," with another mortal born from another line [the Hebrews] "who is adored as Jove," and this is unquestionably an allusion to Christ. Minerva declares that, although this figure will "obtain that place [Jovian stature]

---

[36] Bruno, 1964, 256.

[37] *Hermetica* 484–85; Garin, 1975, 149–50; Yates, 1969, 215–17. If Bruno knew Doni's *Mondi*, he might have drawn this notion of inverting appearances from Doni. On Doni and Bruno, see Omodeo, 2016.

[38] "In Christum fortasse" (Bruno, 1927, 208n1). As for the overbearing presence of Orion (or Christ), earlier in the "Explanatory Letter" to Sidney, Bruno says of Orion: "Divine and Miraculous Orion disconcerts the Divinities with Imposture, Profitless Courtesy, Vain Prodigy, Prestidigitation, Sleight of Hand, and Knavery, which, as guides, conductors, and doorkeepers, serve Boastfulness, Vainglory, Usurpation" (Bruno, 1964, 86). Given the depictions of Orion (as Christ) as a trickster, deceiver, and impostor in the *Expulsion*, it is no surprise that some would see this work as one and the same as the infamous Tale of the Three Impostors (see below).

The Execution of Giordano Bruno   133

or throne," he only "serves as the ape and mockery of blind mortals," an extremely anti-Christian statement upon which the anonymous annotator oddly neglects to comment.[39]

Jove does not accept Momus's recommendation that Orion be sent down to confuse and misdirect mortals from their true promise of greatness, heroism, and magical access to the divine. Instead, he will send him to earth stripped of all of his power in order to assure that he not diminish human agency:

I want him [Orion] to go down to earth; and I shall command that he lose all power of performing bagatelles, impostures, acts of cunning, kind actions, and other miracles that are of no worth, because I do not want him together with the other [the Christ figure to whom Minerva refers] to be in a position to destroy whatever excellence and dignity are found and exist in things necessary to the commonwealth of the world.[40]

The anonymous annotator marks this passage as voicing "vain complaints of atheistic men against Christianity."[41] Bruno seems to want to depict God as rewriting Christian history by not doing what Momus suggested, by not sending down a figure "superior to himself … by whom everything will be depreciated, slighted, confused, and thrown into disorder, ignorance being placed by the latter where knowledge is customary."[42] Minerva assents, and thus Orion will be dispatched from his place in heaven to be replaced by "Industry, Military Training, and Military Art, through which the peace and authority of the fatherland may be maintained, barbarians be fought, beaten, and converted to civilized life and human society, and inhuman, porcine, savage, and bestial cults, religions, sacrifices, and laws be annihilated."[43] At the passage regarding the replacement of Orion with "Military Training," the annotator remarks that "in the place of true Christianity the Nolan [Bruno] puts the Military

[39] Bruno, 1964, 257, 308n6.
[40] Bruno, 1964, 257.
[41] "Vana querela atheorum hominum in Christianismum" (Bruno, 1927, 210n1).
[42] Bruno, 1964, 257.
[43] Bruno, 1964, 257–58.

134   *Doubting the Divine in Early Modern Europe*

Art."[44] In all of these comments by Momus, Jove, and Minerva regarding Orion, Bruno presents a striking attack on Christ and his role in the world. Furthermore, like Alberti – whose *Momus* Bruno appears to have read – he frames some of this conflict between the divine and human as a struggle between the agency and industry of humans and the malice and insecurity of gods (God). Where Bruno goes beyond Alberti is in his denigration of Christ, a figure virtually absent (pro or con) in Alberti's works.

Other parts of the inflammatory ending of the *Expulsion* include further assaults on Christianity. When Momus raises the issue of what to do with Centaur, he frames the question of hybridity as a spoof of the dual nature of Christ: "Now what do we wish to do with this man inserted into a beast, or this beast imprisoned in a man, in which one person is made of two natures and two substances concur in one hypostatic union? Here two things come into union to make a third entity; and of this there is no doubt whatsoever."[45] At this comment the annotator notes: "Again, against Christ under the persona of the Centaur, just as above, under Orion."[46] Jove tells Momus that he should not try to understand this matter, but simply believe it. Like the Jove of Doni's *Mondi* who could not understand the mystery of Christ, Bruno's Jove likewise insists on a non-rational belief. Of course, this could reveal on the part of both authors a nod to fideism, but Momus's concession is rather caustic: "And to please you, oh Jove, I want to believe that one sleeve and one trouser leg are worth more than a pair of sleeves and a pair of trousers; and I want to believe much more still, that a man is not a man, and that a half of beast is not a half beast, that a half man and a half beast are not an imperfect man and an imperfect beast, but rather ... a god."[47] Momus's skepticism appears to overpower his will to believe.

Finally, Bruno even mocks the Eucharist. When Jove turns to review the status of the "Hare, whom I want, through

[44] Bruno, 1927, 210n3, my trans.
[45] Bruno, 1964, 268.
[46] Bruno, 1927, 223n4, my trans.
[47] Bruno, 1964, 269.

The Execution of Giordano Bruno   135

Contemplation of Death, to be the prototype of Hope and Confidence, the contraries of Fear," Bruno likely intends to invoke Christ's role as conqueror of the fear of death. Inappropriately enough, Momus responds with an obviously satirical riff on the theology of Communion:

> I understand, oh Jove, that he who eats hare becomes beautiful. Let us then bring it about that whosoever will eat of this animal, be he male or female, shall change from one who is ugly to one who is well formed, from one who is graceless to one who is graceful. And may the belly and stomach of him who contains, digests, and is converted to it, be blessed.[48]

Not only does Bruno mock the transformative power of eating the Hare, but also the theological debates regarding the presence of the body and blood of Christ in the bread and wine of the sacrament: "'I shall tell you,' said Momus, 'a way in which the entire world will be able both to eat and to drink of her, without her being eaten and drunk, without there being a tooth that will touch her, a hand that will feel her, an eye that will see her, and perhaps, even a place that will contain her.'"[49]

A treatise that begins as a rather benign piece of moral philosophy depicting the expulsion of vices with a playful mythological framework becomes a serious assault on theology by the end. The anonymous annotator was not overreaching when he noted the scurrilous analogies to and ridicule of Christ. Most of these blasphemous comments are voiced by the figure of Momus. While he plays the Lucianic and Albertian role of erstwhile exile and rehabilitated courtier in the *Expulsion*, he is also given the unusual distinction of being the synderesis, the conscience that enables humans to right their moral course. This elevation of Momus in the "Explanatory Letter" to Sidney makes all the more potent his cynical depiction of the function of Christ and the Eucharist. Moreover, this denigration of Christ conforms with Bruno's earliest flirtation with Arianism in Naples in the 1570s and the charges leveled against him the interrogations in the 1590s

---

[48] Bruno, 1964, 259–60.
[49] Bruno, 1964, 260, 308n7, 47.

136   *Doubting the Divine in Early Modern Europe*

up through his execution. In a Venetian interrogation of June 2, 1592, he confesses his doubts as to how Christ was incarnated but claims that he has never denied it.[50] The record of his condemnation on February 8, 1600, in Rome cites his denial of transubstantiation, alleges (but does not identify) eight heretical propositions, and mentions that while in England "he was held to be an atheist and had composed a book on the *Triumphant Beast*."[51]

That some incorrectly thought that this "beast" was the pope is evident in a letter written on the day of Bruno's execution on February 17. A recent Catholic convert from Lutheranism, Caspar Schoppe, wrote a Lutheran acquaintance, Konrad Rittershausen, of Bruno's execution. In regard to the *Expulsion*, he comments on "the book he wrote on the Triumphant Beast, that is, the Pope, whom your people [the Lutherans] are accustomed to honorarily call the beast."[52] This assumption was mistaken: Bruno's stated beast was vice and his likely subtext was Christianity itself, not the pope or the Catholic Church. Other parts of Schoppe's letter, however, offer plausible reasons for Bruno's condemnation. He specifies Bruno's doctrines regarding infinite worlds and the transmigration of souls; his belief that magic is legitimate and that Moses was a magician; his views that the world is eternal, that the Holy Spirit is merely the "*anima mundi*," that "Christ is not God but was an extraordinary magician," and so on.[53] Most famous in his letter is the report of Bruno's spurning of the crucifix just before his death: "Today therefore, led to the funeral pyre, when the image of the crucifix of the Savior was shown to him as he was about to die, having spurned it with a savage expression, he rejected it."[54] Having confessed to his doubts about Christ from the age of 18, his last act was to reject his image.

Certainly, there was a matrix of offensive views that led to Bruno's execution, and Schoppe lists other works besides the

[50] Stampanato, 1933, 97.
[51] Stampanato, 1933, 191, my trans.
[52] Stampanato, 1933, 200, my trans.; Blum, 2012, 109; D. Berti, 1868, 181.
[53] Stampanato, 1933, 200–1, my trans.
[54] Stampanato, 1933, 202, my trans.

The Execution of Giordano Bruno

Expulsion in naming his "dreadful and utterly absurd" matters.[55] Still, the *Expulsion* contained unmistakably blasphemous comments regarding Christ that were evident to the anonymous annotator. The sections on Capricorn, which affirmed Hermetic magic, and those on Orion, the Centaur, and the Hare, which depicted Christ's role on earth in either perverse or destructive terms vis-à-vis mortals, clearly represent heterodox and even anti-Christian views. Bruno's Momus is at the center of these exchanges involving the affirmation of Hermetic naturalism and the ridicule of Christian belief. Whereas Lucian used Momus to mock Jove, and Alberti used him to mock the pope and God, Bruno used him to mock Christ.

How central was the *Expulsion* in Bruno's execution? Unfortunately, the eight doctrines named by his examiner, Cardinal Bellarmino, are not named in the condemnation. If the inquisitors, like Schoppe, mistook the "triumphant beast" for the pope, then they were misled by the work's ambiguous, yet sensational title. In fact, the treatise's real affront was much deeper than that. Domenico Berti links Bruno's views to the religious relativism famously voiced over two centuries earlier in Boccaccio's "Tale of the Three Rings" in *Decameron* 1.3, in which a father (God) constructs three identical rings (Judaism, Christianity, Islam) to be given to his three sons as equally legitimate heirs of his estate.[56] Others have gone much further and linked the *Expulsion* to the infamous *Treatise of the Three Impostors* (Moses, Jesus, and Mohammed), a work that had a mythical origin from the thirteenth century until its eventual publication in Latin and French versions in the seventeenth and early eighteenth centuries.[57] As Silvia Berti and Georges Minois

---

[55] Schoppe (Stampanato, 1933, 200) lists the *De umbris idearum*, the *De immenso et infinito*, and the *De innumerabilibus*, in the last two cases jumbling the *De l'infinito universo e mondi* and the *De immenso, innumerabilibus et infigurabilibus* (on which see Yates, 1969, 245–46).

[56] Boccaccio, 1995, 41–44; D. Berti, 1868, 183–84.

[57] On the Latin *De tribus impostoribus* (printings of which first began to be reported in the 1660s) and the *Traité des trois imposteurs* (1719), see Minois, 2012; S. Berti, 1992.

138   *Doubting the Divine in Early Modern Europe*

have shown, this treatise – incorporating material from the likes of Giulio Cesare Vanini (1584–1619), Machiavelli, Pierre Charron, Hobbes, and particularly Spinoza – represents the culmination of a skeptical, materialist view of the origin of religion (in fear and superstition) and its misuse for political and social reasons.[58] The English freethinker John Toland is likely the source of the belief that the *Expulsion* was actually the *Three Impostors*.[59] At least two of his contemporaries testified to this, as did Prosper Marchand later, who also attributed the 1713 English translation of the *Expulsion* to Toland: "If one is able to believe Toland, the work so renowned for so long a time under the title *De tribus impostoribus* is none other than the *Spaccio de la bestia trionfante*: and that fact, which would have deterred every honorable person from reproducing it is precisely that which determined him to translate it into English."[60] Toland had ties with various figures involved with the circulation of manuscripts of the *Three Impostors* treatise and may have played a part in revising it for its 1719 publication.[61]

[58] S. Berti, 1992; Minois, 2012, 163–89.

[59] Champion, [1990?], 4.

[60] Marchand, 1758–59, 318; my trans; Marchand goes on to identify the 1713 London translation as this translation (on the disputed authorship of which see Bruno, 1964, 281n4; Aquilecchia, 1975). On earlier testaments of Toland's promoting the *Spaccio* as the *Three Impostors*, Mathurin Veyssière de la Croze reported that in conversation in 1702 "Monsieur Toland, qui a ses raisons pour faire beaucoup de cas de cet ouvrage, croit que c'est celui qui est si fameux dans la monde, sous le titre de Traité des trois imposteurs" (cited in Champion. [1990?], 4; also see Champion, 1992, 150–54; Minois, 2012, 55–56, 160–61; Jacob, 1981, 37–38, 220). The interest in and outrage at the *Spaccio* in early eighteenth-century London is clear from an entry in the *Spectator* on May 27, 1712 by Eustace Budgell, who, remarking on the high price a copy of the *Spaccio* brought at a recent auction, condemns Bruno as "a professed atheist, with a design to depreciate religion" (Budgell, 1853, 464) and describes the work as appealing to atheists' proclivities: in it, he says, "Momus tells [Jupiter] that the [great decay of the worship of the gods] is not to be wondered at, since there were so many scandalous stories of the deities, upon which the author takes occasion to cast reflections upon other religions." As a result, this treatise has "recommended itself wholly by its impiety to those weak men [whom he goes on to identify as atheists] who would distinguish themselves by the singularity of their opinions" (465).

[61] Champion, [1990?]; Minois, 2012, 157–61.

In a 1720 treatise entitled *Discourses Concerning the Ever-Blessed Trinity*, Thomas Brett opens with a chapter "On the Folly of Atheism" in which he attacks Bruno and particularly the *Expulsion*, assigning it an argument from the *Three Impostors* that it does not contain. First, he clarifies that the Inquisition was wrong to think that the target of the treatise was the Catholic Church:

The *Roman* Inquisitors however mistook him in the Title of the Book, which has given me Occasion to mention him here; by which it is pretty plain, he does not so much mean their Religion, as the Christian [religion] in general, and any other whatsoever. It is a most Enthusiastick Atheistical Satyr against all Religion; being a feigned Conference between *Jupiter, Momus,* and the *Constellations*: Wherein he represents *Jupiter* as complaining of the Decay of the Worship of the Gods amongst Men; and *Momus* as casting the Blame of it upon their Amours and Misgovernment. Whereupon the *Constellations* being advised with, it is decreed that all Religions shall be abolish'd, and the Moral Vertues set up in their room; with such Stuff. Horrid Comparisons are therein made between the Fables of the Poets, and the Sacred Histories of the Bible.[62]

And then he imports the Three Impostors: "and Moses, and our Blessed Saviour being shuffled in with Mahomet, are styled Impostors; as God generally in the Writings of this Brute is called Nature."[63]

That the French version of the *Treatise of the Three Impostors* first appeared under the title *L'Esprit de Spinoza* bespeaks Spinoza's major presence in its content: indeed, one chapter largely reproduces the Appendix to Part 1 of his *Ethics*.[64] But Spinoza is also particularly relevant to our study of Momus, because he represents an important terminus of materialist currents found in several of the early modern Momus authors – and, conversely, he argues that Momus found his way into the Bible in disguised form. As to materialism, a presupposition that underlay Democritean and Lucretian thought, we have seen

[62] Brett, 1720, 9–10.
[63] Brett, 1720, 10.
[64] Minois, 2012, esp. 169 and appendix 1; S. Berti, 1992; Spinoza, 2000, 107–12; Anderson, 1997, ix, 8–11; Jacob, 1981, 215–24.

140   *Doubting the Divine in Early Modern Europe*

this theme developed somewhat in Alberti's *Momus*: especially in regard to his references to the world as a "machine," to the logic of worshipping natural forces (such as the sun), and to Democritus' challenge to Apollo concerning any plan to destroy the material world. In Anton Francesco Doni's *I mondi* – whose very title may have emboldened Bruno's advancing his cosmology of infinite worlds – the material view is concretized by his image of the mill continuously churning out hours, generation and corruption, corporeal intake and excretion.[65] In one section of the Wise and Mad World, moreover, in which Jove and Momus discuss the magical power of statues, Doni draws on a recent translation of Lucian's *Syrian Goddess* (1539) and Hermetic themes in Ottone Lupano's *Torricella* (1540).[66] In Bruno, the Hermetic triumph over the traditional Greek gods and Christianity culminates in a pantheistic natural religion that points toward Spinoza's *Deus sive natura*.[67] While Spinoza lacks the Hermetic dimension found in Bruno, he certainly furthers the identification of God and nature. The authors of the *Treatise of the Three Impostors* enlist Spinoza's *Ethics* as a contemporary complement to Lucretius' materialism and turn Spinoza's position to polemical ends.[68]

As Spinoza demystified God with nature, he also demystified Scripture with reason. In his *Theologico-Political Treatise* of 1670, published anonymously, he applied a critical, skeptical analysis to the composition of the Bible – discounting, for instance, the possibility that Moses was the author of the Pentateuch. This investigation led him to consider the Book of Job, which posed Scripture's most substantive treatment of

---

[65] On multiple worlds in Doni and Bruno, cf. Omodeo, 2016.

[66] Doni, 1994, 174–87, 174n1; Masi, 1992.

[67] On the identification of God and nature, see the *Ethics* (Spinoza, 2000, 226, 231).

[68] While Spinoza's Preface to his *Theologico-Political Treatise* of 1670 shows that he certainly shared Lucretius' view that fear has provoked superstitious forms of religion, he does not go to the atheistic ends of the author(s) of the *Three Impostors* (Spinoza, 1951, 3–11).

The Execution of Giordano Bruno 141

theodicy. And, here, Spinoza offers an astute theory on the possible relevance of Momus to scriptural tradition:

> The book and personality of Job have caused much controversy. Some think that the book is the work of Moses, and the whole narrative merely allegorical ... Aben Ezra ... affirms, in his commentaries, that the work is a translation into Hebrew from some other language; I could wish that he could advance more cogent arguments than he does, for we might then conclude that the Gentiles also had sacred books. I myself leave the matter undecided, but I conjecture Job to have been a Gentile, and a man of very stable character, who at first prospered, then was assailed with terrible calamities, and finally was restored to happiness.[69]

Then, Spinoza proposes the true identity of the Adversary in the book:

> I should also be inclined to agree with Aben Ezra that the book is a translation, for its poetry seems akin to that of the Gentiles; thus the *Father of Gods summons a council, and Momus, here called Satan, criticizes the Divine decrees with the utmost freedom*. But these are mere conjectures without any solid foundation.[70]

In speculating that Momus might be Satan, Spinoza make a connection that Milton may have envisioned in *Paradise Lost*, published three years before the *Theologico-Political Treatise*.

Deploying Momus as divine advisor and a divine critic, Bruno had Lucian's Momus as a ready model. He also, however, surely drew upon Alberti's novel, as he depicts Momus as a one-time exile banished to the region of the Caucasus Mountains. This Promethean identification signaled Alberti's attempt to heroize this god as a martyr for the cause of a dynamic mankind. Similarly, Bruno signaled his regard for Momus not merely by this Promethean allusion but also by declaring in his "Explanatory Epistle" to Sidney that Momus was the symbol of human conscience: "a certain light" in the "stern of soul" that can lead the way to virtue.[71] This privileging of Momus makes

---

[69] Spinoza, 1951, 149.
[70] Spinoza, 1951, 149–50, emphasis added.
[71] Bruno, 1964, 79.

142 *Doubting the Divine in Early Modern Europe*

all the more telling Bruno's use the impish god, which would be the most radical of the sixteenth century. Where Erasmus avoided reviving Lucian's Momus dialogues and the Spanish translator of Alberti's *Momus* unpersuasively took pains to protect the innocence of the novel, Bruno represents the further extension of the Momus trope into blasphemous territory. Franco and Doni before him used Momus in tamer ways – to challenge divine justice, to mock efforts at Church reform – but Bruno uses him to propose a naturalist, Hermetic religion in concert with Jove and Isis and to flagrantly denounce the function of Christ in the figure of Orion. In this, Bruno was as radical as Alberti, though in slightly different terms. Alberti's Momus put forward Lucretian, atheistic arguments, and the figure of "Gelasto" (or Alberti himself) confessed to unbelief. Bruno's depictions of Orion, the Centaur, and the Hare disparage Christ and the Eucharist. Even worse, Momus's proposal that Orion be sent down to confuse mankind and militate against Nature suggests overtly hostile views of Christianity's relationship to reason and the natural world. In fact, this sentiment adumbrates the view in the *Treatise of the Three Impostors* that when humans embraced religion "they no longer had anything but contempt for nature, and respect only those pretended beings, which they named Gods."[72] One can see how some, like John Toland, were apt to associate the *Expulsion of the Triumphant Beast* with the *Three Impostors*.[73] In the speech on Orion, Bruno (via Momus) basically proposes that Christ be deployed as an impostor to keep mortals from realizing their true potential vis-à-vis the gods. Bruno of course had no part in the *Three Impostors*, though he almost certainly influenced the naturalism and pantheism of Spinoza, under whose "spirit" the atheistic treatise first appeared. The nexus between the idea of naturalism and the deployment of Momus was evident in Alberti, Doni, and Bruno. All of these thinkers, via the Momus meme,

[72] Anderson, 1997, 14.
[73] Cf. in the *Expulsion* the comment that "natura est deus in rebus" (Bruno, 1964, 235) to the comment in the *Three Impostors* regarding "God, as we have seen, being but nature" (Anderson, 1997, 33).

independently or as a collective, led to Spinoza's formulation of *Deus sive natura*. Perhaps these influences help to explain why, in his textual analysis of Scripture in the *Theologico-Political Treatise*, Spinoza is the one to identify the greatest challenge to God in the Bible – the Adversary in Job – as Momus. As for Bruno, his Arian doubts about the nature of Christ, which dated from his early years, crystallized in the *Expulsion*. His detractors were wrong to think that the Beast was the pope. His anonymous annotator, however, was right to see that his Momus was a blasphemer.

5

Milton's Lucifer

As Bruno proved, befriending Momus could be dangerous. Alberti avoided this liability by hiding the theological critique more deeply within his text. Another solution – witting or unwitting – was to incorporate the Momus meme into analogous archetypes from the Judeo-Christian tradition: specifically, Lucifer and the Adversary in Job. In this part of the story Momus proceeds often in disguise, sprinkling fairy dust of doubt in occasional passages or remaining completely hidden as a silent conspirator in an author's challenge to traditional belief. In 1667, just a few years before Spinoza posed his theory that the Satan figure in Job may have been Momus, Milton published the initial ten-book version of his epic treatment of Satan in which, I will argue, Momus lurks as a figure skulking around the edges, whispering doubts about divine justice and offering a template for Lucifer's rebellion.[1]

Lay readers and literary critics have long been struck with the rather obvious fact that Lucifer is the most compelling character in *Paradise Lost*. As in Milton's war in heaven, critics have waged their own pitched battle regarding the depiction of Lucifer: the pro-Satanists (emphasizing Lucifer's heroic, complex interiority) vs. the anti-Satanists (stressing his self-denigration and willful malevolence). Romantics recognized

---

[1] In 1674, the year of his death, Milton published the revised twelve-book version of *Paradise Lost* (Parker, 1968, 1:595–605).

144

Milton's Lucifer

the attraction and power of Milton's antihero, Blake claiming that Milton was "of the Devil's party without knowing it" and Shelley seeing in Lucifer a heroic analogue to Prometheus.[2] Orthodox readers insist that the lesson is clear: C. S. Lewis points to the poem's opening line, which speaks of "man's first disobedience."[3] Stanley Fish split the difference in his influential 1967 *Surprised by Sin*, saying that both readings are legitimate. That is, Milton wanted the reader to fall for Satan's argument (and thereby participate in mankind's sin and Fall) and then be chastened and redeemed by the truths of orthodox characters such as Raphael and Michael.[4]

I do not presume here to enter the lists of a centuries-long debate among the Miltonists, but I do want to propose that another factor be considered. In a wonderful chapter John Carey argues that "no convincing single source for Milton's Satan has been found."[5] In part this may be due to the originality of the text. But in part it may also be due to Satan's trimorphic nature: Archangel in Heaven, then King of Hell, then Tempter on earth. Some critics see fluctuating traits of Milton's Lucifer according to his changing roles: more positive features when he is leader of the rebel angels; more negative ones when tempting Eve; overall, a lack of unity in the character.[6] One way out of the thicket of criticism is to expand the models on which Milton may have drawn. Most

---

[2] For the full version of Blake's famous statement see his *Marriage of Heaven and Hell*, where he states "the reason Milton wrote in fetters when he wrote of Angels & God, and at liberty when of Devils & Hell, is because he was a true Poet and of the Devils party without knowing it" (Blake, 1982, 35); Shelley, 1989, 472–74.

[3] Lewis, 1942, 69–70; Bryson, 2012, 10.

[4] The critical debate on Milton from Dryden and Addison to the present is of course voluminous. For sample summaries see Fish's "Preface to the Second Edition" of *Surprised by Sin* (Fish, 1997, ix–lxix); Empson, 1965, 9–35 (forgiving his personally polemical intrusions); Bryson, 2012, 1–15 (forgiving his sensational title); Revard, 1980, 15–27; Forsyth, 2003, 69–76; Dobranski and Rumrich, 1998, 1–17.

[5] J. Carey, 1989, 160.

[6] Kastor, 1974, 15–31; J. Carey, 1989; though see criticism of this view in Forsyth, 2003, 25.

146   *Doubting the Divine in Early Modern Europe*

attention has been paid to religious archetypes found in such sources as the Old English "Caedmon" poems, Hugo Grotius's *Adamus Exul* (1601), Giovan Battista Andreini's *L'Adamo* (1613), and Joost van den Vondel's *Lucifer* (1654).[7] Some have looked to Prometheus (another god who was punished for transgressing the divine order) and to more recent models of antiheroes or tragic figures such as Marlowe's Faust or Shakespeare's Macbeth, Iago, or, as an example in "revenge tragedy," Hamlet.[8] David Quint's *Inside Paradise Lost* offers a thoroughgoing reading of the poem through the lens of classical models – such as Homer, Hesiod, Virgil, Euripides, Lucretius, and Ovid – though not Aesop and Lucian (both of whom communed with Momus) even though Milton apparently knew the first and certainly the second.[9]

In fact, no one to my knowledge has ever suggested the archetype of Momus as a template for Lucifer, even though the mythic parallels, especially as detailed in Alberti's *Momus*, are striking: a god exiled from Olympus for insubordination and treachery goes to earth to cause trouble among mortals through dissimulation and brings the order of heaven and earth into near collapse. He is a character now envious and hateful, now genuine and perceptive: a Lucifer in Olympian dress. Perhaps these similarities are not coincidental. Milton's classical interests, his travels, and his religious and political views suggest that they are not. In particular, Milton had three likely exposures to the Renaissance revival of Momus: via Thomas Carew, Giovan

---

[7] For translations and a compilation of possible such sources for Milton, see Kirkconnell, 1967. It is debated whether the Old English *Genesis A*, *Genesis B*, and *Christ and Satan*, dubiously attributed to Caedmon and published by Franciscus Junius in Amsterdam in 1654, were known to Milton, whose facility in Old English is questioned (Krapp, 1931; Revard, 1980, 141–43, esp. note 27; Forsyth, 2003, 50–54).

[8] Forsyth, 2003, 316–17. Those who would tie Lucifer to Prometheus in his role as "trickster" god and "culture hero" on behalf of mankind (Forsyth, 2003, 312n19; Werblowsky, 1952) would find an analogy in Momus's identification with Prometheus (Alberti, 2003, 22–23, 30–31, 276–77).

[9] Quint, 2014; Boswell, 1975, 3, 160; Milton, 1953–82, 1:701, 834.

Milton's Lucifer   147

Battista Andreini, and Alberti – the last two resulting from his trip to Italy in 1638–39. This story has several twists and turns.

Milton's interest in classical mythology is evident in his various academic *Prolusions* written during his university days at Cambridge in the 1620s and early 30s. In fact, his very first such oratorical exercise, "Whether Day or Night is the More Excellent," is replete with mythology, including the list of the many children of Night, one of whom was Momus, or, in the Latin of the *Prolusion*, "Querela."[10] Night – the child of Earth or, alternatively, of Chaos (which figured prominently in *Paradise Lost*) – was described as engaging in a war with Day. Aside from the sad truth that Night's assault over Day – or darkness over light – would intensify in Milton's writing with the onset of his blindness in 1652, there is posed here the template of a cosmic battle, though he transforms the various physical revolts of lesser gods against greater ones into a rhetorical one: "Her [Night's] thoughts now turn to complaint [here, significantly, "*querela*"] and accusations, and, womanlike, after a brave fight with tooth and nail, she proceeds to argument or rather abuse, to try, I suppose, whether her hands or her tongue are the better weapon. But I will soon show how unadvised, how arrogant, and how ill-founded is her claim to supremacy."[11] Already, then, in his university days Milton had begun to transform the cosmic battle of Hesiod's *Theogony* into a rhetorical agon. And Momus's eponymous role of lodging a "*querela*" (complaint) was thus present in this, Milton's first public literary performance. But Momus himself, in truer Greek form, was to be found in a work written considerably later: in, appropriately enough, a response to his presumed critic Alexander More, whom he incorrectly thought to be the author of *Clamor … Against the Parricides [of Charles I]*. In his *Defense of Himself Against Alexander More* (1655) Milton exploits More's name to ask "Tune Morus es an Momus? An uterque idem est?"(Are you

[10] Milton, 1953–82, 1:225; Milton, 1698, 341.
[11] Milton, 1953–82, 1:222; cf. Milton, 1698, 340.

148   *Doubting the Divine in Early Modern Europe*

More or Momus? Or are they one and the same?).[12] Here obviously Momus appears in his role as unreasonable critic. These two citations – as Latin Querela, child of Night, and as Greek Momus – are to my knowledge the only two direct citations of Momus in Milton's corpus.

But this does not mean that Momus would not be a silent presence in Milton's writings, as there would be other avenues that could have piqued Milton's interest in the impish god. In 1634, on the heels of his college days and scholarly *Prolusions*, Milton likely learned of a recent appearance of Momus in a court masque, performed on February 18 and published that same year.[13] This play, the *Coelum Britannicum* of Thomas Carew, is a playful version of Bruno's *Expulsion of the Triumphant Beast*, whose currency in England was no doubt assured by its dedicatee Philip Sidney. Like Bruno, Carew casts Momus as a starring figure in a work detailing the reform of the heavens, but he has lightened the tone and turned the play to safely political ends as a praise of the monarchy of Charles I, at whose court at Whitehall it was performed. In this masque, the virtues of the Stuart monarchy were to be a template to reform the world of the gods and the constellations – thus, the "British Heavens." Momus appears during the festivities of Carnival as the light-hearted bane of the gods identifying his "Offices and Titles [as] the Supreme Theomastix [divine scourge], Hupercrittique of manners, Protonotarie of abuses, Arch-Informer, Dilator Generall, Universal Calumniator, Eternal Plaintiffe, and perpetual Foreman of the Grand Inquest."[14] (For Inigo Jones's aptly impish design of Momus for the play, see Fig. 2.)[15] He proclaims himself a scourge of all the gods and "bird of the [same] feather" with Pietro Aretino and Rabelais, the most famous literary

---

[12] Milton, 1838, 749.
[13] The seeming discrepancy between the date of the performance on "Shrove Tuesday Night, the 18 of February, 1633" and the publication date of 1634 is owing to the Old-Style dating in which the new year began on March 25 (Carew, 1634, title-page).
[14] Carew, 1634, 5.
[15] Orgel and Strong, 1973, 2:590.

FIGURE 2 Sketch of Momus for Production of Thomas Carew's *Coelum Britannicum* at Whitehall, London, 1634. Inigo Jones. Courtesy of Chatsworth House, Devonshire.

scoundrels of their respective countries in the sixteenth century. Momus and Mercury will undertake a benign reform of the heavens – for instance, Jove will cease his philandering, Cupid his public nudity – and vices enshrined in the stars will be replaced by worthy candidates.

How did this likely come to Milton's attention? Henry Lawes, the musician who wrote the music for Carew's masque, similarly collaborated with Milton in the writing of his *Masque at Ludlow Castle*, performed later that year at Michaelmas (September 29). Milton wrote the masque to celebrate the appointment of John Egerton, Earl of Bridgewater, to his post as President of Wales. The starring character in the masque was Comus (the name by which the masque has subsequently become known). Two of the leading actors in the play, both sons

150   *Doubting the Divine in Early Modern Europe*

of Egerton, had earlier appeared in the *Coelum Britannicum*, as had Lawes himself. Structural similarities between the *Comus* and the *Coelum* and the obvious overlap of Lawes in both productions make it almost certain that Milton was familiar with Carew's masque.[16] It is also probable that Milton's featuring of Comus in his masque was in part inspired by Carew's prominent depiction of Momus in his. Aside from the phonetic similarity, both figures represented forces of disruption: Momus of the divine order, Comus of the moral. With his "crew" of wild followers representing licentiousness, Comus tries to seduce the Lady of the masque (Alice Egerton) to forsake her chastity.[17] Comus was a god of Late Antique origin depicted first in Philostratus' *Imagines* of the third century CE and had some resurgence in the mid sixteenth and early seventeenth century, including a non-speaking appearance in Ben Jonson's *Pleasure Reconciled to Virtue* of 1619, which Milton likely knew.[18] Still, his interest in this character could have been stoked by Carew's Momus. Though obviously not proving Milton's connecting the two figures, a link between the two appeared later in the century in an anti-Catholic drollery entitled *Democritus Ridens: or Comus and Momus* (1681).[19] In the nineteenth century the two characters migrated to the United States, as both had their own "crews" in Mardi Gras parades in New Orleans. Milton's role

[16] On the production of and similarities between the two masques, see Evans, 1966.

[17] On cultural and political themes in *Comus* (especially its critique of court mores), see Marcus, 1986, 169–212; Entzminger, 1991; and Hill, 1977, 43–49, who argues that the disreputable Comus in the masque has the same ironic prominence as Satan in *Paradise Lost* (46).

[18] Comus appears in Vincenzo Cartari's 1556 *Images of the Gods of the Ancients* (Cartari, 2012, 326–27; Hiltner, 2003, 68–69). Aside from Jonson's *Pleasure Reconciled to Virtue*, not published until 1641 but possibly circulating in manuscript (Jonson, 1903; Marcus, 1986, 108–27), Milton may also have drawn on a Latin play by the Dutch writer Hendrik van der Putten (Erycius Puteanus) entitled *Comus* written in 1608 and performed in Oxford in 1634 (Singleton, 1943; Merritt Hughes in Milton, 1953–82, 3: 87).

[19] The subtitle of this two-man comic dialogue is "A New Jest [Comus] and Earnest [Momus] Pratling Concerning the Times" (in this case, the Exclusion Controversy of James II). The two-page piece was published in London in 1681 (*Democritus Ridens*).

Milton's Lucifer

in popularizing Comus is evident in the first appearance of the Misticke Krewe of Comus on February 24, 1857, in which the cast of demons in *Paradise Lost* is listed as Comus's crew.[20] Regardless of the exact relation between Milton's Comus and Carew's Momus, Milton's almost certain familiarity with the *Coelum Britannicum* offered him a recent model of the spirited god of criticism.

A few years after composing the *Comus*, Milton embarked on his Grand Tour of the Continent, during which he spent about a year in Italy in 1638–39. Upon returning to England in mid 1639 he shortly thereafter (until about mid 1641) made drafts of possible tragedies, including one entitled "Paradise Lost" and another "Adam Unparadiz'd."[21] Although never completed, these tragedies of course adumbrated his great epic. The impact of the Italian journey may have been even more pronounced than scholars have recognized: first in the unrealized tragedies and later in *Paradise Lost*. One particular Italian drama, *L'Adamo* by Giovan Battista Andreini, was a major inspiration for Milton's contemplation of the theme of the Fall. Voltaire is the witness here. In his *Essay Upon the Epick Poetry of European Nations, From Homer to Milton* (1727), Voltaire gives this account of part of Milton's stay in Italy:

Milton, as he was travelling through Italy in his Youth, saw at Florence a Comedy called *Adamo*, writ by one Andreino a Player ... The subject of the Play was the Fall of Man; the Actors, God, the Devils, the Angels, Adam, Eve, the Serpent, Death, and the seven mortal Sins. That topick so improper for a Drama, but so suitable to the absurd Genius of the Italian Stage, (as it was at that Time) was handled in a Manner entirely conformable to the Extravagance of the Design. The Scene opens with a Chorus of Angels, and a Cherubim thus speaks for the Rest. "Let the Rainbow be the Fiddlestick of the Fiddle of the Heavens, let the Planets be the Notes of our Musick, let Time beat carefully the Measure, and the Winds make the Sharps, etc." Thus, the lay begins, and every Scene rises above the first in Impertinence.

Milton pierced through the Absurdity of that Performance to the hidden Majesty of the Subject, which being altogether unfit for the

---

[20] Storyvilledistrictnola.com.
[21] Lewalski, 2000, 123.

152   *Doubting the Divine in Early Modern Europe*

Stage, yet might be (for the Genius of Milton and for his only) the foundation of an Epick Poem.[22]

In later French versions of this *Essay*, Voltaire remarks that Milton saw the play in Milan, that he conceived the idea of writing a tragedy on the theme and wrote an act and a half, and that he learned all of this from literati who had it from Milton's daughter in London.[23] Despite Voltaire's inconsistency as to whether Milton saw the play in Florence or Milan, his testimony is supported by the textual similarities between the *Adamo* and the later *Paradise Lost* (which themselves suggest that Milton may even have seen a written version of the play). Presumably the act and a half of a tragedy that Voltaire claims Milton wrote refers to the drafts of plays found in manuscript in Cambridge's Trinity College.[24]

The dramatic format would naturally have encouraged Milton to experiment with types of rhetorical agon: between Lucifer and his colleagues, Lucifer and himself, and Lucifer and Eve. Andreini's influence on Milton is generally, though not universally, acknowledged, but what has not been examined is how Andreini's own treatment of Lucifer had parallels in his depiction of Momus. The year before he published his *L'Adamo*, Andreini wrote a *Dialogo fra Momo e la Verità, spettante alla lode dell'arte comica*. This dialogue, actually performed in Ferrara by Andreini (as Momus) and his wife Virginia Ramponi (as Truth), was a full-throated defense of modern comedy against the attacks of conservatives who thought it obscene and corrupting. Andreini had ample reason to defend the art, as his mother Isabella Andreini of the Gelosi company was one of the most famous actresses of the day.[25] He uses Momus as a straw man, who unfairly criticizes comedy as decadent only to be corrected by Truth, who proclaims that modern comedy has remedied such features of ancient comedy and can even

[22] Voltaire, 1760, 66–67.
[23] French, 1966, 1:378–80.
[24] Milton, 1931–38, 18:228–25, 511–14.
[25] On the fame of Isabella, see Garzoni, 1996, 1182; Richards and Richards, 1990, 72–76, 223–25; McClure, 2004, 193–95.

be morally instructive. Most telling are some of the parallels between Momus in this dialogue and Lucifer in *L'Adamo*. In the *Dialogo*, Momus opens by saying "sated and tired of having until now contradicted celestial things and contending with the gods, I descend to the earth to exercise my office among mortals, and I have done this by force, shoved out by the wrath of Jove who ... has wished to relegate me to the center of Hell."[26] This last phrase reveals that Andreini has perhaps blended the Lucifer story into the Momus myth, as the classical Momus was never banished *to Hell* like Lucifer, but simply expelled from the heavens.[27] Furthermore, Andreini refers to Jove at one point as "*sommo Padre*," just as he refers to God as the "*Padre Eterno*" in *L'Adamo*.[28] Finally, he has Jove dispatch Truth to correct mortals from error and to show his pity for their miserable lives that need "honest respite."[29] This sending down of Truth as a theological favor or counter-stroke certainly evokes the role of Virtue in Alberti's *Momus* and Michael in Milton's *Paradise Lost*.

If Andreini "elevated" Momus in the *Dialogo* to assume a quasi-theological stature, so in *L'Adamo* he assigns Lucifer some of the more worldly, carping role of Momus. In the first prologue to this work "Al benigno lettore," Andreini opens with the same two words ("sazio e stanco") that opened Momus's first speech in the *Dialogo*. Andreini states that he is "sated and tired" of dealing with worldly matters, so he will tackle some heavenly ones.[30] He is, however, very nervous about mixing the sacred and the profane. In a second prologue to the reader, he apologizes that his *L'Adamo* opens up with a reference to Iris – goddess of the rainbow or heavenly "fiddlestick" as cited by Voltaire above – and that some readers may find it discordant that he puts mortal speech in the mouths of God

[26] Andreini, 1612, [A2r].
[27] Granted that miscreants were often banished to Tartarus in the classical world, but Andreini does embellish this part of the Momus story and even uses the phrase "centro dell'Inferno" (Andreini, 1612, [A2r]), suggesting Dante's placement of Satan.
[28] Andreini, 1612, [A2r]; Andreini, 2007, passim.
[29] Andreini, 1612, [A3r].
[30] Andreini, 2007, 8.

154   *Doubting the Divine in Early Modern Europe*

and other divine figures. He argues that the paucity of scriptural material – for instance, regarding the Serpent's temptation of Eve – necessitates that he do this.[31] Andreini thus presents the defense of crafting a worldly-wise agon between God, Lucifer, Eve, and other principals in Genesis.[32]

The result in Andreini is a rhetorical encounter between God and Lucifer that has many of the markings of a highly anthropomorphic and secular exchange between an imperious Jove and resentful Momus such as took place in Alberti's epic. Unlike some of the other works that Milton may have drawn upon – Grotius's *Adamus Exul* or Vondel's *Lucifer* – which open with Satan or other fallen angels lamenting their displacement by newly created mortals, Andreini's *L'Adamo* opens with God virtually taunting Lucifer to rise out of the depths and admire the brilliance of the sun, stars, all of his handiwork:

> Lift your dreadful face from the dark horror,
> Grievous Lucifer, to behold such great light!
> Be blinded by the flash of the shining stars,
> Yearn for the rays of the mild Sun.
> In the works of the sky read
> The great marvels of the celestial hand.
> Marvel, insane Rebel
> How easy the process is
> To the grand Artisan of worlds.[33]

God created man to replace the proud rebels with a humble admirer. In the spirit of the Aesopian Momus critiquing divine creations, Lucifer's first statement is a critique of this wondrous creation. Rising from his Hell-hole, he asks

> Who calls me from my dark redoubt
> To gaze at such light?

[31] Andreini, 2007, 8–14. His sensitivity to this issue is evident in the *Dialogo*, which also contains an appendix of theologians' rulings on the legitimacy of comedy – interestingly enough, from the likes of some of the same people Luther vied against in the previous century – Prierias and Cajetan – in which he argues that what comedy must not do is mix in sacred words and themes. Andreini, 1612, D1r.

[32] Cf. Arthos, 1968, 29–31.

[33] Andreini, 2007, 25; my trans.

> What new marvels
> Do you invent today, O God?
> Perhaps you are weary of your abode in the sky?
> Because now you create on earth
> This lovely Paradise
> In order to replicate yourself in human flesh two worldly Gods?
> Tell me, vile Architect
> What works you have fashioned from mud
> What will become of this man poor, nude
> Lonely inhabitant of woods and forests?[34]

Lucifer here is not simply the envious or proud rebel. He is a critic. So, you are bored with your heavenly home, God? Trying again with a second Paradise? Whipping up a new creation out of mud, oblivious as to what will come of this defenseless creature in the wild? What Andreini presents is a rhetorical challenge to and rational critique of the divine Architect. The template of Momus's descent and critique of human comedy in the *Dialogo* of the previous year has been transposed to Lucifer's ascent and critique of divine creation. God's taunting of the rebel and Lucifer's bold response certainly offered Milton an apt model for the agon between God and Satan in *Paradise Lost* – especially in giving Lucifer rational criticisms not found in the one-dimensional figure in Grotius and Vondel, who is simply embittered, hateful, and envious. This rational critique of God's plan – a challenge of *logos* to *mythos* – occurs later in *L'Adamo*, when Lucifer exposes the contradiction and regret inherent in God's creation of man. Let me understand, he muses: you create mortals with a need for food to live and then forbid their eating from a particular tree? This makes Lucifer's temptation of them *too* easy. Maybe God had second thoughts and decided to sabotage his new creation:

> Perhaps God, now irritated
> For having placed and dirtied both hands in the mud
> Recognizing the nature of Angels and Man
> *Fully regretted that he exists*
> And with the sweet bait of the desired strategy
> He decrees to him the prohibition: whence that one sinning

---

[34] Andreini, 2007, 34–35; my trans.

156 *Doubting the Divine in Early Modern Europe*

> With some reason, *albeit a tyrannical one*,
> Demolisher of this world though he be,
> He again returns the mud [mankind] to vile mire.[35]

Like the Jove of Alberti's *Momus*, who regrets the paradisiacal world he gave mankind and visits hardship upon mortals as an afterthought, Andreini's God changes his mind, regrets his creation, and plots mankind's downfall. Like the Lucifer of *Paradise Lost*, who accuses God of needing to construct a second paradise on earth "built / With second thoughts" (Book 9:100–1) – a sign of a fickle Creator – Andreini's Lucifer criticizes God for being fickle in needing a new paradise and for his mistaken creation of mankind. These rational challenges to God the Creator suggest that Andreini has gone beyond the traditional model of a merely proud and envious Lucifer to a cerebral critic in the spirit of the Momus of Aesop, Lucian, and Alberti. He thus intellectualizes Lucifer by endowing him with *parrhesia*, rather than simply bile. There can be little doubt that Andreini's figure was an inspiration for Milton's own antihero.[36] The *Dialogue Between Momus and Truth* of 1612 either wittingly or unwittingly informed the encounter between Lucifer and God in the *Adam* of 1613. The *Adam*, in turn, inspired Milton's earliest thoughts on a tragedy, or as it turned out, an epic on Paradise Lost. But I would argue that the influence of the Italianate Momus on Milton went much deeper than this. Crucial bits of textual evidence suggest that Milton knew Alberti's *Momus*.

To my knowledge, Milton never cited Alberti in his writings, nor does Jackson Boswell include any of Alberti's works in his

---

[35] Andreini, 2007, 41; my trans. and emphasis.

[36] For textual similarities between *L'Adamo* and *Paradise Lost*, cf. Andreini's Lucifer declaring that he would be "maggior contento / Vivere in libertà, tutti damnati / Che sudditi beati" (Andreini, 2007, 158) and Milton's proclaiming "Better to reign in Hell, than serve in Heav'n" (*PL* 1:263); also, Lucifer's feat of bringing a third of the stars to his cause (Andreini, 2007, 223) and *PL* 5:710, where Lucifer claims he brought a third of the angels over to his side (though elsewhere he claims "well nigh half," *PL* 9:141). The influence is unquestionable.

reconstruction of Milton's library. Still, several circumstances make it likely that Milton would have been aware of Alberti's novel. In his sojourn in Italy Milton spent about four months in Florence, from July to mid September in 1638 and again from mid March to mid May the following year.[37] Here he spent considerable time with various academies: the Svogliati, the Apatisti, the Crusca, and the Florentine Academy. Minutes of the Svogliati indicate his reading of Latin poetry at three meetings, and a record of the Apatisti indicates that in 1638 one of the inductees in the academy was "Giovanni Milton inglese."[38] In his *Second Defense of the English People* (against the anonymous *Clamor ... Against the English Parricides*), Milton recounts his Italian journey, naming several of the literati he befriended.[39] Given the fame of Alberti – both for his Italian and Latin works, as well as his architecture, including the striking facade of Florence's Santa Maria Novella – and given that the Florentines claimed him as one of their own, it would be surprising that he would not be among the modern Italian writers whose works Milton encountered.

Indeed, the first named of the Florentine friends he lists in the *Second Defense*, Jacopo Gaddi, the founder of the Svogliati, may well have introduced Milton to Alberti. Gaddi – at whose home, some have speculated, Milton might have stayed – was an ardent bibliophile.[40] In 1648 he published a massive catalogue, *De scriptoribus non ecclesiasticis, graecis, latinis, italicis*, in which he included an entry on Alberti, whom he hailed as the "Florentine Vitruvius" celebrated by poets, historians, and by Gaddi himself in a history of his own family and in an unpublished work on notable Florentine families. In listing Alberti's many writings, in which Gaddi clearly favors the Latin works over the vernacular

---

[37] Lewalski, 2000, 90; Parker, 1968, 1:169–82; 2:818–31.

[38] He may also have been inducted into the Svogliati (Haan, 1998, 10–37).

[39] These figures included Jacopo Gaddi, Carlo Dati, Pietro Frescobaldi, Agostino Coltellini, Benedetto Buonmettei, Valerio Chimentelli, and Antonio Francini (Milton, 1953–82, 4.1:614–20, esp. at 616–17).

[40] Arthos, 1968, 19–20; Haan, 1998, 12.

158   *Doubting the Divine in Early Modern Europe*

ones, *Momus* is listed third after Alberti's well-known treatise on architecture and his Aesopic fables: "Momum dialogum summae gratiae cum priscis opusculis conferendum exaravit" (He produced *Momus*, a dialogue of the highest charm comparable to ancient works).[41] Given Gaddi's regard for Alberti and the *Momus* itself, it is plausible that this work would be a likely recommendation for a visiting writer interested in classical culture and Renaissance Florence – especially one such as Milton, whose Latin was better than his Italian, as he revealed in a letter to Benedetto Buonmattei in 1638.[42] Alberti's name also came up in records of the Florentine Academy in 1639. The official who recorded events that year was Filippo Pandolfini, who commemorated his ancestor Agnolo Pandolfini (long mistakenly thought to be the author of Book 3 of Alberti's dialogue *On the Family*), remarking that Alberti and Matteo Palmieri were two writers who praised Agnolo.[43] In collecting these accounts of the Florentine Academy, Salvino Salvini also included an account of Cosimo Bartoli's 1568 translation of Alberti's Latin works, which "from the lower world almost lost he recalled to life."[44] Clearly, Alberti was a presence among Florentine intellectuals in the later sixteenth and early seventeenth century.

In sum, although there is no hard evidence that Milton read Alberti while in Italy, there are circumstantial clues that he may have done so. Aside from Alberti's fame in Florence, would not an avid book-lover such as Milton – who was interested in classical mythology, who had purchased a book on Homer's allegories on the gods in 1637, who sprinkled mythological allusions in his Latin poems during his Italian journey, who relished the Italian epics of Tasso and Ariosto, who was more comfortable in Latin than Italian – have been interested in the first Renaissance Latin novel featuring a classical god?[45]

[41] Gaddi, 1648, 1:21.
[42] Milton, 1953–82, 1:331–32.
[43] Salvini, 1717, 498.
[44] Salvini, 1717, 79–80.
[45] On Milton as bibliophile, when he made his way to Rome, he was graced with a tour of the Vatican library by Lucas Holste (Haan, 1998, 103; see

Milton's Lucifer 159

Textual similarities between Alberti's *Momus* and *Paradise Lost* suggest that he was. Milton may have read the *Momus* during his 1638–39 stay. Or possibly later: letters of 1647 reveal that he maintained contact with Carlo Dati via booksellers.[46] He may have read it before or after seeing Andreini's *Adam*. Whatever the case, key passages in *Paradise Lost* suggest that Milton gleaned ideas from Alberti's novel that he did not draw from Andreini, from earlier theological dramas of Grotius and others, or from Lucian. Scholars have noted the residue of the Italian journey in other ways – references to Galileo, with whom he met, allusions to Fiesole and Vallombrosa (*PL* 1:288–304), and the influence of *Gerusalemme liberata* and *Orlando furioso* – but have not explored this crucial one that could elucidate many of the contested issues regarding Milton's view of the divine.[47]

Aside from the obvious similarity of a rebellion by an exiled malcontent, the two epics work on both a political and theological level. Alberti claims that his work is a political allegory, though, I argue, it also has a theological subtext. Milton claims his work is a theological one, though it has a political subtext: it is rife with allusions to tyrannical monarchy, rebellion, and warfare that all reflect the Civil War of the 1640s, the Interregnum, and Restoration. And although Vondel's *Lucifer* may also roughly reflect the Dutch Revolt of the sixteenth century, the political machinations of *Paradise Lost* are far more detailed

---

Milton's letter of thanks to Holste in Milton, 1953–82, 1:332–36). While Holste's collection was highly theological and philosophical, it did contain some literary and humanist works (e.g., of Plautus, Valla, Poliziano, Bembo, and Sannazaro), but did not include any works of Alberti (Alfredo, 2000, 213, 327, 338, 357). On Milton's mythological interest, he bought a copy of Heraclides of Pontus' 1544 *Allegoriae in Homeri fabulas de diis* in 1637 (Lewalski, 2000, 65; French, 1966, 1:304). In a letter to Milton in 1647 Carlo Dati mentions Lilio Gregorio Giraldi's *De deis gentium* (Milton, 1953–82, 2:771), and this may also have been a work Milton could have known (Boswell, 1975, 112, lists it as a "doubtful work" in Milton's library. On his literary endeavors while in Italy, see Haan, passim, who suggests (at 48–51) that Milton may have even recycled or circulated some of his highly classical *Prolusions* from the Cambridge days.

[46] Milton, 1953–82, 2:762–77, esp. at 765.

[47] On the impact of the Italian journey in general, see essays in Di Cesare, 1991.

160   *Doubting the Divine in Early Modern Europe*

and share many features of the *Momus*.[48] In both works, the authors depict the nature of imperious authority (Jove and God) and an obstinate, freedom-loving courtier who suffers exile and sows dissension. Both works deal with the rivalry among divine forces that leads to the creation of mortals as a political counter-weight. In Book 1 of *Momus*, Jupiter creates mortals to discomfit the other gods: Momus proclaims, "At first, of course, Best and Greatest Jupiter was overjoyed that he had created men: if he became angry, rightly or wrongly, with us gods, he could push them forward as our rivals to excite our envy."[49] In *Paradise Lost*, God creates mankind as a counterweight to the contingent of rebel angels. Lucifer describes this as God's attempt to replenish the depopulation of heaven that Lucifer's revolt had effected:

> I in one night freed
> From servitude inglorious well nigh half
> The angelic name, and thinner left the throng
> Of his advisers: he to be avenged,
> And to repair his numbers thus impaired,
> Whether such virtue spent of old now failed
> More angels to create, if they at least
> Are his created, or to spite us more,
> Determined to advance into our room
> A creature formed of earth, and him endow,
> Exalted from so base original,
> With Heav'nly spoils, our spoils: what he decreed
> He effected; man he made, and for him built
> Magnificent this world, and earth his seat
> Him lord pronounced.
>
> (PL 9:140–54)

As Jupiter created mortals to beat back uppity gods, God created them to repopulate his forces against rebel angels. In both cases, the deity is depicted as making a political calculation to protect his power. This political triangulation between divine elements (gods vs. gods, or God vs. angels) and mortals certainly is a particularly striking feature of *Paradise Lost* for which I know of no other precedent than Alberti's *Momus*.

[48] Dijkhuizen and Helmers, 2011.
[49] Alberti, 2003, 27.

Milton's Lucifer

161

In both works, furthermore, the chief deity displays a fickle or perverse attitude toward the newly created mortals. In *Momus*, when the other gods become jealous of the idyllic life of mortals, Jupiter changes course and visits misery upon them: this, according to the narrative. The figure of Momus adds another twist:

> But when he [Jupiter] realized it would be better for heavenly homes to be occupied by their old inhabitants rather than by an upstart crowd of mortal gods, he decided to keep men down there, to pour out his raging floods of anger on their heads, and to run riot against them with his bestial savagery. Hence he heaped up lightning, thunder, pestilence and everything wretched human souls find harsh and unbearable, also anxiety and fear and every evil that can be devised and fashioned, and inflicted them all upon mankind at once.[50]

In Milton's epic God arguably treats mortals in a rather callous way by orchestrating the Fall and thus introducing the woes of humanity. When Eve is persuading Adam to eat the forbidden fruit, she reasons that God surely would not be so fickle as to destroy what he had created. This would be the sign of a flawed, improvident creator (a typical Momus trope):

> So God shall uncreate,
> Frustrate, do, undo, and labour lose,
> Not well conceived of God, who through his power
> Creation would repeat, yet would be loath
> Us to abolish, lest the Adversary
> Triumph and say; Fickle their state whom God
> Most favours, who can please him long? Me first
> He ruined, now mankind, whom will be next?
> (*PL* 9:943–50)

Andreini's *Adam* had broached this same theme of God repenting of his creation and engineering mankind's Fall and return to "vile mud." Granted that Milton's God arranges the Fall in order to enable the glory of a future redemption, but is even that eventual end implicitly framed as yet another assertion of a lust for power, glory, and a willingness to manipulate a weaker creature? In any case, Alberti's Jupiter and Milton's God both

[50] Alberti, 2003, 27.

162   *Doubting the Divine in Early Modern Europe*

display an imperious and rather hard-hearted stance in creating and punishing mortals.

A third major similarity between the two works concerns the interiority of the antihero. Lucifer's soliloquies are arguably the most intriguing parts of Milton's epic – and certainly the reason for "pro-Satanists" to claim him as the hero, or at least tragic victim, of the story. Where else can such layered introspection be found in the speeches of a damned and damnable character: in his recognition of his ingratitude toward his master; in his understandable assertion that "I 'sdained subjection" (*PL* 4:50), especially to an imperious God who hid his true power to tempt rebels to revolt?[51] An eighty-one-line speech in Book 4 (lines 32–113) and a seventy-nine-line rumination in Book 9 (lines 99–178) depict Lucifer engaged in morose, tormented reflections on his (legitimate) desires for freedom and resentment of subjection and his (illegitimate) motives driven by overweening ambition, pride, and need for face-saving among his confederates. The likes of such inward torment might have had a precedent in saints' lives (in narratives of self-renunciation such as Augustine's *Confessions*), but not in a scoundrel's inner struggle. In drama the closest precedent, which indeed was likely influential to some degree, was Marlowe's *Doctor Faustus*, whose antihero shows moments of wavering and eventual regret.[52] But in Faust

---

[51] On the resentment of subjection, some hints of this can be found in the Old English "Caedmon" poems (*Christ and Satan*, *Genesis A*, and *Genesis B*) in terms more of a medieval vassal begrudging submission to his lord, where Lucifer asks if he should be so weak as to "bow down before Him and fawn as a vassal," but this is largely an angry complaint rather than a moral reflection. Kirkconnell, 1967, 26; Forsyth, 2003, 50–54.

[52] See Faustus's speeches in the 1604 A-Text in 2.1, lines 1–14; 2.3, lines 18–37; and his closing speech in 5.2, lines 65–123 (Marlowe, 1993, 138, 150–52, 194–97). One particularly clear influence is Mephistopheles' claim that Hell in an internal state (A-Text, 1.3, lines 78–82 [Marlowe, 1993, 130]), a concept also found in *Paradise Lost* when Lucifer says, "The mind is its own place, and in itself / Can make a Heav' n of Hell, a Hell of Heav'n" (*PL* 1:254–55) and later "Which way I fly is Hell; myself am Hell" (4:75). Discussing other possible models scholars have cited – Iago, Macbeth – Forsyth sees Hamlet as an apt forerunner of Lucifer for his soliloquies (though it should be noted that Hamlet is a fully sympathetic victim and in no way an antihero) (Forsyth, 2003, 56, 316–17; Gardner, 1965, 99–120; Werblowsky, 1952, 100–2).

there is no sense of the rebellion against a tyrannical, unfair, or fickle God. For that, the best precedent is Alberti's *Momus*.

Momus has several soliloquies in Alberti's novel: some quite lengthy, such as a sixty-three-line speech in Book 1 and a fifty-eight-line soliloquy in Book 2, and other shorter but equally revealing accounts of a figure reckoning with his own character.[53] Although Lucifer is clearly a figure with a higher conscience and deeper regret about his rebellion against God, he and Momus both share a capacity to address their own nature. Momus's essence is to be unreservedly free, "immoderately free" as Lady Fraus (Fraud) accuses him.[54] In his first soliloquy, after fleeing heaven following his conviction for treason, he says that he will have to change his nature and be submissive and agreeable when met by a divine ambassador, the goddess Virtue. This capitulation goes against his very nature, but is necessary: "Don't think it dishonorable to do what honor requires you to do ... If conforming and acting as a suppliant will lead to bigger and better things, then Momus is prepared to adapt. Now you will say: 'I cannot *not* be Momus, and I cannot *not* be who I have always been without sacrificing my freedom and consistency.'"[55] Lucifer's soliloquy in Book 4 also deals with the issue of freedom, though more theologically so, as he castigates himself for having the free will to resist ambition, but still choosing to rebel, because he "'sdained subjection" (*PL* 4:50), as Momus disdained courtly deference. Both characters lament their descent: Momus into servile flattery, Lucifer into the serpent. For the latter, this violation of his dignity is particularly stinging:

> O foul descent! That I who erst contended
> With Gods to sit the highest, am now constrained
> Into a beast ...
> But what will not ambition and revenge
> Descend to?
>
> (*PL* 9:163–69)

---

[53] Alberti, 2003, 45, 60–64, 100–4, 202–4.
[54] Alberti, 2003, 20.
[55] Alberti, 2003, 45.

164   *Doubting the Divine in Early Modern Europe*

Aside from self-reflection, both antiheroes share similar missions of self-actualization. Exiled from the heavens, Momus goes to Tuscany to stir up trouble against Jupiter, just as an exiled Lucifer goes to earth (by way of Hell) to do the same. And both self-consciously employ artifice and dissimulation to exact revenge on an overbearing master. Scholars have observed the courtly depiction of Satan's appearance in *Paradise Regained*, as he enters to tempt Christ in the wilderness (*PR* 2:298–301).[56] Also like a courtier, Lucifer in *Paradise Lost* disguises his angst from his confederates with studied artifice: "Each perturbation smothered with outward calm, / Artificer of fraud; and was the first / That practiced falsehood under saintly show" (*PL* 4:120–22). The rhetoric of dissimulation he used to tempt Eve is like that of a sophist, resembling that of "old some orator renowned / in Athens or free Rome" (*PL* 9:670–71). As I showed in Chapter 2, at the heart of Alberti's *Momus* was a cynical reflection on the art of simulation and dissimulation. In fact, one could argue *that* was Alberti's version of the original sin. And whereas Lucifer went to earth to sow the *theological sin* of disobedience, Momus's act of apostasy was to corrupt mortals through the *courtly vice* of dissimulation.

What tied these epic missions together was the common hatred of or contempt for authority. Momus could not abide being told by Jupiter to create a gift for the newly created world, nor could he stomach Jupiter's indecisive beneficence and then malice toward mortals. Lucifer's resentment of monarchy, the "tyranny of Heav'n" (*PL* 1:124) ruled by an "angry Victor" with "ministers of vengeance" (*PL* 1:169–70), permeates *Paradise Lost*. Like any courtier, he bitterly resents the fact that a newcomer, Christ, is peremptorily elevated "viceregent" (*PL* 5:609) holding authority over all others; is this not an injustice toward angelic powers "if not equal all, yet free, / Equally free" (*PL* 5:791–92)? He is angry that an entire new (human) race was created to repopulate the depleted heavens and regaled with "Heav'nly spoils, our [angels'] spoils" (*PL* 9:151). David

---

[56] Lewalski, 2000, 516.

Milton's Lucifer

Quint thinks that this reading of God as a tyrant arrogantly corralling his courtiers is merely the perspective of the rebel angels and that "this temporal, political understanding of a spiritual relationship is the essence of the fallen angels' irreligion and sin."[57] Not so. If that were the case, why does Milton describe God "smiling" when he saw the rebellion mounting, and informing Christ that "Nearly it now concerns us to be sure / Of our omnipotence, and with what arms / We mean to hold what anciently we claim / Of deity or empire" (*PL* 5:721–24). Christ approves:

> Mighty Father, thou thy foes
> Justly hast in derision, and secure
> Laugh'st at their vain designs and tumults vain,
> Matter to me of glory, whom their hate
> Illustrates, when they see all regal power
> Giv'n me to quell their pride.
>
> (*PL* 5:735–40)

This political arrogance is not merely a misperception, but, for Milton, an essential feature of the deity. And whereas Alberti's Jupiter was usually more inept, myopic, and bumbling, he and God shared one perverse attribute: namely, hiding their power to encourage or allow weaker foes or subjects to struggle on in vain. More than once in *Paradise Lost*, Milton's rebel angels suspect this manipulation. At the opening council in Book 1, Lucifer depicts God as a (perhaps Stuart)

> Monarch in Heav'n, till then as one secure
> Sat on his throne, upheld by old repute,
> Consent or custom, and his regal state
> Put forth at full, but still his strength concealed,
> Which tempted our attempt, and wrought our fall.
>
> (*PL* 1:638–42)

In this speech he is rehearsing Beëlzebub's suspicion that God "hath left us this our spirit and strength entire / Strongly to suffer his vengeful ire, / Or do him mightier service as his thralls / By right of war" (PL 1:146–50). Of course, Yahweh had done

---

[57] Quint, 2014, 135.

166   *Doubting the Divine in Early Modern Europe*

similar things in Exodus, hardening the heart of Pharaoh, provoking the Egyptian pursuit of the Hebrews, only to vanquish them and affirm His glory. But Milton's language of monarchy, custom, and old repute certainly suggests the recent turmoil of the Civil War and Stuart Restoration. Milton's comments here thus seem more aimed at indicting political or theological tyranny than affirming divine benevolence and glory. This divine plan to orchestrate rebellion and resistance only to overcome it with inestimable power is played out in the war between the loyalist and rebel angels in Book 6.[58] God allows two days of carnage before sending in Christ on the third day to triumph and confirm his power and right of succession. While perhaps a metaphor of the Resurrection, consider how Milton plays it out. As God tells Christ – who is "full of wrath bent on his enemies" (*PL* 6:826) and will receive a Roman general's triumphant entry – he will infuse him with "power above compare, / And *this perverse commotion governed* thus, / To manifest thee worthiest to be heir, / Of all things, to be heir and to be King / By sacred unction" (*PL* 6:705–9, my emphasis). Certainly, this language implies a secular political calculus with dire implications.

This plan for a deity with matchless power to arrange "perverse commotion" and tragedy has a telling counterpart in *Momus*. In response to the Olympian gods' jealousy of mortals' newly created utopian world, Jupiter with "bestial savagery" rained down upon them "lightning, thunder, pestilence and everything wretched human souls find harsh and unbearable."[59] He gave mortals two options to contend with such misery: death or a rather unfair struggle. The former is the easiest; the latter the harder, more inequitable agon of man against a too-powerful Jupiter. As Alberti puts it, "if ... it avails them [mortals] to fight [against these evils], O heedless Jupiter, *you have not refused these little men the patience to beat you, the angry and heavily*

---

[58] Forsyth (2003, 28–35) discusses classical combat myths (e.g., Zeus and the Titans, and Zeus and Typhoeus in *Theogony* 820–85) on which Milton drew, but these lack any meaningful depiction of motive, moral struggle, or political coloration.

[59] Alberti, 2003, 27.

Milton's Lucifer

armed prince of the gods."[60] This grant of minimal "patience" sounds much like Beëlzebub's and Satan's complaints about a God perversely hiding his power against weaker foes or subjects endowed with barely enough "spirit and strength" to mount a resistance. In Alberti, I believe, this is a theological complaint to God (not Jupiter) about the travails of the human condition and the unlikely possibility of a benign providence; in Milton, a charge against a manipulative God who is a perverse tyrant. These are perhaps the most severe attacks on divine governance by both authors. In terms of the specific charge of the deity's staging an unfair fight, it does seem quite possible that Milton drew this theme from Alberti.

There are then several compelling reasons to suspect Milton read *Momus*, either during his trip to Italy or sometime later. Proving textual influence is elusive, especially in the realm of myth criticism and theology, as themes can have potentially universal origin and coincidental occurrence. Still, the many textual similarities suggest something more at work than happenstance, just as they explain something about the secular origins of Milton's Lucifer. Aside from these major similarities, there are numerous minor overlaps which are less telling; these may be simply coincidental, or they may be further evidence of influence. Momus is identified as the smartest god in Jupiter's court, just as Lucifer was once the pre-eminent angel in God's.[61] Momus assumes two of Lucifer's three roles – those of rebel in heaven and tempter on earth – and he and Lucifer are both shape-shifters.[62] Alberti satirically attacks votive prayers and statues of the gods (*read* Christian icons), and Milton flagrantly attacks Catholic practices in *Paradise Lost* 3:478–97 and 12:507–37. The elaborate theater (or temple) in Book 4 of *Momus* shares some of the monumentalism of the palace of Satan in Pandaemonium (*PL* 1:710–37), and both likely reflect papal rebuilding programs in Rome (that of Nicholas V for Alberti, that of St. Peter's basilica for Milton). The "high-arched" bridge the devils build from hell

---

[60] Alberti, 2003, 29, emphasis added.
[61] Alberti, 2003, 205, although at 225 Apollo is also so identified.
[62] Cf. J. Carey, 1989, 162, 170.

168   *Doubting the Divine in Early Modern Europe*

to earth (*PL* 10:301) may have been influenced not only by the bridges of Xerxes and Augustus as Quint observes but also by the vainglorious arch Juno built in Book 2 of *Momus*.[63] Both works display a thoroughgoing misogyny (though most early modern male writings do), especially in the case of Alberti's female arch-villain, Fraud, who resembles the destructive Eve, but also in rape scenes resulting in the birth of monsters.[64] The strong Lucretian presence in *Momus* has a counterpart in the Lucretian description of Chaos in Book 2 of *Paradise Lost*.[65] Finally, in the preface to Book 3 of *Momus*, Alberti boasts of the same cosmic scope (albeit in satirical terms) as Milton's epic, as he promises that in it "You will see how the salvation of mankind, the majesty of gods and the government of the world were brought almost to a final crisis."[66] In all, the accumulation of textual evidence – both the probable major similarities and the possible minor ones – points to the likelihood that Milton drew on Alberti's *Momus*, just as he was certainly inspired by Andreini's *Adam*, which itself reflected the Momus trope in its depiction of Lucifer.

What do these similarities tell us about Milton's purpose in his great epic and in his own religious thought? The standoff between the pro-Satanists and anti-Satanists in Milton criticism has to some degree resulted from the assumptions that Lucifer could not be simultaneously hero (championing freedom) and antihero (deserving damnation). The Momus archetype as fully realized by Alberti was in fact a precedent for a figure equally wicked (hateful and discordant) and heroic (candid and independent). How could both sides of such a figure reflect Milton's religious beliefs? Rather than seeing Milton as fully orthodox

[63] Alberti, 2003, 176–79; Quint, 2014, 204–5.

[64] Momus rapes Praise to produce the "loquacious" "monster" Rumor (Alberti, 2003, 69–73), and in *PL* 2:757–96 Death, the incestuous product of Satan and Sin, rapes his mother to produce "yelling monsters," the dogs of Hell.

[65] *PL* 2:896–97, 932. Quint has difficulty reconciling the materialist view found here with Milton's proposed theism and suggests that it perhaps represents his materialist and mortalist "doubts and fears" (Quint, 2014, 63–92, esp. at 85).

[66] Alberti, 2003, 199.

Milton's Lucifer

169

(as C. S. Lewis did) or as a closet "atheist" (as Michael Bryson has recently proposed), reading Milton through the lens of Momus helps contextualize his larger interests in "frank speech" in regard to religious orthodoxy.[67]

There are two preoccupations consistent throughout much of Milton's enormous corpus: the desire for freedom(s) and a fascination with Job or Job-like victims. As for the first, at a most primal level – that of vocational choice – Milton bridled at his father's desire that he enter clerical life. Perhaps this rejection of the clergy fueled the raft of anti-prelatical writings he issued against the Anglican Church in 1641. In his *Reason of Church Government Urg'd Against Prelaty* he reveals this personal and ecclesiastical nexus, referring to the Church "to whose service by the intentions of my parents and friends I was destin'd of a child, and in mine own resolutions, till comming to some maturity of yeers and perceaving what tyranny had invaded the Church."[68] In this same work he declares that "no free and splendid wit can flourish" under the "yoke of prelaty" with its "inquisitorius and tyrannical duncery."[69] William Parker argues that it was at this time, when in a contentious mood regarding the Church, that Milton decided on opening his never completed "Adam Unparadiz'd" not with Gabriel or Moses but with a speech from Satan that later became the beginning of Lucifer's soliloquy in *Paradise Lost* 4:32–41.[70] Assigning Lucifer these opening lines was likely also inspired by Andreini's opening in the *Adam*. This suggests a confluence of the ecclesiastical rebellion with an emerging theological one, fueled by his exposure to Andreini's play with its own Momus influence.

With the publication of his *Areopagitica* in 1644, Milton entered the fray against political tyranny and the state's licensing

---

[67] Bryson's title, *The Atheist Milton*, is something of an exaggeration, as he defines Milton's position to be "atheist" by the standards of the early modern period: that is, adhering to Arianism, materialism, and mortalism.

[68] Milton, 1953–82, 1:822–23.

[69] Milton, 1953–82, 1:820.

[70] This story concerning the origin of this speech comes from Milton's nephew Edward Phillips. Parker, 1968, 1:224–25; French, 1966, 2:50–51.

170   *Doubting the Divine in Early Modern Europe*

laws regarding publication. Having recently been lumped with atheists and other subversive authors because of his divorce tracts, Milton had ample motivation to write this first great defense of freedom of speech.[71] Tellingly, the treatise's title-page carried an epigraph from the greatest Greek tragedian of "frank speech," Euripides.[72] Later, in 1654, in his *Second Defense of the English People* Milton in fact categorizes his writings of the 1640s as reflecting a trajectory in pursuit of different types of freedom: "I observed that there are, in all, three varieties of liberty without which civilized life is scarcely possible, namely ecclesiastical liberty, domestic or personal liberty [as in divorce], and civil liberty."[73] Of course, there is a seeming contradiction in such a republican defender of regicide incarnating his champion of freedom as Satan. Scholars who see Milton as a political leftist struggle to explain this in various ways: for Christopher Hill, Milton's Lucifer represents a failed revolutionary and even displays some of the flaws of aristocratic rule that the Stuarts embodied. Hill claims that Milton did not identify with Satan.[74] I disagree: both are ardent opponents of submission, both are freedom fighters, both represent (after the Restoration, and especially with Milton's own imprisonment) a lost cause. But does it make sense for Milton to implicitly demonize Cromwell or any of the revolutionary party? Yes, because the point is not to demote Cromwell but to elevate Satan in his struggle against an unfair, omnipotent God who hides his power. Milton's embrace of freedom on so many levels – vocational, ecclesiastical, marital, civil – also filtered to the theological realm, as he began to embrace Arminianism, a defense of free will against the strident predestinarianism of Calvinism.[75] Such a position would be laid out in his *On Christian Doctrine* (c. 1658–74)

---

[71] On Milton's divorce tracts and his involvement in the Toleration Controversy, see Lewalski, 2000, 178–79, 202.

[72] He cites from the *Suppliant Women* 437–41.

[73] Milton, 1953–82, 4.1:624; Lewalski, 2000, 154–56.

[74] Hill, 1977, 365–67.

[75] On this connection, see Lewalski, 2000, 422.

Milton's Lucifer

and in *Paradise Lost*, whose compositions partly overlapped. The affirmation of human freedom – also a Momus hallmark – was clearly a key thread in Milton's rejections of all types of supernal authority.

If God did not absolutely *predetermine* all things, the deity was not completely exempt from *enabling* all things. This is a dour feature of *Paradise Lost*, and one which posed serious doubts about the benign nature of God's Providence. Like Erasmus before him, Milton's theological solution lay in God's capacity of foreknowing our (bad) use of free will, not his firmly preordaining it.[76] But what does his foreknowledge envision? In Milton's epic, Satan has the right to choose good or evil, but he does so in the framework of a God who foreknows how he likely would act, given the alienation of the rebel angels. In this challenge to God's goodness it would seem that Milton is more intent to justify the ways of Satan to man than to accomplish his proposed purpose to "justify the ways of God to men" (*PL* 1:26). Likewise, Eve and Adam have the freedom to choose, but they do so in the face of God's foreknowledge of their entrapment by a guileful rhetorician. Human freedom in this setting is simply the freedom to be victims.

This gloomy view dovetails with Milton's other longstanding interest in Job. As Barbara Lewalski observes, as early as 1642 in his *Reason of Church Government* Milton identified Job as a potential model for an epic poem.[77] That Job had such literary potential is especially relevant given the depiction of God in the prose preface, which together with the prose epilogue scholars generally believe to have been added later to the verse core of the book. In this preface God accepts a dare or bet from Satan to test the piety and patience of Job, who is subjected to all manner of physical and psychological torment. This "secular" contest

---

[76] Cf. Erasmus's *On the Freedom of the Will* in his debate with Luther and the latter's *On the Bondage of the Will* (Erasmus, 1999, esp. at 48–52).

[77] Lewalski, 2000, 512; Milton, 1953–82, 1:813; for a similar reading of Milton's challenge to theodicy, see Herman, 2005, esp. 110–14, who also notes the proliferation of commentaries on Job in seventeenth-century England.

172   *Doubting the Divine in Early Modern Europe*

with Satan obviously bears a resemblance to the secular agon with him in *Paradise Lost*, especially in regard to the victims Adam and Eve, who are subjected to an unnecessary trial and testing. This template is repeated in *Paradise Regained*, which centers on Satan's temptation of Christ. Doubling down on the wager with the Adversary in Job, God reveals that he will now expose to Satan another man, it would seem, in a spirit of competitive and martial arrogance:

> He [Satan] now shall know I can produce a man
> Of female seed, far abler to resist
> All his solicitations, and at length
> All his vast force, and drive him back to Hell
> Winning by Conquest what the first man lost
> By fallacy surpris'd.
>
> (*PR* 1:150–55)

The reference to Christ's origin from female seed here only reinforces the Arian position that Milton had taken by the time he wrote his epic poems and *On Christian Doctrine* – and only reinforces the secular promotion of Christ in the court in Heaven *at a specific moment in time*. And as in *Paradise Lost*, God discloses a political purpose for his son: "His [Christ's] Mother then is mortal, but his Sire, / He who obtains the Monarchy of Heav'n, / And what will he not do to advance his Son?" (*PR* 1:86–88). Milton's Arianism and his politicizing of God's purposes for Christ confirms the epic worldliness of the story and stresses Christ's human qualities (like Job, Adam, and Eve) while virtually ignoring his divine powers.[78]

Finally, the archetype of Job is re-figured yet again in *Samson Agonistes*. He too is largely a victim of the divine plan. Though it was his mission to infiltrate the Philistines, his efforts were not recognized by the Elders. Though reluctant to dignify the Philistines' celebration of Dagon with his presence, divine impulse led him to do so – and thereby led him to his death. Blessed with preternatural strength, Samson questions a divine justice that toppled him from divine heights to misery: "Why was my

---

[78] Cf. Lewalski, 2000, 511.

Milton's Lucifer 173

breeding order'd and prescrib'd / As of a person separate to God, / Design'd for great exploits, if I must die / Betray'd, Captiv'd, and both my Eyes put out ...?"(*SA* 30–33). The Chorus functions like Job's Consolers, proclaiming the justice of God's ways. But even they articulate the possibility of doubt: although claiming that there has never been a "School" of those "who think not God at all," they acknowledge that "yet more there are who doubt his ways not just, / As to his own edicts, found contradicting" (*SA* 293–301). This position goes to the heart of Milton's belief: a questioning of a harsh, even perverse divine order, though obviously not a denial of God. Certainly, Samson sees himself as someone who has been set up by a divine plan for a tragic end: "to those cruel enemies, / Whom I by his appointment had provok't / Left me all helpless with th' irreparable loss / Of sight" (*SA* 642–45). The personal dimension is accentuated, of course, by the fact Milton is, like Samson, blind. Thus, Milton's choice of Samson for his tragedy could simply have been a tailoring of the Job archetype to his own circumstances. In any case, his interest in Job as the foundational text on theodicy clearly infiltrated all three of his epic poems. The fall from heights of power and greatness (or piety) links the fates of Job, Lucifer, and Samson in the Judeo-Christian tradition to those of Prometheus and Momus in the classical tradition. Indeed, it is possible that Alberti's *Momus* could have had some influence on Milton's reading of the Samson story. Both heroes fell from divine favor, suffered loss of virility (Momus literally his manhood, Samson his strength), and both were undone by women (Fraud and Delila). Most telling, both works end in the toppling of a theater filled with false idols: in *Momus*, a "theatrum" filled with statues of gods collapses to the distress and detriment of the gods; in *Samson*, a "theater" is pulled down by Samson, destroying himself and the idolatrous Philistines with him.[79] Perhaps Alberti's epic may have conspired with Milton's blindness to draw his attention to the Samson story.

---

[79] Milton uses the term "theater" at *SA* 1605 as well as "temple" at 1370 and 1378.

174   *Doubting the Divine in Early Modern Europe*

An insistence on personal freedom, a resistance to authority, and a disbelief in divine and worldly justice link various strands in Milton's thought. The Momus tradition may be the secular source that informed these sentiments, even when they are voiced in ecclesiastical or theological contexts. In some cases, Milton may have drawn Momus themes directly from Lucian. Certainly, Lucian's *Zeus Refuted* deals with the subordination of Zeus to Fate, which might be said to parallel Milton's disbelief in divine predestination and his lack of confidence in even a looser notion of benign Providence.[80] Joseph Frank has suggested that Milton moved toward deism in later life and that all three epics reflect this shift. I would qualify his argument. Yes, Milton wanted to accent human freedom against a theology of Calvinist predestination, but contrary to deist thought, his divine "watchmaker" *does* intervene in human history, now creating mortals for political reasons and orchestrating their temptation, now injecting Samson into tragic circumstances. Milton goes beyond Lucian's questioning of Zeus's power vis-à-vis the fates; more cynically, his God *enables* the conditions for human misery – much as Zeus *creates* those conditions, as an afterthought, in Alberti's *Momus*.

Another possible echo of Lucian might be found in Milton's Arianism. Lucian's Momus raised the troubling issue of demigods in the *Parliament of the Gods*, complaining that such half-breeds had made their way into the Olympian ranks. This criticism or skepticism of the stature of the pantheon possibly coincided with Milton's doubts about the divinity of Christ. Of the three faces of Milton's heterodoxy – Arianism, Arminianism, and mortalism – this one is obviously the most radical challenge to Christianity (as opposed to theism in general).[81] Milton was a close reader of Cicero's *On the Nature of the Gods*, which recounted the Euhemerist theory that the classical gods derived from prominent mortals (1.42.119).[82] Lucian's Momus lays out in strident

---

[80] In his marginalia on Pindar, Milton cites the *Timon* and alludes to the 1619 edition of Lucian edited by Johannes Benedictus (Milton, 1931–38, 18:277).

[81] On Milton's heterodoxy, see Frank, 1961; Bryson, 2012; Maurice Kelley in Milton, 1953–82, 6:74.

[82] On certain or possible citations of *De natura deorum* see Boswell, 1975, 61.

Milton's Lucifer

parrhesia the various impostors such as Dionysus, Asclepius, and Heracles who with semi-mortal origin have crashed the heavenly gates. In exposing Dionysus and mentioning the sad fate of his mortal cousin (*Parliament of the Gods* 4–7), Lucian implicitly resurrects the horrible tale of the *Bacchae*, in which the disbelieving, rationalist Pentheus was brutally torn apart for questioning Dionysus' stature. As Milton's marginalia reveal, Euripides, in turn, was clearly one of his favorite authors.[83] In one of the Latin poems written while in Rome, Milton refers to "Dircean Pentheus," and his capacity to comparatively navigate the classical and Christian traditions is evident in the controversial Book 1, Chapter 5, of his *On Christian Doctrine*.[84] In his treatment here "Of the Son of God," Milton parses the Hebrew and Greek uses of the words "god(s)" and "lord" in metaphorical or elastic contexts to refer to angels or men: he cites three of Euripides' plays (including the *Bacchae* 1028) to show how "*despoton*" can simply refer to a master.[85] Clearly, Milton had carefully read Euripides with an eye for the language of god and master, and used this in a chapter challenging Christ's parity with God. The ancient Euhemerist views could have influenced him more than has been recognized – as might have the tragic story of Pentheus.

In Euripides, Cicero, and Lucian, Milton had several classical sources that may have shaped his religious views, but Lucian's use of Momus especially could have infiltrated Milton's views of the Arian, Socinian currents of his day. Early modern intellectuals certainly knew the dangers of Lucian. This is probably why Erasmus did not translate into Latin Lucian's Momus dialogues, and the first two English translations did not include these dialogues or the *Passing of Peregrinus* (which mocked Christianity).[86] In a third English translation in 1638,

---

[83] After Pindar, Euripides was most heavily annotated by Milton; Milton, 1938, 18:304–25, 566–68; Kelley and Atkins, 1961.

[84] On the Roman poem, see Haan, 1998, 188–89.

[85] Milton, 1953–82, 6:235–36.

[86] Craig, 1921, 142–43; Anselment, 1979, 169–70n45.

176   *Doubting the Divine in Early Modern Europe*

Jasper Mayne did include the Momus dialogues, but he felt the need to defend Lucian from anachronistic charges of Arianism and Arminianism. Recounting the contemporary brief against Lucian in his dedication, Mayne says:

> But Lucian wrote against the Christians. 'Tis more tolerably spoken, and with lesse Ignorance then [than] his, who sayd, Lucian was an Aerian and wrote against Bishops. He might as well have said, that he wrote in Defense of Antichrist; Or that by the Figure of wild Anticipation, He was an Arminian, because, In his Jupiter Confuted [*Zeus Refuted*], he wrote against Stoicisme, in the point of Fate, and Absolute Decree.[87]

This is a revealing criticism of the porous boundaries between ancient and contemporary religious thought. If people can read Arianism and Arminianism back onto Lucian, Milton may have been able to read Lucian forward in his embrace of these positions. Some Catholics, like Dryden, would see their way clear to accept Lucian as an aid in the attack on pagan polytheism, but even in the 1711 English translation of Lucian, to which Dryden appended a "Life of Lucian," the *Passing of Peregrinus* was omitted from the collection.[88] In short, if Lucian was still a controversial figure in early modern England, Milton would have been reluctant to cite the Momus dialogues – just as he might have hesitated to cite or acknowledge the key Renaissance reappearance of Momus in Alberti's novel.

All of these examples invite a more searching analysis of Milton's application of classical religious thought to Christian forms of belief and doubt. In his very orthodox reading of *Paradise Lost*, C. S. Lewis objected "Milton has failed to disentangle himself from the bad tradition ... of trying to make Heaven like Olympus."[89] And, this, he continues, is why God comes off poorly in the epic: "It is these anthropomorphic details that make the Divine laughter sound merely spiteful and the

---

[87] Lucian, 1664, A7v. In his 1634 translation of Lucian, Francis Hickes also tried to defend Lucian somewhat from his reputation as an atheist (Hickes, 1663, B2v–B3r). On Swift and Lucian, see Chapter 6.

[88] Craig, 1921, 152.

[89] Lewis, 1942, 127.

Milton's Lucifer

Divine rebukes querulous."[90] Andreini apologized for a similar transgression in the *Adam* – putting very human words in the mouth of God and Archangel Michael – and Milton followed suit in his version of the tale.[91] Milton's purpose in incorporating the classical elements, however, should not be seen as a literary defect, but rather as an attempt to understand divine history – or better, as a "secular" objection to God's exemption from rational criticism.

In his otherwise splendid study of *Paradise Lost*, David Quint strains to understand why Milton includes Lucretian currents in his epic, as if they are only the residue of reluctant doubts. Perhaps these doubts are not so reluctant after all. Similarly, the references to Galileo and the discussion between Adam and Raphael on the heliocentric theory should also be seen as aggressive reactions to religious dogma. Given his meeting with Galileo in Florence and his condemnation of the suppression of Galileo's thought in the *Areopagitica* – in which he depicts him as "grown old, a prisner to the Inquisition, for thinking in Astronomy otherwise then [than] the Franciscan and Dominican licensers thought" – it is unlikely that Milton truly thought that mortals should avoid questioning such matters as geocentrism, as is proposed in Book 8.[92] These scientific undercurrents simply reinforce Milton's strategy of depicting doubt in the face of ecclesiastical and divine authority. Reading Milton only in the light of pure unquestioned orthodoxy inhibits a full probing of his criticism of the Catholic and Anglican Church and his attack on divine justice.

In fact, the search for God-like knowledge – which Satan urges – and the image of bearing the light of knowledge and civilization explain why Romantics such as Shelley would connect Lucifer (the "light-bearer") with Prometheus, who stole fire from the gods and bore it (and civilization) to humans.[93]

---

[90] Lewis, 1942, 127.

[91] Andreini, 2007, 10–12.

[92] Milton, 1953–82, 2:538; *PL* 8:159–68.

[93] Werblowsky, 1952, esp. 54–63; Forsyth, 2003, 312n19. Milton's early attitude toward Prometheus is, like that to Satan, ambivalent. In one of his university *Prolusions* he condemns him as a thief, whose action indirectly

178   *Doubting the Divine in Early Modern Europe*

Alberti's Momus, who always questioned and tried to counsel a benighted Jupiter, was for his efforts bound to a rock in the manner of Prometheus. This Promethean image is another facet that joins Momus and Lucifer as heroic figures in their quests. How else could the author of the *Areopagitica* be read in the discussion of the geocentrism/heliocentrism controversy in Book 8, but as a closet supporter of the Promethean Galileo?

Milton's Italian journey and its literary aftermath were more consequential than scholars have realized. Milton the Italian visitor: a scholar steeped in classical lore and interested in viewing and acquiring new texts, who is more proficient in Latin than Italian, who is recently familiar with Momus's lively appearance in Carew's masque. While in Florence for four months, would he not be interested in a prose epic on this character written by one of the luminaries of Florentine culture? As an archetype of personal freedom, cherishing *parrhesia*, challenging the judgment of a monarchical Jupiter, Momus would surely stay in his mind long after his journey. And Andreini's *L'Adamo* – with its unspoken incorporation of Momus – certainly sparked Milton's earliest conception of a Paradise Lost in the early 1640s. Alberti's *Momus* supplies many of the missing pieces for those puzzled (or entranced) by Milton's antihero. The secular, political setting of Jupiter's court – with its envious courtiers,

led to the unleashing of evils from Pandora's box upon mankind; in another one, he praises him as the wisest of gods, giving advice to Jupiter from the retreat on the Caucasus Mountains (Milton, 1953–82, 1:238–39, 289). More telling, in his poem *Ad Patrem* (To His Father), defending poetry, he proclaims that poetry is part of the "Promethean fire" (Milton, 1953–82, 3: 83). On sun and light imagery, Satan's address to the Sun (starting at *PL* 4:33) has been compared to Prometheus' similar one in Aeschylus' *Prometheus Bound* (lines 88–126, Aeschylus, 1922, 224–27; Hale, 1991, 563–64). As for Shelley, he clearly now turned Christian (or anti-Christian) thought back onto the pagan myth in his celebration of Prometheus: in the preface to his *Prometheus Unbound* he compares him to Satan: "The only imaginary being resembling in any degree Prometheus, is Satan" though he is somewhat better for being free of such faults as ambition and envy, "which, in the Hero of *Paradise Lost*, interfere with the interest" (Shelley,1989, 472). Shelley praises Milton as being a welcome product of an era "which shook to dust the oldest and most oppressive form of the Christian religion" (474).

Milton's Lucifer

179

exiled hero, triangulation of political power vis-à-vis mortals, and flawed sense of justice – was a perfect model for Milton's depiction of God's court. Both epics worked on the political and theological levels to convey a rejection of authority and a manifesto of liberty with all of its personal costs.

With its unabashed speeches of Lucretian atheism, Alberti's text revealed the more profound doubt. But the iconoclastic elevation of Lucifer in Milton's text revealed doubts as well, though subtler ones. In the end, Milton seems to have most questioned the reality of a benign Providence. God's initial interference in human affairs callously enabled the opportunity for human failure and misery. The choral statement in *Samson Agonistes* states the case: "more [than the number of pure atheists] there be who doubt his ways are just ... [who] never find self-satisfying solution" (*SA* 300–6). These unpersuasive Job's Consolers only reinforce the unfairness of God's treatment of Samson. It is no accident that Milton makes a distinction between atheists and doubters of providence in the *Areopagitica*. He claimed that the ancients may have censored the likes of Protagoras (who actually was an agnostic and not an atheist), but as for those "denying of divine providence they took no heed."[94] In fact, he argues that if such sentiments were prosecuted the Bible would have to be banned, because "it brings in holiest men passionately murmuring against providence through all the arguments of Epicurus: in other great disputes it answers dubiously and darkly to the common reader."[95] This reference to the "holiest men" could only imply Job. Milton here is implicitly exonerating Job, Samson, himself, and even, in part, Satan for their doubts concerning God's plan. In this regard, the Book of Job is perhaps a foundational text for Milton's theology. In the prose preface – an interpolation that presents an anthropomorphic diminution of God not found in the original verse core of the work – Job is depicted as an undeserving victim of a God who deigns to make a wager with Satan that results in Job's persecution. Satan is the

---

[94] Milton, 1953–82, 2:494.
[95] Milton, 1953–82, 2:517.

180 *Doubting the Divine in Early Modern Europe*

Adversary who challenges God's boast concerning Job's devotion and who exposes God's defensiveness and willingness to persecute mortals in order to confirm his power. This Adversary will be a model for Satan in both *Paradise Lost* and *Paradise Regained*, who challenges God's ways and provokes his perverse treatment of mortals. The Hebrew for "Satan" is "Adversary," as Milton states in *On Christian Doctrine*; the Greek word for "devil" is *"diabolos"* or "slanderer"; in *Zeus Rants* Lucian calls the Epicurean Damis, Momus's mortal counterpart, a *"theos ecthros"* (god-hater) and a *theomache* (god-fighter).[96] In both pagan and Judeo-Christian tradition, the adversarial critic challenged the deity at the most fundamental level. Spinoza may indeed have been correct in arguing that the Adversary in Job was in fact Momus.

---

[96] Milton, 1953–82, 6:350; Forsyth, 2003, 36–37; Lucian, *Zeus Rants* 43, 45; Lucian, 1931–67, 2:154–55, 158–59.

6

God of Modern Criticks

As was evident in the classical world, Momus was a critic not only of the gods, but also of authors. This chapter will pick up the thread of his alternate biography as the god of literary criticism in the early modern period. In some ways these two biographies – of Momus as Agnostic and Momus as Critic – are parallel. At times, however, they intersect, especially when the persona of the cultural critic is elevated with the status and hubris of the agnostic. *Lèse-majesté* could affront authors, texts, and intellectual traditions as well as gods. In all cases, the targets are authority and legitimacy. In the course of the early modern era, Momus's function as Agnostic will yield to his role as Critic. What does this reveal about the larger process of the secularization of culture? How do perceptions of cultural criticism mirror those of religious criticism? In the particular area of authors and texts, some revealing parallels emerge: writers as gods, readers as devotees, critics as priests (or heretics), literary canon as divine pantheon. At times Momus was a bridge between these two realms. By the time of Jonathan Swift's famous *Battel of the Books* (1704), Momus moves from episodic literary critic to newly enshrined patron deity of "Modern Criticks" and leader of the forces of modernism against tradition. This playful, literary elevation of Momus and his human counterpart Zoilus will intersect with – and possibly intensify – the professionalization of the critic in the writings of Swift, Pope, and Thomas

182   *Doubting the Divine in Early Modern Europe*

Parnell. In the transference of piety from the divine to the aesthetic realm, it may be no coincidence that Momus's affronts overlap with Lucifer's cardinal sins of envy and pride.

Tomaso Garzoni's *Piazza universale di tutte le professioni del mondo* (1585)

The transition in Momus's role is best seen in the writings of Tomaso Garzoni (1549–89) and Jonathan Swift (1667–1745). Both figures were *professionally* tied to the clerical realm, but also at times more *vocationally* drawn to the literary one, a dual identity that facilitated their sometimes controversial movement between the religious and secular realms. In fact, both authors saw fit to issue apologies defending their piety.[1] Garzoni was heir to the tradition of *poligrafi* pioneered by Niccolò Franco and Anton Francesco Doni; indeed, given the enormous success and output of his works, he arguably represents the highpoint of this tradition in late Renaissance Italy. The great range of his publications, which also included works on psychological types, madness, natural wonders, and other topics, was aided by the fact that he was a habitual plagiarizer.[2] His most popular work, the *Piazza universale di tutte le professioni del mondo*, went through twenty-nine Venetian editions between 1585 and 1683.[3] This almost 1,000-page encyclopedia covered over 150 categories of profession, offering a history and a praise and blame of each, from theologians, princes, poets, to latrine-cleaners and chimneysweeps. Dated from Treviso in the environs of Venice, the work clearly mirrors the expansiveness and professional diversity evident in Venice's piazza San Marco.[4]

---

[1] Garzoni presents an apology for his *Piazza universale* at Garzoni, 1996, 10–11; Swift "anonymously" apologizes for his "anonymous" *Tale of a Tub* at Swift, 1958, 3–21.

[2] Cherchi, 1980; McClure, 2004, 71, 77–78, 275n60.

[3] Garzoni, 1996, cxxiii–cxxiv; on Garzoni, the *Piazza*, and his various other works, see Cherchi, 1980; Simonini, [1990]; McClure, 2004, 70–140.

[4] On allusions to piazza San Marco in the *Piazza universale*, see McClure, 2004, 79–80.

God of Modern Criticks

183

Garzoni wanted his readers to realize that there were two particularly new features of his work. One was the inclusion of the lowliest professions. In his "Author to the Viewers" in the second edition (1587), he boasts that his catalogue will include "all the professions of the world, *both honored and neglected*," the last phrase a change from "*both noble and ignoble*" in the first edition.[5] In this change, he may have wanted to tone down the traditional legal and social categories of professional classification and aim for a more neutral categories of "honored and neglected," the latter able to encompass a range including the respectable but not commonly described pursuits (engineers), the largely unacknowledged manual workers (seat-bearers, porters), and the criminal class (prostitutes, procurers, fake beggars). He had some precedent in discussing this last underworld group, as Cornelius Agrippa von Nettesheim had treated certain of these in his *De incertitudine et vanitate scientiarum* (1526), but Garzoni offers the widest imaginable panorama of all the lower, often invisible professions. A second, but related, distinction that Garzoni assigns to his work concerns its organization or, better, lack thereof. Rather than treating professions in any particular order – such as alphabetically or in descending hierarchy from "high" to "low" – he jumbles them up. The result is a sometimes jarring juxtaposition: for instance, the chapter on physicians immediately follows one on butchers (possibly with facetious intention), and gravediggers succeed musicians.[6] The general point in this disorder is to democratize the professions, a point mirrored in the content of the chapters, which often assigns – sometimes satirically, sometimes not – intricate arcana to even the lowliest of pursuits.

---

[5] Garzoni, 1996, 63, emphasis added; the title of the 1585 edition and its 1596 reprinting was *La piazza universale di tutte le professioni del mondo e nobili et ignobili* (ibid., cxxiii).

[6] McClure, 2004, 84–85; there is some precedent in Agrippa for sarcastic juxtapositions: in his *De incertitudine et vanitate scientiarum*, seven chapters on the church and clergy are immediately followed by chapters on prostitutes, procurers, and beggars, often drawing connections between these realms (130).

184   *Doubting the Divine in Early Modern Europe*

In disregarding or flouting professional hierarchy and authority, Garzoni invokes Momus in order to identify and defend this potential slight to the political and religious elite, the learned, and the well-born. In a "Prologo Nuovo" (Novel Prologue) he stages a trial of his work before the gods, in which his chief prosecutor is Momus, who assumes his customary role as critic and trouble-maker. Garzoni's use of him, however, is ironic. He has him criticize the book in such a manner as to anticipate criticisms that the book might receive, accomplishing two goals: he blunts future critics by stealing their thunder, and he points out the unique features of the book to which the small-minded or conservative might object (or the dense might not appreciate).

Garzoni's Momus, like Alberti's, is something of an anti-hero, but his gaze is directed toward an author (Garzoni) rather than a god (Jupiter). His attacks are persuasive and threaten to discredit the text, and yet they offer stirring insights into the nature of criticism and the significance of Garzoni's work. Momus appears before the assemblage of the gods to accuse "a subject [Garzoni] too audacious, who disturbs the world and the elements with his work, material of a thousand complaints regarding all the professors of the sciences and arts, which by your high judgment are constituted in the worldly globe not only for the ornamentation of that realm, but also because they make with their talent in their principal efforts every possible type of honor."[7] This haughty author, Garzoni, roils the stable universe of professions, exposing defects in pursuits tradition-ally decreed to be sources of worldly honor. Momus charges that he dares to "submerge the whole world with his tongue" and to "aggravate with his words all types of people, without regard more for one than another."[8] Assuming the power of gods and demigods – wielding Hercules' club, Neptune's tri-dent, Jove's thunderbolt – he raises himself above all and levels all classes of people. Because of this author's mortal hubris,

---

[7] Garzoni, 1996, 29, my trans.
[8] Garzoni, 1996, 30, my trans.

God of Modern Criticks

the gods should appreciate Momus's role: after all, he says, the whole world respects his truth-telling, saying to him: "'Momus, you are the freedom of the world (*libertà del mondo*), you the true scourge of unjust writers.'"[9] Here Garzoni thus identifies the heroic charge of Momus as scourge not of unjust gods, as in Lucian, Alberti, or Doni, nor unjust princes, as in Aretino, but of unjust writers.

Momus's attack on Garzoni's text frames the *Piazza* as an affront to the gods who are the creators and patrons of the arts and sciences both generally and specifically. This divine role in human endeavor makes this writer's hubris all the more offensive. Momus tells the gods:

> It is up to you, immortal gods, to vindicate these common outrages and repress as great a license as any mortal could exercise, particularly in your disrepute. Are you not the inventors of the sciences and arts that he treats so vividly – rather, that he strikes and injures with his words? You, sacred Pallas, have you not been the inventor of select and elegant disciplines? You, blissful Mercury, have you not founded rhetoric? You, glorious Apollo, have you not been the inventor of poetry?[10]

And so on he goes, plagiarizing from Jean Tixier's *Officina* (1520), to identify the traditional association of classical gods with various pursuits: Ceres with agriculture, Aesculapius with medicine, Minos with law, Vulcan with smithery, and on down even to the lower trades of gravediggers and latrine-cleaners.[11] In gathering all of these professions under his pen, Garzoni indirectly brings all the gods under his control. Although the divine tribunal is merely a literary device, the larger point is that, particularly in regard to the higher professions, Garzoni is affronting intellectual and cultural authority as surrogates for divine authority, a

---

[9] Garzoni, 1996, 30, my trans.

[10] Garzoni, 1996, 30, my trans.

[11] The *Officina historicis poeticisque referta disciplinis* of Jean Tixier (Joannes Textor), a book of lists, first appeared in 1520 and was added to in subsequent editions; by the time of the *Piazza*, the work had also appeared in several Venetian editions; I am indebted to the remarkable efforts of Paolo Cherchi and Beatrice Collina to identify plagiarisms in their superb edition of the *Piazza* (Garzoni, 1996).

186   *Doubting the Divine in Early Modern Europe*

gesture made even more relevant by the fact that Christian saints replaced ancient gods as patron saints of professions.

Garzoni's intentional displacement of cultural hierarchy is more explicitly identified in another of Momus's criticisms: namely, the random order of professions in the *Piazza*. In this (non) scheme, Garzoni drew on recent mnemonists, Giulio Camillo and Alessandro Citolini, who in constructing their memory schemes jumbled up the traditional hierarchy (based on intellectual and social criteria) and organized the arts along new celestial or naturalistic schemes. Garzoni further extended this trend by having *no* clear organizational plan.[12] Although the first half of the treatise dealt relatively more with the learned professions and the second half with manual ones, there are some jarring juxtapositions, and Momus objects to such a flagrant disregard for social gradations: "Why not give yet some order, as to the person considered, to his [Garzoni's] professions, as it appears Citolini did in his *Tipocosmia* [1561], and as it seems Giulio Camillo intended to do in is *Teatro* [1550], departing from that common alphabetical path in order to gain, at least in some way, praise for a judicious and unique intellect?"[13] This criticism from "Momus" illustrates well Garzoni's paradoxical use of the Momus trope, as he is in fact alerting the reader to the impressive iconoclastic feature of his encyclopedia.

Momus then enumerates a range of flaws critics could find in the *Piazza*: that Garzoni is "ostentatious" to try to rival Pliny (in his *Natural History*); that the style in not elevated enough like that of a Marsilio Ficino or Poliziano; that he mixes Latin and vernacular passages; that he has not spent long enough on the project; that the book is a mish-mash of jokes, stories, bagatelles; that it includes two prologues; that he is a plagiarist; and so on. In short, Garzoni's use of Momus reflects an almost postmodern self-consciousness of the writer's process of writing. Two or three criticisms in particular further develop the

[12] On the structure of Garzoni's treatise and other works (beside those of Camillo and Citolini), such as Polydore Vergil, Leonardo Fioravanti, Agrippa, and Barthélemey de Chasseneuz, see McClure, 2004, 70–89.

[13] Garzoni, 1996, 35, my trans.

controversial, anti-conventional nature of the work. The first is that his subject matter does not befit a canon, who should be writing on religious subjects: who should be a "theologian among pagans," rather than, as he is here, a "pagan among theologians."[14] This is a fair criticism of an author who clearly identified more with writers than clerics, who showed inordinate interest in the secular professions relative to religious ones, and who displayed too much knowledge of the culture of prostitutes and pimps. Moreover, seamlessly moving between the Christian and the pagan, Momus points out that Garzoni insults the pagan gods: rather than celebrating Jove with hymns and psalms, he writes of "the pimping of Venus, the amorous wars of Cupid, the brazen impudence of Flora, the excessive intemperance of Bacchus."[15] Garzoni was both irreverent Christian and irreverent pagan.

Second, Momus chides Garzoni for leveling more blame than praise in his survey of professions, a rather ironic charge coming from Momus. In fact, Garzoni is much influenced in this regard by Agrippa von Nettesheim's *De incertitutine et vanitate scientiarum* (1526), an Italian translation of which appeared in 1547 from the hands of another polygrapher, Ludovico Domenichi, and served as a key source for Garzoni to plagiarize. As Charles Nauert has shown, Agrippa's work is the most influential statement of skepticism in sixteenth-century Italy, proclaiming the hubris and corruption to be found in approximately a hundred professions.[16] In the front matter of the text, an epigraph, presumably supplied by the original publisher, contains a list of skeptical and cynical archetypes with whom Agrippa is associated. Heading the list is Momus: "Among the gods Momus reprehends everyone."[17] He is followed by such figures as Democritus (who laughs), Heraclitus (who cries), Pyrrho (who knows nothing), and Diogenes (who scorns all). Agrippa is hailed as

[14] Garzoni, 1996, 33.
[15] Garzoni, 1996, 33, my trans.
[16] Nauert, 1965.
[17] Agrippa, 2004, 10, my trans.

one with these doubters: "Agrippa does not spare anyone. He despises, he knows, he does not know, he weeps, he laughs, he persecutes, he reprehends everything."[18] Momus is thus identified as the Ur-Critic in this first major skeptical manifesto of the sixteenth century.[19] Decrying human learning in a theological context of the Fall – for eating from the Tree of the Knowledge of Good and Evil – Agrippa presents a fideistic denial of human wisdom.[20] Garzoni rejects this theological perspective and praises the arts and sciences as affirmations of human greatness, making "man similar to his maker God, full of infinite wisdom and intelligence."[21] In this sense, he would reject Agrippa's religious renunciation of learning with a more positive affirmation of man's divine-like wisdom, stealing liberally from Barthélemey de Chasseneuz's *Catalogus gloriae mundi* of 1529.[22] Thus, while he follows Agrippa in skeptically exposing and criticizing the arts, he does so not so much as a theological statement regarding the hubris and vanity of human wisdom, but as a betrayal of man's divine-like promise. Similarly, when Momus accuses Garzoni of criticizing the arts, which have various gods as their patron deities, he can reasonably charge that Garzoni is affronting the gods. Certainly, in adducing criticisms especially of elite, learned, and religious professions, the *Piazza* might be faulted for insolence. Indeed, one of Momus's key criticisms is that Garzoni has tilted the epideictic rhetoric of praise and blame too much to the negative. Momus asks: "Why not attend equally to the praises without describing the tedious and strange defects of all the

---

[18] Agrippa, 2004, 10, my trans.

[19] Agrippa himself, I believe, refers to Momus only once in the treatise: in the note "To the Reader" he predicts that will be attacked by various types in the coin of their trade, including the "dazed poets [who] will drag me in their verses through Momus" (Agrippa, 2004, 16, my trans.).

[20] Yet, because Agrippa also criticized institutional religion – ceremonies, images, clerics, inquisitors – the work was condemned by theologians at Louvain and the Sorbonne, and for this reason, even Garzoni referred to him as "sacrilego" (Garzoni, 1996, 10, 323; Nauert, 1965, 165–66, 314.

[21] Garzoni, 1996, 68, this and all the following translations of Garzoni are my own.

[22] Garzoni, 1996, 66–75.

God of Modern Criticks 189

professions?"[23] In short, why is this author so critical, asks Momus the Ur-Critic?

Finally, Momus charges Garzoni that, by "insult[ing] some people covertly, knowing that the jokes are understood," he will acquire the "name of Zoilus or Aretino among magnates and tyrants of the world."[24] I will return to Zoilus later, but Aretino, the famous pornographer, purveyor of pasquinades, and "scourge of princes," was arguably the human embodiment of Momus in sixteenth-century Italy. Once again, Garzoni strikes satirical gold by having Momus accuse him of being an Aretino – which Momus himself is and which in many ways Garzoni is also in his irreverent encyclopedia. Thus, time and again, in Momus's prosecution of Garzoni before the gods, he emphasizes the *Piazza*'s challenge to authority and tradition, whether it be the reputation of legitimate professions and disciplines, the divinities associated with such pursuits, the proper literary organization of such an encyclopedia that should respect hierarchy, the cultural preference for praise over blame, the reputation of the elite who should not be subject to insult, or the impropriety of a canon writing such a secular book.[25]

After the prosecution rests, the defense begins. Minerva, goddess of wisdom, now steps up to rebut Momus and advocate for Garzoni. Her first task is to remind the council of gods that Momus is the origin of all the scandalous stories about the gods: "Tell me, supreme gods, who has revealed to the world the infamous rape of Ganymede by the supreme Jove, if not Momus? Who has made known (if it indeed is true) that under

---

[23] Garzoni, 1996, 35.

[24] Garzoni, 1996, 35–36.

[25] As for the religious perils of his book, Garzoni includes a letter "To Readers" that is, in effect, a letter to censors and inquisitors, in which he professes his complete orthodoxy, apologizes if any minor lapses remain that are inappropriate to the "person of the author" (i.e., as a canon) or to the doctrines of the Church, and regrets if he has omitted any deserving epithets for wicked authors such as he has assigned to "l'infame Aretino" and "sacrilego Agrippa" (Garzoni, 1996, 10). He also points out (to the censors?) his fawning chapter "On Heretics and Inquisitors," which is a shamelessly unbridled attack on the one and defense of the other (855–68).

190   *Doubting the Divine in Early Modern Europe*

the form of a bull he carried Europa away ... if not Momus? Who showed the conquest of Danae in a shower of gold, if not Momus? Who publicized Mercury as the god of thieves, if not Momus?" and so on she goes at some length, attributing to Momus all the disreputable tales of the gods.[26] Although Lucian's Momus alluded to such scandals, Garzoni's Minerva credits Momus as the source of *all* the negative depictions of the gods: in short, as the greatest enemy of the divine, whose tales led to loss of belief.[27] These are obvious exaggerations, as these tales generally arose from a range of sources from the Greek world, most not originating from Momus's depictions. And yet Garzoni (via Minerva) does choose to portray Momus as a threat to traditional religion – as a "scorner (*sprezzator*) of the gods" – and thus he affirms the connection between Momus the Critic and Momus the Agnostic.

As for the defense of Garzoni, Minerva insists that Garzoni is by no means one who has "that petulant spirit of Agrippa or the infernal language of Aretino, so favored by you [Momus], who would make a profession of speaking ill [of others] well, and who would wish to transform himself into Pasquino and Marforio [the two Roman statues on which derisive verse was posted] in order to make the world laugh at the whips he would give to this and that person."[28] Minerva thus fully addresses the charge that Momus hurls – and that Garzoni clearly believes – that his book is in the tradition of sixteenth-century skeptics like Agrippa and libelers like Aretino. Momus's charge – Garzoni's admission – is of course generally true: Garzoni's plagiarism of Agrippa's *On the Uncertainty and Vanity of the Sciences* certainly places him in Agrippa's school, even if surreptitiously.[29] Minerva's defense

[26] Garzoni, 1996, 37.

[27] Garzoni cites, for instance, the case of Demonax, who neglected the Eleusinian rites because of Momus's influence (Garzoni, 1996, 38); there is no mythological evidence, however, that Momus had anything to do with the impiety of Demonax, known for his *parrhesia* in Lucian's *Demonax* 11 (Lucian, 1913–67, 1:148–51).

[28] Garzoni, 1996, 39.

[29] See, for instance, his plagiarisms of Agrippa's chapters on prostitutes and procurers; Garzoni, 1996, 951–99; Agrippa, 2004, 287–311.

is that Garzoni's exposé of defects and fraud is not destructive or defamatory, as were Agrippa's or Aretino's, but rather moral and cautionary: that is, it was meant "to exclude vice and help men with notice of evil prudently exposed to all."[30] Minerva then responds to Momus's many other criticisms, offering excuses sometimes rather facetious (that irregularities of style and accents, are more the doing of the corrector or printer than the author), sometimes more serious (that even Virgil and other ancient authors plagiarized).

The trial ends with a verdict from the divine court, which unanimously decrees that "Momus is a beast and wretch, and is unworthy of being allowed to judge anyone, having a public reputation both in the heavens and on earth as a slanderous detractor, sower of discord, and inventor of woes."[31] Garzoni thus turns the motif of Momus's expulsion from the heavens for insulting the gods into a condemnation of him as a critic of texts. This trial of an author for aesthetic transgressions (maybe a first) ends in a condemnation of his critic as an unworthy judge. But, of course, Garzoni is writing this entire scene himself and has reified the critical process, given it some patina of (mock) epic force, and used Momus ironically as a voice of conservative defensiveness against an iconoclastic book. The ultimate irony, then, is that, by pointing out the boldness of his book against these conservative forces, Garzoni uses Momus as a vehicle for a rather proto-modernist defense of bucking traditional intellectual and literary authority.

Moreover, Garzoni's "anatomy of criticism" is not finished. The agon then filters down to the human world in a section regarding the "Conspiracy of Zoilus and the Convent of Detractors, together With the Assembly of Pedants and With the Demonstration of the Buffoons and Ignorant Against the *Piazza* of Garzoni ... and He [Garzoni] Vindicates Himself Against All of These With a Most Beautiful Letter Written at the End to the Council of Gods."[32] In this section Garzoni critiques his own

[30] Garzoni, 1996, 39.
[31] Garzoni, 1996, 44.
[32] Garzoni, 1996, 46.

book through the eyes of different classes of critics that could appraise his book. The first group, the literary critics, is personified by Zoilus, the fourth-century BCE rhetorician famous as the critic of Homer. He is in effect a mortal counterpart to Momus as the Ur-Critic. He chides the council for their poor verdict in favor of Minerva and Garzoni, confirming that worldly critics are in agreement with Momus's criticisms of the *Piazza*. He then reviews the early history and prerogatives of the literary critic. No god (like Minerva) intervened to prevent him (Zoilus) from attacking Homer, nor Bavius and Mevius from critiquing Virgil, nor Quinto Rennio Palemone from attacking Varro. Why does this council of gods listen to Minerva and rule "perfidiously against the truth?"[33] This brief defense of the critic then lifts various examples from Jean Tixier's *Officina*, which contains a chapter "On Free and Troublesome Loquacity," a catalogue of detractors through time, including Momus and Zoilus.[34] Zoilus then discredits the council of gods by rehearsing the litany of their scandalous reputations, thereby suggesting the primacy of truth-telling critics over decadent gods.

In the context of situating his own book as an object of literary criticism, Garzoni thus explores the cultural tradition of criticism. The classical examples cited here, moreover, are complemented by modern ones in a chapter in the *Piazza* entitled "On Slanderers, Detractors, and Murmurers." Here, he portrays the office of critic in wholly negative terms, calling it a "shameful profession" and bringing it up into the sixteenth century:

There is a profession of some uncivil and ill-bred men, even infernal demons, who do not do anything else from morning till night than, with the worst tongue, lacerate this person and that, haunt the shops, hold court in the piazzas and public and private assemblies, showing themselves to be of the academy of Aretino, Burchiello [Domenico di Giovanni, a fifteenth-century burlesque poet], [Francesco] Berni and Franco, not to mention the school of Pasquino and Marforio.[35]

[33] Garzoni, 1996, 47.
[34] Tixier, 1600, 777–79.
[35] Garzoni, 1996, 1052.

God of Modern Criticks   193

Whereas Zoilus's speech in the "Novel Prologue" offers a praise of the critic, this chapter provides the blame, especially as it reflects the contemporary climate of the irreverent pasquinade of figures such as Aretino – a particular feature of Renaissance Italy that Jacob Burckhardt rightly identified in his classic study from the nineteenth century.[36] Once again plagiarizing Tixier's chapter "On Free and Troublesome Loquacity," this time he emphasizes all the punishments befalling those who speak against authority.[37] Given Garzoni's own challenge to literary and intellectual authority in the *Piazza*, this could be seen as exceptionally hypocritical or, more likely, deliciously ironic.

Following Zoilus's affirmation of Momus's judgment on the *Piazza* and his defense of the tradition of critics, the pedants and buffoons take their turn, each representing opposite poles of culture: the pedants attacking from the vantage point of high culture, the buffoons from that of low. Mosco, a spokesman for the learned, castigates Garzoni, who with his "petulant speech has slandered our common honor, insanely adopting satirical eloquence against everyone, with respect to the world of so many Ciceronian luminaries who light up our age with eloquent and clever speech."[38] Garzoni naturally would not simulate this criticism if it was not substantially true. He also has Mosco attack the *Piazza* for all manner of scholarly deficiencies in conventional literary techniques, "grave examples, profound sentiments, cheerful urbanity, congruent order" in favor of "scurrility and silliness."[39] As a work aiming for a middlebrow audience, the *Piazza* would come under fire for such failings, especially since it does include learned disciplines among its purview. Again, then, Garzoni is constructing reasonable

---

[36] Burckhardt, 1990, 114–19; on Aretino, see Waddington, 2004.

[37] Such figures include Theocritus, put to death by King Antigonus for the "extreme license of his biting comments," and Archilochus, banished by the Spartans for his "unrestrained sharpness" (Garzoni, 1996, 1057; cf. 47; Tixier, 1600, 77–79).

[38] Garzoni, 1996, 49. And later he even says that Garzoni is a "butcher of our honor, who mocks the mass of so many erudite men" (52).

[39] Garzoni, 1996, 52.

194   *Doubting the Divine in Early Modern Europe*

criticisms from a certain audience that would find this book unconventional.

At the other end of the cultural spectrum, Proto, representing the buffoons and the ignorant, criticizes the *Piazza* for its lack of social realism. If Garzoni intended to construct a truly accurate piazza, why has he left out so many details? How about the street vendor like Gambarin the leather-strap man, Baraso the jokester, Mattia the madman, Menega the fritter-lady, and others? How about the mechanics of commerce in a real piazza: "If this (as he says) is a piazza, on what day is the market? If there is a market, where do the goods come from? And if these good come in, where do you pay the gabelle? And if the gabelle is paid, where is the customs office?"[40] Because the *Piazza* does include a chapter on charlatans, buffoons, quacks, and street performers (ch. 104), it is reasonable to assume that his text should face criticism from this class.[41] On the one hand, this criticism that Garzoni places in the mouth of buffoons mocks their naïveté in completely conflating the metaphorical and literal piazzas on which his book is constructed. On the other, however, his book does indeed exploit the actual features of Piazza San Marco and does aspire to a social comprehensiveness: thus by posing this self-criticism, he reveals his awareness of the nitty-gritty of that world and, as an author, forestalls such "realistic" critics.

At the end of these assaults by the literary critics, pedants, and buffoons, Garzoni includes a "Letter of Garzoni to the Supreme Chorus of the Gods." As Minerva rebutted Momus in the first round of the critical agon, Garzoni rebuts his mortal detractors in the second; in effect he arrays the chorus of gods, Minerva, and himself on one side and Momus, Zoilus, pedants, and buffoons on the others. He protests to the gods that the "extreme liberty of reasoning" of these worldly critics detracts from both the gods' honor and his own.[42] Implicitly equating blasphemy of the gods with criticism of the author, he cites cases of poets (Homer

---

[40] Garzoni, 1996, 54.

[41] For this chapter, "De' formatori di spettacoli in genere, e di' ceretani o ciurmatori massime," see Garzoni, 1996, 1188–97.

[42] Garzoni, 1996, 57.

and Hesiod) and mortals (Tantalus) who have been punished for their critical revelations of the gods' defects or secrets. The pedants he counters in their own terms, facetiously detailing how they are deficient in all ten of Aristotle's logical *Categories*. Similarly, he mocks the buffoons at their level, saying that they should not dare broach the realm of learning but should only be talking of jugs, kettles, buckets, urinals, and such matter.

What Garzoni does in this extended Momic analysis of his own work is to provide a template for the contentious terms of literary criticism. He channels the barbs of his potential critics from high to low culture. He covers the whole essence of a literary work: its ambition, structure, content, style, potential reception. As a self-reflexive analysis by an author of his process and reception, the "Novel Prologue," twenty-one pages in the 1587 edition, has an eerily postmodern ring.[43] Doubly so, in that Garzoni constantly shifts between irony and seriousness. Is he really arraying himself on the side of decadent, defensive gods who cannot take criticism? Not really; but only insomuch as he wants to equate the author and his dignity with the gods and their dignity. Some of Momus's criticisms – such as his jumbling of the order of professions – are in fact praises of his work as a modern departure from authority. In this sense, Momus as architect of authorial self-criticism is both antihero and hero in ushering in the terms of modern literature and criticism. There is no evidence that Garzoni read Alberti's *Momus* – rather he has read Lucian and Doni's *I mondi* – but it is interesting to see how he has created an analogous antihero, though one who is moving away from divine criticism to literary criticism. And, as his trial illustrates, Garzoni accomplishes this transition through an (admittedly playful) divine tribunal.[44]

That Garzoni's attitude toward literary criticism is serious becomes evident in the massive chapter "On Poets in General, and Of the Forming of Epitaphs and Pasquinades in Particular,"

---

[43] Damrosch, 2013, 134, makes a similar point about Swift's many prefaces and preliminaries in the *Tale of a Tub*.

[44] See his citations of *I mondi* and *Gli inferni* at Garzoni, 1996, 1165, and 1488.

196   *Doubting the Divine in Early Modern Europe*

which in the original 1585 edition was the last chapter in the work.[45] This chapter assesses poetry at its most sublime – as a craft inspired by the gods and voiced by the poet as *vates* – and at its most destructive – as a weapon in the pasquinade of the likes of Aretino and Franco.[46] Truly a "pagan among theologians," Garzoni also inserts himself into the discussion as he invokes a range of classical gods to inspire him in his effort in prose to discuss poets. Clearly striving doubly for irony here, he says "I make a new invitation in prose to Mercury of the winged sandals that he enable me to fly so high that I resemble Jove, when in the form of an eagle he raped Ganymede on top of Mount Ida," and so on, invoking Phoebus, Pan, Minerva, Bacchus, and many others.[47] Momus appears twice in this chapter, in ways that reflect both his destructive and constructive personas. In one case, he is cited as a pejorative counterpart to Pasquino.[48] In another, he is invoked more neutrally, as the reminder that he must include at least some criticism of poets as a class in his chapter: "But because Momus would grieve if I did not discuss the coarseness of many [poets] and the inept weavings that some anatomists of poetry make, it is necessary that I say almost in a breath all the censures that have been given to poets."[49]

Most notable, however, in this chapter is the staging of a literary "duel" (*duello*), featuring the writing and analysis of a Latin poem. In some ways, this replicates the literary trial in his "Novel Prologue," in which critics (Momus, Zoilus, and others), defenders (Minerva, the Chorus of Gods), and the author's

---

[45] Garzoni, 1996, 1472–525. In the second edition, Garzoni added a brief chapter "On Humanists" that followed the one on poets, which, at thirty-seven pages in the 1587 edition, is one of the longest in the book.

[46] On the pasquinade, see Garzoni, 1996, 1481–82; in the section on epitaphs, he cites a similar discussion in Doni's "Laughable World" at 1488–89.

[47] Garzoni, 1996, 1474.

[48] Garzoni, 1996, 1481.

[49] Garzoni, 1996, 1492; for instance, he cites Plato's banishment of poets from his Republic. Cf. Agrippa's comment that the poets would attack him in the name of Momus for criticizing them (Agrippa, 2004, 16). This example may have influenced Garzoni, as I believe that it is the only time in the *Piazza* that he invokes Momus as the inspiration for his enumeration of professional defects or bad reputation.

response are recorded. In this case, the agon involves a poem written by a jurist and chancellor of the Venetian state, Lorenzo Massa, which is criticized by a Paduan humanities professor, Antonio Riccobono, whose critique in turn is anonymously rebutted (probably by the Venetian humanities professor, Fabio Paolini). This is a truly real-time publishing event. Garzoni's first edition of the *Piazza* appeared in late 1585, with a dedicatory letter dated December 5, 1585; Riccobono's critique is dated October 4, 1585. In fact, in the rare 1585 edition this section, clearly added at the last possible moment, is not even paginated.[50] Garzoni boasted that the publication of this critical debate was singularly new: "The duel is truly unique, and the matter, in my judgment, worthy of being publicized to the world."[51] The exchange, waged in Latin, Greek, and Italian, was certainly quite scholarly – even pedantic, despite Garzoni's scorn for the pedants in the "Novel Prologue." What it demonstrates, however, is that Garzoni has self-consciously given criticism a dramatically visible platform. To be sure, there was already in place in Renaissance Italy a sophisticated tradition of literary criticism (on Dante, Ariosto, Tasso), philological analysis (Lorenzo Valla's exposé of the forged Donation of Constantine), and endless literary in-fighting among humanists hurling invectives at each other (Poggio vs. Valla, Poggio vs. Filelfo, Filelfo vs. everyone, etc.).[52] What Garzoni has done, however, is to elevate the concept of criticism to a self-conscious level (for the art) and self-reflexive meaning (for the author).

Quite industrious, quite popular, and quite self-aware as a "writer of books," Garzoni the polygrapher is an ideal figure to fully resurrect Momus's persona as the literary critic. He assigns Momus his most extended speech in this capacity in the "Novel Prologue." Much of Garzoni's own task in the *Piazza*

---

[50] This is probably one reason this was the last chapter in the first edition of the *Piazza*; on this duel, see McClure, 2004, 102–3.

[51] Garzoni, 1996, 1495.

[52] On literary criticism in Renaissance Italy, see Weinberg, 1961; Valla, 1993; on humanist invectives, see Erasmus's comment in his 1515 letter to Martin Dorp (Erasmus, 1989a, 230; Filelfo, 2013; De Keyser, 2015).

198   *Doubting the Divine in Early Modern Europe*

is in fact Momic criticism of learning and cultural authority. Much as Garzoni pretends to cast Momus as his and society's enemy in the *Piazza*, much as he deems him a powerful enemy of the gods and of the author, he deploys him ironically as a figure identifying the iconoclastic and modern features of his work. His Momus in this sense is not truly a critic of the author but rather, by inversion, a mocker of the stodgy traditions of a hierarchical society and of the requirement that a book fit into only one (learned) niche of that society. Thus, his Momus archly praises via blame. Finally, Garzoni's seriousness about the legitimacy of criticism and literary debate is evident in the very contemporary controversy commanding the last pages of the 1585 edition. He has truly elevated criticism to a discrete, high art. And while generally playful in doing so in the "Novel Prologue," he equates the author with the gods, who must deal with the nettlesome challenges of an antihero such as Momus.

Jonathan Swift's Momus: Hero of the Moderns

Over a century after Garzoni published his *Piazza*, Jonathan Swift wrote two quasi-anonymous works in which Momus makes an appearance: *A Tale of a Tub* and the adjoined *Battel Between the Antient and Modern Books in St. James's Library.*[53] Swift's treatment of Momus reveals no influence by Garzoni, and yet the writers reveal some parallel developments in the early modern ascent of Momus as literary critic. Swift further reifies Momus's status and history as Ur-Critic and, in doing so, signals the triumph of Criticism that flowers in Dryden, Pope, and Thomas Parnell: Swift's use of Momus represents this trope's minor, yet imaginative, role in the "invention of English criticism," to borrow Michael Gavin's phrase.[54] Second,

---

[53] These works, probably written in the second half of the 1690s, were not published until 1704. I will be citing the facsimile edition edited by A. C. Guthkelch and D. Nichol Smith in 1958; on dating, see their comments in Swift, 1958, xliii–xlvii.

[54] Gavin, 2015.

like Garzoni but even more explicitly and less ironically, Swift deploys Momus to herald the disruptive forces of the "moderns." Third, just as Garzoni charts the transformation of Momus from critic of gods to critic of authors, Swift employs a mock-epic use of Momus that likely informed his coevals Pope and Parnell in their porous imagery linking religious heresy to aesthetic heresy, a linkage presaging – not necessarily intentionally – the secularizing ascent of texts over deities.

In 1709 Swift wrote an "Apology" published at the beginning of the 1710 edition of the *Tale of a Tub* and *Battel of the Books*. In this "Apology," written in the third person, he declares that his goals in the two works are linked: "he thought the numerous and gross Corruptions in Religion and Learning might furnish Matter for a Satyr ... The Abuses in Religion he proposed to set forth in the Allegory of the Coats, and the three Brothers ... Those in Learning he chose to introduce by way of Digressions."[55] His critical and satirical eye surveyed both religious and literary realms, and although the settings were differentiated into the "Tale" and the "Digressions" we might consider whether there were implicit connections between the two realms. Scholars disagree on this issue. Some, such as Phillip Harth, see the two parts as unconnected owing to slightly different periods of composition: the religious tale written in 1695–96 when Swift served his first brief stint as a cleric in Kilroot, Ireland; the discussion on literature and learning begun in June 1697, once Swift had returned to the service of Sir William Temple.[56] Others, such as Howard Weinbrot, see the *Tale* (and its "Digressions"), the *Battel of the Books*, and an adjoined fragment, *A Discourse Concerning the Mechanical Operation of the Spirit*, as being all of a piece thematically.[57] Swift's intersplicing the *Tale* with the "Digressions" does suggest that, at least in terms of literary structure, he intended to link critics of religion and critics of literature.

The *Tale of a Tub* is a religious allegory regarding the divergent paths of Catholicism, Anglicanism, and Calvinism. A father

---

[55] Swift, 1958, 4.
[56] Harth, 1961, 6–7.
[57] Weinbrot, 2005, 119–21.

(Christ) bequeaths coats to his sons Peter (Catholicism), Martin (Anglicanism), and Jack (Calvinism), who use or abuse this bequest in various ways. Because Martin makes the fewest alterations to the coat – as opposed to Peter, who dresses it up far too much, and Jack who strips it down too far – he is the least objectionable. Thus, Swift mildly endorses Anglicanism, which befits his career in that Church. The weight of scholarly opinion favors the view that Swift is generally in the camp of conservative Anglicanism, opposed especially to the Puritans and various currents of Deism or atheism afoot. There are problems with such a view or any monochromatic view of Swift, who is devilishly sly in his literary maneuverings. There are many hints in the *Tale* that suggest a far more skeptical view of religion in general.[58] The motif of the inheritance of the three brothers recalls Boccaccio's radical "Tale of the Three Rings" (*Decameron* 1.3), which implies the equal validity of Judaism, Christianity, and Islam.[59] Beyond that motif of religious relativism, one of religious imposture could also be at work, as Swift at one point compares preachers orating from on high to mountebanks and charlatans.[60] In introducing his three clerics, moreover, he characterizes all three as gambling, whoring types variously drawn to the Duchess d'Argent (Greed), Madame de Grands Titres (Ambition), and the Countess d'Orgueil (Pride).[61] He mocks the Trinity at one point, and Prosper Marchand later even charged that the work was so anti-religious as to rival that other infamous story of Three, the *Treatise of the Three Impostors*.[62] All of this, in addition to the frequency of quotations from Lucretius' *De rerum natura*, needs

---

[58] Damrosch, 2013, 135–40.
[59] Boccaccio, 1995, 41–44.
[60] Swift, 1958, 56–60.
[61] Swift, 1958, 74.
[62] In his chapter "De tribus impostoribus" in his *Dictionnaire historique*, Marchand condemned the *Tale* to be "as criminal and perhaps even more pernicious than [the *Three Impostors*], because it proposes nothing less than to turn cruelly to ridicule the three principal sects of Western Christianity" (Marchand, 1758–59, 326, my trans., Minois, 2012, 157–58). He goes on to acknowledge that certain Anglicans see it as a defense of the Anglican Church, but he thinks otherwise.

God of Modern Criticks

to be accounted for in claiming a fully conservative position in Swift. William Wotton, a contemporary rival, condemned the *Tale* as "one of the Prophanest Banters upon the Religious of Jesus Christ, as such, that ever appeared," citing the ridicule of the Trinity and the comparison of preachers to mountebanks.[63] Later, Samuel Johnson speculated that the tale kept Swift from gaining a bishopric in England, consigning him to the deanery of St. Patrick's in Ireland.[64] In short, both internal textual evidence and external contemporary reactions suggest that the *Tale* likely had motives beyond weakly defending Anglicanism, which, as the text implies, was simply the least bad of institutional alternatives.[65]

As is evident, despite Swift's interest in Lucian (a three-volume French translation of whom he bought as a gift for his beloved Stella), Momus figures nowhere in the religious sections of the

---

[63] See Wotton's *Observations Upon the Tale of a Tub* (1705) in Swift, 1958, 322, 324.

[64] Swift, 2010, 728, 731.

[65] As for Swift's views on religion (his "Thoughts on Religion," not published during his lifetime), several comments suggest a rather detached view of belief: "To say a man is bound to believe, is neither truth nor sense," and more telling: "I am not answerable to God for the doubts that arise in my own breast, since they are the consequence of that reason which he hath planted in me, *if I take care to conceal those doubts from others, if I use my best endeavors to subdue them*" (Swift, 2010, 710, emphasis added; Damrosch, 2013, 148–49). This last rumination follows a rather odd admission about his clerical career: "I look upon myself in the capacity of a clergyman, to be one appointed by providence *for defending a post assigned me*" (Swift, 2010, 710, emphasis added). It is telling that he never published any of his sermons (Damrosch, 2013, 271). His *Argument Against Abolishing Christianity* (written in 1708, published in 1711) is a facetious simulation of a secularist defense of *institutional religion* (vs. belief) grounded in purely worldly arguments: for instance, that, without religion to rail against, wits like John Toland would have no target and people would turn their scorn on the government (Swift, 2010, 137–38). Less ironic, however, may be Swift's having his freethinker avow, "not that I am, in the least of Opinion with those, who hold Religion to have been the Invention of Politicians, to keep the lower Part of the World in Awe, by the Fear of Invisible Powers" (Swift, 2010, 141) – an argument perhaps too redolent of Lucretius and views that would find their way into the *Treatise of the Three Impostors*.

202 *Doubting the Divine in Early Modern Europe*

Tale.[66] Instead, he appears in the first of many digressions, this one entitled "A Digression Concerning Criticks." This digression is the opening salvo against the "Moderns," whom he will ridicule in the *Battel of the Books*, a controversy between the Ancients and the Moderns arising out of his acquaintance with Sir William Temple, a retired diplomat whom he served as secretary.[67] This debate, which has its true origins in the Italian Renaissance, blossomed in full in the seventeenth and eighteenth centuries, one of the English principals being Temple, who wrote an *Essay Upon the Ancient and Modern Learning* (1690) in response in part to Bernard de Fontenelle's praise of the moderns in his *Digression sur les anciens et les modernes* (1688).[68] In his zeal to proclaim the superiority of the ancients, Temple proved himself to be an ardent and rather dull-witted traditionalist, minimizing modern gains in science (aside from the Copernican system), condemning the modern "itch" for satire in literature (accusing *Don Quixote* of ruining the Spanish monarchy), and bewailing the rise of pedantry in modern learning. Most unfortunate was his claim that the very earliest pieces of prose literature, Aesop's *Fables* and the spurious *Letters of Phalaris* (fifth-century BCE Greek tyrant), surpass anything written in their genres up through the modern world.[69] Temple's treatise launched a prolonged battle. William Wotton responded with his *Reflections Upon Ancient and Modern Learning* (1694), in which he argued that recent advances in "Mechanical Philosophy" had unearthed truths proving how God works through Nature: Deist arguments that presumably inspired Swift's *Discourse on the Mechanical Operation of the Spirit*.[70] After Charles Boyle's weak effort to provide a critical edition of the *Letters of Phalaris*, Richard Bentley, the librarian of St. James's, weighed in with a *Dissertation Upon the Epistles*

---

[66] On the never-delivered gift of the Lucian translation for Stella, see H. Williams, 1932, 24–25, 46.
[67] On Swift's long service to, and somewhat troubled relationship with, Temple, see Damrosch, 2013, 37–61, 79–93.
[68] For a superb account of the debate, see Levine, 1991.
[69] Temple, 1963, 56–70.
[70] Wotton, 1694, A5v.

God of Modern Criticks
203

of Phalaris (1697), in which he proved the collection to be forgery.[71] Poor Temple had not only made a naïve claim about the unmatched superiority of the letters, but his claim was based on a forgery. As Temple's amanuensis who helped prepare Temple's *Essay*, Swift was fully versed in controversy and chose to mock the Modern camp in his "Digressions" in the *Tale* and in the *Battel of the Books*.

In the "Digression Concerning Criticks," Swift opens by defining three types of critics. First are those who draw up aesthetic rules and should both praise and blame (and not just blame). Second are those who restore ancient manuscripts: in effect, those humanists beginning in the Italian Renaissance who compiled critical texts. These two classes, seriously described, are worthy. Then comes the satirical treatment of the most prominent class of critics:

> The Third, and Noblest Sort, is that of the TRUE CRITICK, whose Original is the most Antient of all. Every True Critick is a Hero born, descending in a direct Line from a Celestial Stem, by Momus and Hybris, who began Zoilus, who begat Tegillius, who begat Etcaetera the Elder, who begat B-tly [Bentley], who began Rym-r [Thomas Rymer], and W-tton [Wotton], and Perrault, and [John] Dennis, who begat Etcaetera the Younger.[72]

This class thus has pseudo-divine lineage, is mock-heroic, and has as its progenitors Momus and Hybris, a new genealogy not found in Hesiod or Alberti.[73] This line of heroic critics, stretching down to the present day, has been deified by mankind because of their Herculean efforts in slaying "Monstrous Faults … [and] Errors like Cacus."[74] From the ancient critics Zoilus (scourge of Homer) and Tegellius (would-be critic mocked in Horace's *Satires*), Swift brings the tradition down to the contemporary figures such as Wotton and Bentley.[75] Swift's lineage is somewhat paradoxical. On the one hand, he assigns the propensity to excessive criticism and hubris as a particular feature of modern critics;

[71] Bentley, 1874; Levine, 1991, 49–50; Grafton, 1990, 73, 98.

[72] Swift, 1958, 93–94.

[73] Ehrenpreis, 1962, 231, suggests that the "heroic" attribute is intended to mock the deluded hubris of the modern scholars.

[74] Swift, 1958, 95.

[75] On Tegellius, see Ullman, 1915.

204   *Doubting the Divine in Early Modern Europe*

on the other, his speaker, self-identified as a Modern, shows that the phenomenon of criticism has a hoary tradition among the Ancients, beginning with the god Momus and the mortal Zoilus. Albeit in satirical terms, he offers a history of the cultural dynamic and profession of criticism. Critics have been deified by their admirers like the demigods of old. Ancient writers feared critics and could allude to their power only in metaphorical or mythological terms or through satirical prefaces or fawning praises of critics.[76] (In fact, as previously noted, Garzoni for one exemplified this use of the defensive and satirical preface.) Like fiddlers, architects, or tailors, critics have sought to justify their existence in the state by creating a profession, "set[ting] up with a Stock and Tools for his Trade, at as little Expense as a Taylor."[77]

Two of his points address claims made by the modern critics Wotton and Bentley. The former argued that it is the *Modern* philological critic who can truly authenticate the treasures and facts of the *Ancient* world: "They [citing Wotton in the marginalia] have proved beyond contradiction, that the very finest Things delivered of old, have long since been invented, and brought to light by much later Pens, and that the noblest Discoveries those Ancient ever made, of Art or of Nature, have been produced by the transcending Genius of the present Age."[78] This sarcastic rendering of Wotton's serious argument, addresses a signal feature Joseph Levine finds in the debate between the Ancients and Moderns: namely, that the real (vs. forged) artifacts of Antiquity are reified only by the authentication of the modern critics through philological and historical analysis.[79] Swift also cites Bentley's argument that critics improve and shape learning:

A certain Author [Bentley identified in the marginalia], whose Works have many Ages since been entirely lost [a Swiftian insult], does in

---

[76] He fabricates fantastical interpretations from Pausanias and Herodotus to argue the metaphorical recognition of critics (Swift, 1958, 98–99).

[77] Swift, 1958, 101.

[78] Swift, 1958, 96.

[79] Presumably, Swift is alluding chiefly to Wotton's chapter "Of the Philological Learning of the Ancients" in his *Reflections Upon Ancient and Modern Learning* (Wotton, 1694, 310–21); Levine, 1991, 2–3, 45–46.

God of Modern Criticks

his fifth Book and eighth Chapter, say of *Criticks*, that their *Writings are the Mirrors of Learning*. This I understand in a literal Sense, and suppose our Author must mean, that whoever designs to be a perfect Writer, must inspect into the Books of *Criticks*, and correct his Invention there as in a Mirror.[80]

Granted that he does so with an eye toward satirizing modern hubris, Swift thus incorporates two serious claims by modern scholars regarding the constructive forces of criticism. The "Digression" ends on a fully derisive note, prescribing procedures for the "True Modern Criticks": namely, that they act on first impression, pick at the best authors, and fight over literary scraps like dogs at a feast.[81] In assigning Criticism a mythology, history, professional standing, and intellectual claims, Swift offers a template for the cultural status of the critic which, despite its satirical features, was not to be found in Antiquity.

This and another "Digression in the Modern Kind" in the *Tale* were a prelude to his full-fledged satire on the Modern Criticks in the *Battel of the Books*. Swift's battle is a mock-epic on the battle of the Ancient and Modern books (or authors) in St. James's Library. Ostensibly it defends Temple's position, as the Ancients vanquish the Moderns. Swift did not, however, publish the work until well after Temple's death in 1699, possibly, as Damrosch argues, because Temple had expressed his distaste for the modern "itch" of satire.[82] In staging the conflict,

---

[80] Swift, 1958, 102–3.

[81] Swift, 1958, 103–4. As Guthkelch and Smith point out (Swift, 1958, 103n2). Charles Boyle presents a similar discussion of good and bad critics in his 1698 *Dr. Bentley's Dissertation on the Epistles of Phalaris and the Fables of Aesop Examined* (Boyle, 1698, 223–29). Boyle (1698, 228–29), in turn, cites a recent treatment on Critics from Jean Le Clerc's 1697 *Ars Critica* (Le Clerc, 1698); on the rage of criticism in the late seventeenth and eighteenth century, see Patey, 2005, 3. Because Swift began writing the sections on learning starting in June 1697 and possibly up through and after Temple's death in 1699, it is possible that he drew on this discussion, though livening it with humor (Harth, 1961, 6–7). As for terminology, Dryden refers to "Ancient [and] Modern Critics" in his *Essay of Dramatick Poesy* (Dryden, 1956–2000, 17:76) and is credited with being the first to use the term "criticism" in the literary sense (Gavin, 2015, 2).

[82] Damrosch, 2013, 89; Temple, 1963, 70.

206   *Doubting the Divine in Early Modern Europe*

Swift lines up the two sides when books in the library begin to jockey for space. The Moderns include, among others, Tasso, Milton, Dryden, Descartes, Guicciardini, Buchanan, Bentley, and Wotton; the Ancients Homer, Pindar, Euclid, Plato, Aristotle, Herodotus, Hippocrates, Phalaris, Aesop, Temple, and Boyle.[83] When Fame alerts Jupiter to the impending battle he convenes a divine council to deal with "a bloody Battle just impendent between two mighty Armies of Antient and Modern Creatures, call'd Books, wherein the Celestial Interest was but too deeply concerned. *Momus*, the Patron of the *Moderns*, made an Excellent Speech in their Favor, which was answered by Pallas the *Protectress* of the *Antients*."[84] With Swift, as with Garzoni, literary debates have claimed the attention of the gods, albeit in mock-epic terms.

When the council deadlocks, Momus seeks help from a demonic goddess, Criticism, who is described in terms of epic malevolence: "MEAN while, *Momus* fearing the worst, and calling to mind an antient Prophecy, which bore no very good face to his Children the *Moderns*; bent his Flight to the Region of a malignant Deity, called *Criticism*."[85] Sitting among half-eaten volumes, she is surrounded by family members who included her father and husband Ignorance, her mother Pride, her sister Opinion, and a brood of children, "Noise and Impudence, Dullness and Vanity, Positiveness, Pedantry, and Ill-Manners."[86] A. C. Guthkelch and D. Nichol Smith rightly observe that the depiction of Criticism resembles Milton's portrayal of Sin in Book 2 of *Paradise Lost*: like Sin, whose father and husband was Satan, Criticism's father and husband was Ignorance. Also, Swift

---

[83] As for Swift's inclusion among the Moderns of his relative Dryden, with whom he had a somewhat troubled relationship (Damrosch, 2013, 84–86), Dryden had recently provided some precedent for the *Battel* in his 1688 *Essay of Dramatick Poesie*, in which four figures discuss the merits of the Ancient and Moderns and of French and English authors (Dryden, 1956–2000, 17:7–81, 332–33).

[84] Swift, 1958, 238–39.

[85] Swift, 1958, 240.

[86] Swift, 1958, 240.

depicts her as having a ravenous "Crew of ugly Monsters ... greedily sucking" at her teats, just as Milton's Sin has a brood of "yelling monsters" (bred of rape by Death) that "howl and gnaw / My bowels."[87] Albeit satirically, Swift thus may have implicitly assigned Criticism the status of Sin. If it is true that Milton drew on Momus for his depiction of Lucifer, Swift closes the loop by drawing on Milton for his depiction of Momus's sovereign demonic deity Criticism. In any case, the battle of the books is invested with an imagery similar to and likely reliant upon that found in Milton's cosmic battle between Lucifer and Christ. Reaching her on top of a snowy mountain, Momus entreats her:

Goddess, said *Momus, can you sit idly here, while our devout Worshippers, the* Moderns, *are this Minute entering into a cruel Battel, and, perhaps, now lying under the Swords of their Enemies; Who then hereafter, will ever sacrifice, or build Altars to our Divinities? Haste therefore to the* British Isle, *and, if possible, prevent their Destruction, while I make Factions among the Gods, and gain them over to our Party.*[88]

His message delivered, Momus departs and an enraged Criticism presents a soliloquy of ironic self-praise that resembles that of Erasmus's Dame Folly but also has some of the defiance and resentment of Lucifer's bitter soliloquy in *Paradise Lost* 4:35– 113. In Swift's epic, Momus's agency stirs the new goddess to proclaim her greatness in a fit of "Rage" and "Resentment":

MOMUS having thus delivered himself, staid not for an answer, but left the Goddess to her own Resentment; Up she rose in a Rage, and as it is the Form upon such Occasions, began a soliloquy: *'Tis I* (said she) *who give Wisdom to Infants and Idiots; By Me, Children grow wiser than their Parents. By Me,* Beaux *become Politicians; and* School-boys, *Judges of Philosophy. By Me, Sophisters debate, and Conclude upon the Depths of Knowledge; and Coffee-house Wits instinct by me, can*

---

[87] Swift, 1958, 240 and note 2 therein; Milton, *Paradise Lost* 2:757–802. Weinbrot, 2005, 187, notes that in Spenser's *Fairie Queen* 1.14–15, the figure Foule Errour also has monsters feeding on her breasts (Spenser, 1995, 5).

[88] Swift, 1958, 240–41.

208 *Doubting the Divine in Early Modern Europe*

*correct an Author's style and display his minutest Language. By Me,
Striplings spend their Judgment, as they do their Estate, before it comes
into their Hands. 'Tis I, who have deposed Wit and Knowledge from
their Empire over Poetry, and advanced my self in their stead. And
shall a few upstart Antients dare to oppose me? — But, come, my aged
Parents, and you, my Children dear, and thou my beauteous Sister; let
us ascend my Chariot, and hast to assist our devout Moderns.*[89]

Like Momus in Alberti's epic and Lucifer in Milton's, Swift's
Criticism soliloquizes in proud, resentful tones. The battle is
then engaged, in which Temple and Boyle and the Ancients
defeat Bentley, Wotton, and the Moderns.[90]

What was Swift doing in the *Battel*? What does it mean that
Momus is the Patron of the Moderns? Is there a thematic relationship between the religious parts of the *Tale* and the discussions
of literature and criticism in the "Digressions" and the *Battel*?
Howard Weinbrot sees clear parallels in Swift's criticism of religion and learning. For him and others, Swift is a defender of tradition, mocking religious dissenters (the Puritans), who threaten
the stability of the Anglican Church, and the literary dissenters
(Bentley, Wotton), who threaten the literary authority of Homer
and other ancients.[91] In this interpretation, Swift is simply a foe
of the Moderns and his Momus a demonic force undermining
the literary authority of the ancient world. Momus is thus the
herald of a skeptical and destructive "modernism," a term Swift
himself was the first to coin in pejorative terms in a letter to
Alexander Pope in 1737.[92] I am not convinced, however, that
Swift is merely the doleful towncrier of modernism, but rather
may also be its wily practitioner. That is, while he may be parodying the Moderns in both works, he also seems to be using this

[89] Swift, 1958, 241.
[90] Ehrenpreis, 1962, 228–31, charts the precedents in the *Iliad* and *Aeneid* and
in some mock battles depicted in seventeenth-century literature.
[91] Weinbrot, 2005, 141–42; Damrosch, 2013, 88–89; Levine, 1991, 115–20.
[92] Damrosch, 2013, 134, points out that the *OED* lists this letter as containing
the earliest usage of the term modernism(s). It is quite negative, as Swift
refers to "the corruption of English by those Scribblers who send us over
this trash in Prose and Verse, with abominable curtailings and quaint
modernisms" (www.oed.com.libdata.lib.ua.edu/view/Entry/120622?redire
ctedFrom=modernism#eid).

satire as a disguise to mock (as Swift) both religion and contemporary learning. How else can we explain the mockery of clerics and the Trinity that gave contemporaries fodder to accuse him of blasphemy? As for writing the *Battel* fully to support Temple, this argument strains credulity. Temple and Boyle embarrassed themselves in the debate regarding the *Letters of Phalaris*, and Temple's *Essay* generally reveals him to be both a dullard and one averse to satire, complaining that "ridiculing all that is serious and good ... 'tis the itch of our age and climate."[93] Swift is the very champion of such satire, and by Temple's definition would be the emblem of the *modern* age. As for the battle between the ancients and moderns, would a mind like Swift's seriously have rated Temple over Milton? When he names the Ancients, why does he not include the edgier ones such as Lucian, Aristophanes, and Lucretius, all of whom were found in his library at auction?[94] It would seem that he has set up a rather artificial battle between ancients and moderns – and in fact is just lampooning the pedantry and pettiness of a contemporary squabble. His unhappy first clerical appointment in Kilroot and his grudging dependence on a pompous Temple may have made of him a rather skeptical, reluctant member of both of these professional worlds (as cleric and secretary): the *Tale* and *Battel* written in this early period may reveal his disillusionment, even while they appear to support both Anglicanism and Temple.[95]

Swift possibly offers a hint about his literary identity at one point in a "Digression in the Modern Kind" in the *Tale*, where he labels himself the "freshest Modern," a post-Modern. And while he does this in the context of explaining why he will

---

[93] Temple, 1963, 70. For a fuller and somewhat more sympathetic view of Temple's contribution to literary theory, see Wellek, 1941, 32–33, 41–44.

[94] H. Williams, 1932, 43, 45–46.

[95] Ehrenpreis, 1962, 91–108, 169–82, depicts Swift's relationship with and regard for Temple in very positive terms. Damrosch, 2013, 44–50, however, agrees with others' view that Swift's service and dependence on the vain and pompous Temple at Moor Park was marked by considerable resentment. As for Swift's clerical career, Damrosch, 2013, 70–78, argues that this life-choice may have been more practical than spiritual – certainly, his first appointment in Kilroot drove him back to Moor Park in quick order.

210   *Doubting the Divine in Early Modern Europe*

upstage his fellow moderns by putting his digressions in the middle of his text rather than at the beginning, there could be another meaning, resonant of Garzoni's boast (via Momus) that his *Piazza* subsumes all disciplines: "But I here think fit to lay hold on that great and honorable Privilege of being the *Last Writer;* I claim an absolute Authority in Right, as the *freshest Modern*, which gives me a Despotick Power over all Authors before me."[96] Perhaps this is also the real Swift (and not just his Modern speaker) revealing his license as the ultimate modernist, a literary despot ridiculing *all* the combatants in the battle of the ancients and moderns and mocking *all* three of the Christian denominations. Furthermore, his experimentation with literary form in the *Tale* makes him a modernist in the true sense of that word. The chaos of multiple voices makes it difficult to determine when Swift is speaking or when a "Modern" is speaking.[97] The layers of satire create uncertainty in the reader as to when Swift subscribes to a view and when he is simply parodying it: the *Tale* is constructed as a set of nested boxes, an image he actually deploys in his "Digression in the Modern Kind."[98] As a cleric, his position on religion had to be the most occluded; the overt and covert presence of Lucretius is a telling example. Lines from the *De rerum natura* are cited six times in the *Tale*, and allusions to Lucretian materialism and even the *clinamen* (swerve) appear in his "Digression on Madness."[99] One could assume that these Lucretian elements are included only as a parody of dangerous materialist currents of the day,

[96] Swift, 1958, 130.

[97] Anselment, 1979, 129; Atkins, 1913, 49; on views of the *Tale*, see Quintano, 1965; on darker views of Swift's penchant for negation and even nihilism, see Leavis, 1952; Adams, 1958, 146–79, who also notes that the *Tale* "stands at the head of a file of volumes profoundly expressive of an even more troubled 'modern' spirit than that which the *Tale* seems to take as its most hated target" (167).

[98] He says that "I have known some Authors inclose Digressions in one another, like a Nest of Boxes" (Swift, 1958, 124); and later in the Tale he includes such a "Digression in Praise of Digressions" (143–49). I believe that the nesting occurs at the both the thematic as well as the structural level in his works.

[99] Swift, 1958, 166–67; and Lucretian materialism presumably also informs the *Discourse on the Mechanical Operation of the Spirit*.

though Swift's interest in Lucretius (whom he read three times in 1696–97) might suggest a too-fervid interest for a new clergyman.[100] Yet more revealing, however, is his *sub rosa* use of Lucretius. As an epigraph for the *Tale* Swift cites *De rerum natura* 4:3–5, an anodyne line in which Lucretius writes "I love to pluck fresh flowers, and to seek an illustrious chaplet for my head from the fields whence ere this the Muses have crowned brows of none."[101] Although this sounds like an innocent profession of originality in the project (of Lucretius and Swift), it is the following passage in Lucretius, not cited by Swift, that is telling: "first because my teaching is of high matters, and I proceed to free the mind from the close knots of religion."[102] At the end of section 6 of the *Tale*, Swift cites another line from Lucretius (1:934), which follows upon Lucretius' use of the exact same line of hoping to free minds from the bonds of religion.[103] Swift's use of lines twice that abut Lucretius' statement of anti-religious intent suggests the possibility that this could be his own hidden agenda as well.[104]

As for Momus's presence in both the *Tale* and the *Battel*, there are two possible interpretations. One, following the view that the works on religion and learning should be viewed as a piece, is that Momus's presence in the "Digression on Criticks" in the *Tale* may carry only implicit meaning in regard to religion: that is, Swift did not use him overtly as a vehicle for

---

[100] Swift, 1958, lvi–lvii; while it is possible that Swift's interest in Lucretius was inspired by Temple's interest in Epicurus, evinced in his *Upon the Gardens of Epicurus; or, Of Gardening, in the Year 1685*, in which he briefly defended Lucretius (Temple, 1963, 8–9; Damrosch, 2013, 40–41), it may also be true that Swift imbibed something more of Lucretius' suspicions of religion.

[101] Lucretius, 1937, 249.

[102] Lucretius, 1937, 248–49; with alteration of "*religionum*" from "superstition" to the literal "religion." Cf. note of Laude Rawson and Ian Higgins, at Swift, 2010, 127.

[103] Swift, 1958, 142.

[104] His interest in materialist and naturalist views at a later point in his life is also suggested by the presence in his library of a 1726 edition of the deist William Wollaston's *Religion of Nature Delineated* (p. 14 of the *Catalogue of Books* of Swift's library in H. Williams, 1932).

212 *Doubting the Divine in Early Modern Europe*

religious criticism (choosing instead the frame of the three brothers) but only located him there as a silent symbol of religious doubt. The more likely reading, following the view that the religious tale of the brothers and literary digressions were written at slightly different times and then interspliced, is that Swift's placing Momus in the "Digression on Cricticks" shows that he has moved Momus fully from his role as Agnostic to the role of Critic. Assigning him his chief role in the *Battel of the Books*, as patron god of the Moderns and acolyte to the goddess Criticism, Swift anoints Momus the god of modernism. Whether Swift is wholly despairing of these modernist currents or partly also promoting them, he uses Momus to announce – or vaunt – the birth of the forces of modernist disruption.

Swift leaves us no clues as to whether any of his early modern predecessors influenced his iteration of Momus. Based on the catalogue of his books, it appears doubtful that he had Italian, and there is no textual residue in the *Tale* or *Battel* of Alberti, Doni, Garzoni, or Bruno. In the last case, the *Spaccio della bestia trionfante*, which Bruno dedicated to Philip Sidney, would appear in English translation only in 1713 after the publication of the *Tale*.[105] Carew's treatment of Momus in his *Coelum Britannicum* is not in evidence. The most likely sources for a model of Momus for Swift would be Lucian, the brief treatment of him in Erasmus's *Praise of Folly*, and the depiction of Querela (Momus's Latin name) in one of Milton's *Prolusions* – all of which were in his library.[106] Given the fact that he bought a French translation of Lucian for Stella, Lucian might loom large as an influence, despite the fact that he was still reputed

[105] The 1745 *Catalogue of Books* does list four Italian manuscripts, but no printed books other than Florio's Italian–English lexicon; works by Tasso and Sarpi appear only in translation (*Catalogue of Books*; pp. 5, 6, 12, 14 in H. Williams, 1932).

[106] H. Williams, 1932, 1, 2, 8, 13. Another possible English source could be Thomas Lodge's *A Fig for Momus* (1595), in which Lodge flouts his disdain for any criticism Momus may have for his satires (A3r in the 1595 facs. repr. in Lodge, 1963:3), but I find no evidence of Lodge in Swift. On the influence of Lucian and Erasmus, see Damrosch, 2013, 134.

as an atheist in seventeenth-century England.[107] This reputation might explain why one finds no citation of Lucian in the *Tale* or *Battel* – doubly ironic, considering that D'Alembert and Henry Fielding would denote Lucian the Greek Swift.[108] If either Lucian or Erasmus was the chief model, Swift certainly enhanced the persona of Momus as a literary critic rather than Olympian scold. In doing so, he offered new mock-mythological details on him: that Momus united with Hubris to give birth to mortal critics from Zoilus to Wotton, that he was patron of the Moderns on earth, and that in the heavens he was the acolyte of the horrible goddess, Criticism. Clearly, the Momus trope inspired Swift to create this new goddess who enshrined criticism even more fully within an epic mythology with an even more demonic antihero.

Alexander Pope, Thomas Parnell, and *Momus Triumphans*: The Literary Critic as Antihero

Michael Gavin cites Philip Smallwood's perceptive statement that the "birth of criticism out of satire of itself is one of the founding paradoxes of its history."[109] Garzoni and Swift prove this to be true, as they both use satirical frames to criticize

---

[107] On the likely influence of Lucian's *True Story* on *Gulliver's Travels*, see Ewald, 1967, 137–38; H. Williams, 1932, 90. As for Lucian's questionable reputation, in his 1634 English translation of Lucian, Francis Hickes defended his project, but had to admit that Lucian "was a most impious blasphemer of our Saviour Christ, and of his sacred doctrine"(Hickes, 1663, B3r). This statement comes in his prefatory "Life of Lucian the Samosatenian. Wherein, He is in some sort Vindicated from certain gross Aspersions, heretofore cast upon him," in which he says that he "got the sirname of *Atheos*, or *Blasphemus*, and was commonly reputed a mocker and derider both of Gods and men" and denies that he was torn apart by dogs (B2v–B3r); Weinbrot, 2005, 65.

[108] Damrosch, 2013, 134, quotes Fielding as remarking "To translate Lucian well into English is to give us another Swift in our own language." In his English translation of Lucian, John Carr translates a comment from D'Alembert regarding "Lucian, who we may call the Grecian Swift, because, like him, he laughed at every thing, even at those things which did not deserve it" (Carr, 1798, 133); Weinbrot, 2005, 65.

[109] Smallwood, 2011, 2; Gavin, 2015, 1–2.

214   *Doubting the Divine in Early Modern Europe*

critics and thereby reify the craft of criticism. As god of criticism and mockery, Momus was the natural vehicle for this marriage. In his "Digression on Criticks" Swift surveys legitimate and illegitimate types of criticism. While he here mocks Modern Criticks for fighting over scraps like dogs at a banquet, some of his points might be intended in a more serious vein. For instance, he has his Modern speaker present a fantastical metaphorical reading of Pausanias to suggest that pruning the excess is as salutary for texts as for vines. He also has him cite Temple's foe Bentley to argue that Critics offer up a "mirror of learning" against which authors can hold up their work – a point meant to illustrate the hubristic belief of critics that this is only a modern development, but one that nonetheless airs the plausible contention that critics provide constructive standards.[110]

The mixing of the satirical and the serious in discussions of modern criticism would also be found in Swift's friend Alexander Pope. In 1711, the young Pope published his famous *Essay on Criticism*.[111] Here he presents his catechism for criticism – and "catechism" is the proper term, as Pope essentially offers rules for aesthetic worship. Cautioning against any attempt to parse the ineffable and beautiful, he damns the *science* of criticism as an affront to literary creation. At times the analogy is quite direct: "if faith itself has different dresses worn, / What wonder mode in wit should take their turn?"[112] He describes texts as ancient altars to which "the learned their incense bring" and which should be "above the reach of sacrilegious hands."[113] Perhaps not coincidentally for Pope as a Catholic, pride – greatest of the seven deadly sins – is one of the critic's greatest flaws: "Of all the causes which conspire to blind / Man's erring judgment, and misguide the mind / What the weak head with strongest bias rules, / Is *pride*, the never-ending

---

[110] Swift, 1958, 98, 102–3.
[111] On Pope's *Essay*, including its comic dimension, see Smallwood, 2011, 56–89.
[112] *Essay on Criticism*, lines 446–47 (Pope, 1993, 31).
[113] *Essay on Criticism*, lines 181–85 (Pope, 1993, 24).

God of Modern Criticks 215

vice of fools."[114] For his archetypal critic, Pope does not look to Momus but rather to his mortal counterpart Zoilus, but for whom (in lines excised between lines 123–24), "the sense of sound Antiquity had reigned, / And sacred Homer yet been unprophaned."[115] Here again, this sacred analogy between poet and god is affirmed.[116]

If it is unclear whether Swift's "Digression on Criticks" influenced the *Essay on Criticism* – written in 1709, prior to 1713 when Pope, Swift, and others founded the Scriblerus Club – Swift's impact on the *Dunciad* seems certain. Swift visited Pope at his villa at Twickenham in 1726, around the time he launched the *Dunciad*.[117] In fact, Swift stated that "he had reason to put Mr. Pope on writing the poem called the *Dunciad*," and Pope dedicated the work to him.[118] Pope fully re-figures the epic drama that Swift devised regarding Momus and the new goddess Criticism in the *Battel*: the *Dunciad* stars the goddess Dulness (one of Criticism's children in the *Battel*), whom he identifies as the daughter of Chaos and Night.[119] Whereas Momus and Criticism, as patrons of the Moderns, sought to defeat the Ancients, Dulness – the embodiment of bad talent and bad taste – wants to fully restore her empire of literary darkness against all the worthy forces of literature, learning, and piety. Pope claims his work forms a tetralogy with epics of Homer,

---

[114] *Essay on Criticism*, lines 201–4; and this attack on pride continues through line 214 (Pope, 1993, 24). Pope also alludes to envy at lines 30–31 and 466–68, one of Momus's flaws and together with pride one of Lucifer's two greatest sins.

[115] Pope,1993, 22; in the final version of the poem Zoilus appears instead at line 465.

[116] Pope also ties criticism to the conflicts in religion (such as Socinianism) and those who would challenge that "God himself should seem too absolute" and publish their blasphemies; he argues that critics should turn their ire on these apostates, not on authors (lines 544–59; Pope, 1993, 33–34).

[117] Damrosch, 2013, 381–89.

[118] This statement is cited in Pope, 1993, 692; whether or not this is actually the case, Pope wrote to Swift of his plans for the work in October 1725 (ibid.).

[119] See her invocation of and tribute to Swift at *Dunciad* 1:19–28 (Pope, 1993, 435).

216   *Doubting the Divine in Early Modern Europe*

Virgil, and Milton, his poem constituting the satyr play that customarily accompanied a trilogy.[120] The work is a mock epic, parodying the serious struggles depicted by his epic forebears. With its length and imagery, however, it certainly reveals how contemporary matters of literary taste have adapted the epic spectacle to the aesthetic realm.[121] In this work, the generally serious analogy between religion and literature in the *Essay on Criticism* is developed in full comic force.

In Book 1, Pope's key target, Colley Cibber, discouraged by his failure as a writer, creates an altar on which to burn his books and "thereon sacrifice all his unsuccessful writings," but Dulness douses the flames and "initiates him into her mysteries."[122] Whereas Swift structurally separated his religious story of the three brothers from his literary sections (in the "Digressions" and *Battel*), Pope fully unites the aesthetic and the religious. He is not only counteracting critics but also lamenting the triumph of secularism over belief in his contemporary world.[123] Natural explanations (i.e., Deism) have led to a loss of faith:

> All-seeing in thy mists, we want no guide,
> Mother of arrogance, and source of pride!
> We nobly take the high *priori* road,
> And reason downward, till we doubt of God:
> Make nature still encroach upon his plan:
> And shove him off as far as e'er we can.[124]

Dulness's empire is one of bad poets, freethinkers like John Toland, and critics whom she empowers "to cavil, censure, dictate, right or wrong, / Full and eternal privilege of tongue."[125] By

---

[120] Pope, 1993, 425.

[121] For a clear connection to Milton, even robbing Milton's phrase "darkness visible" (*Paradise Lost* 1:63), see the opening of 4:1–4 (Pope, 1993, 514 and 703, note for line 4:3). Aubrey Williams has shown how Pope fully adapts the epic struggle and imagery of *Paradise Lost* into the *Dunciad* (A. Williams, 1955, 131–58).

[122] Pope, 1993, 431; the original target was Lewis Theobald but changed to Cibber in the final version (691).

[123] As for contemporary critics, he cites Lewis Theobald at 1:133 (Pope, 1993, 445, 691–92).

[124] *Dunciad* 4:469–74 (Pope, 1993, 541–42).

[125] *Dunciad* 2:377–78 (Pope, 1993, 486).

God of Modern Criticks

217

the end, Pope presents a lament regarding the triumph of modernity over tradition, secularism over mystery:

> Philosophy, that leaned on heaven before,
> Shrinks to her second cause, and is no more.
> Physic of Metaphysic begs defence,
> And Metaphysic calls for aid on Sense!
> See Mystery to Mathematics fly!
> In vain! They gaze, turn giddy, rave, and die.
> Religion blushing veils her sacred fires,
> And unawares Morality expires.
> Nor *public* flame, nor *private*, dare to shine;
> Nor *human* spark is left, nor glimpse *divine*!
> Lo! Thy dread empire, CHAOS! Is restored;
> Light dies before thy uncreating word:
> Thy hand, great Anarch! lets the curtains fall;
> And universal darkness buries all.[126]

Whereas the Moderns were defeated in Swift's *Battel*, in the *Dunciad* they have won.[127] Part of Pope's pessimism about the modern world is a product of the popular press. In the *Dunciad* he laments that the rise of cheap paper, a too liberal freedom of the press, and publishers who will publish anything that will sell has meant "that a deluge of authors covered the land."[128] Conservative checks on ideas – such as the expense of and access to publishing, and censorship – are weakening, as is the authority of the current elite and ancient canon. These same forces explain Garzoni's deposing of authority in his *Piazza* and Swift's comments that the Ancients are being relentlessly attacked by the Grub Street Moderns.[129]

The triumph of the Modern Critic and Criticism provoked two opposing reactions. Jean Le Clerc, whose *Ars critica* of

---

[126] *Dunciad* 4:643–56 (Pope, 1993, 552–53).

[127] On Pope regarding this comparison, see Atkins, 1913, 9. As for Swift, Weinbrot, 2005, 188–92, argues that by the third part of Swift's trilogy, the *Discourse on the Mechanical Operation of the Mind*, he has also conceded the battle.

[128] Pope, 1993, 420.

[129] On Swift's comments on Grub Street in the "Introduction" to the *Tale*, see Swift, 1958, 63–72; Walsh, 2013, 107–8; "Introduction," in Bullard and McLaverty, 2013, 1–28; Weinbrot, 2005, 129–32.

1697 provided a definition of criticism as an expansive discipline, also promoted the revival of *parrhesia*.[130] His *Parrhasiana; ou Pensées diverses sur des matiéres de la Critique, d'Histoire, de morale et de politique* of 1699 defends "freedom in my thoughts and expressions" and urges that "men carry liberty as high as they please."[131] In regard to literary criticism, he defends Momus's counterpart Zoilus from his detractors. Zoilus's critique of Homer, he argues, illustrates people's intolerance for anyone finding fault with a beloved poet: "this is the reason Zoilus, surnamed the scourge of Homer, made himself a thousand times more detested for having had the presumption to censure his faults, than if he had blasphemed all the Gods."[132] And while Le Clerc mocked any equation of literary apostasy with religious blasphemy, others did indeed view Zoilus in somewhat diabolical terms. As seen above, in his genealogy of the "heroic" critic in the "Digression on Criticks," Swift identified Zoilus as the first mortal generation, bred of the celestial union of Momus and Hybris.[133] It is probably not a coincidence that the first and only substantive biography of Zoilus appeared in this period from Thomas Parnell (1679–1718), a fellow member of Pope's and Swift's Scriblerus Club.[134]

Constructed from brief sketches of Zoilus's life from ancient and medieval sources, Parnell's biography adds colorful, satirical embellishments that make his work the third leg of the stool along with Swift's *Battel* and Pope's *Dunciad*.[135] Parnell appended his *Life of Zoilus* to his translation of the Ps.-Homeric *Battle of the Frogs and Mice* of 1717, which, in turn, Parnell undertook to complement Pope's translation of the *Iliad*.[136] Both translators are obviously proponents of the Ancients in the

---

[130] On the expansion and editions of the *Ars critica* in, e.g., 1697,1698, 1700, and 1712, see Patey, 2005, 3n2.

[131] Le Clerc, 1700, A3r; with alterations in orthography.

[132] Le Clerc, 1700, 13; with alterations in orthography.

[133] Swift, 1958, 94.

[134] Woodman, 1985, 6.

[135] Parnell draws on Vitruvius' *On Architecture* 7:8–9, Aelian's *Historical Miscellany* 11:10 (Aelian, 1997, 338–39), and the Byzantine *Suda* Z 130.

[136] Parnell, 1989, 65.

current debate and view Homer as unassailable. Parnell opens his work by recognizing legitimate critics in Antiquity (such as Aristotle, Cicero, and Longinus) before presenting Zoilus as the anti-model. Zoilus of Amphipolis (fourth century BCE) was a rhetorician associated with the Cynic school – and this is probably why Parnell (via Aelian) refers to him as "The Rhetorical Dog."[137] He charts Zoilus's career as a critic of such figures as Zenophon, Plato, Demosthenes, Aristotle, and Aristophanes – and especially Homer. The latter, his chief target, he critiqued in a work he entitled *Zoilus, Scourge of Homer, Writ this Against That Lover of Fables*.[138] After leaving Thrace, Zoilus went to Greece, where he dared to read his scathing critique of Homer's depiction of Patroclus' funeral games (*Iliad* 23) at the Olympics. His listeners whipped him and, some have thought, he was thrown to his death on the Scyronian Rocks, a fate recalling Aesop's punishment for insulting the stature of Apollo's oracle and the Delphians.[139] Parnell, however, pursues other theories and adds satirical detail that link Zoilus the Critic with Zoilus the Heretic.[140] Making his way to the Alexandria of Ptolemy Philadelphus, he went to the temple of Isis, made a sacrifice and received visions of a horrible monster (akin to Swift's demon goddess Criticism) who was surrounded by snakes and who charged him with his vocation to go forth in the world and criticize all authors. This monster conjures a procession of shades of prose-writers, poets, and sophists whom she invokes in terms recalling the scene in *Paradise Lost* 10:504–9, in which Satan's rebel angels turned into hissing snakes: "Come, my Serpents, applaud him with your Hisses, that is all which can now be done; in modern Times my Sons shall invent louder Instruments."[141]

---

[137] Parnell, 1989, 73; Branham, 1996, 84–85.

[138] Parnell, 1989, 73; for some of Zoilus's criticisms of the *Iliad*, the *Odyssey*, and the spurious *Battle of Frogs and Mice*, and Parnell's rebuttals of the last, see Parnell, 1989, 73–74, 97–108.

[139] Cf. *Suda* Z 130.

[140] In the Preface to Book 7:8–9 of his *On Architecture*, Vitruvius presents theories that Zoilus was killed by Ptolemy Philadelphus in Egypt, that he was stoned at Chios, and that he was burned at Smyrna; Vitruvius, 1934, 69.

[141] Parnell, 1989, 77.

220   *Doubting the Divine in Early Modern Europe*

When Zoilus declaimed on Homer's faults before Ptolemy, he failed to win a pension from him, was ridiculed by others at court, and was burned in effigy as "Zoilus the Homero-Mastix" in the temple devoted to Homer. He then fled to Smyrna, a city laying claim to be Homer's birthplace, where he went into a rage in the Homereum, a "Library, Porch, and Temple erected to Homer," vandalizing Homer's writings and medals and "beat[ing] the aged Priests, and br[eaking] down the altar."[142] Parnell chooses this theological incident of desecration as the cause of the burning of Zoilus's books and Zoilus himself: an end surely meant to emulate the execution of heretics for blasphemy. Parnell's fanciful *Life of Zoilus* thus completes the transference of religious apostasy to literary apostasy, a theme explicitly sounded in Pope's *Dunciad* and, possibly, implicitly recalled in Swift's *Battel* where he depicts the goddess Criticism in terms similar to Milton's Sin. He also completes the identification of Zoilus with his divine counterpart Momus as the personification of Envy, closing his biography with the statement, "ZOILUS is the proper name of *Envy*."[143] This statement recalls the tag line regarding Envy added to Aesop's fable Babrius 59 on Momus's criticisms of the three gods' creations. Zoilus the Ur-critic of Homer is the mortal counterpart of Momus the Ur-critic of the gods. Envy resents and fear the creative power at both the divine and human level. With Parnell's biography, even with its satirical tone, sacrilegious *parrhesia* has been shifted from gods to texts.

To be fair, however, to accuse Momus, Zoilus, and their namesakes merely of envy deprives them of their function as challengers of falsehood, a role that Momus exercised at both the divine and human level in his various incarnations. In the *Battel of the Books*, the issue of exposing forgery was a key factor in the case of the *Letters of Phalaris*. As Kevin Pask has shown in a remarkable article, originality was also an emerging criterion of authenticity in this period that pitted Ancient authority against Modern Critics.[144] Here too Momus had

---

[142] Parnell, 1989, 82.
[143] Parnell, 1989, 83.
[144] I am indebted to Pask's discussion of authentication in regard to both forgery and originality in this period (Pask, 2002, esp. 736–37).

Momus Triumphans:

OR, THE

PLAGIARIES

OF THE

Englifh Stage;

Expos'd in a

CATALOGUE

OF ALL THE

Comedies,	Opera's,
Tragi-Comedies,	Paftorals,
Mafques,	
Tragedies,	Interludes, &c.

Both Ancient and Modern, that were ever yet Printed in Englifh. The Names of their Known and Suppofed Authors.
Their feveral Volumes and Editions: With an Account of
the various Originals, as well Englifh, French, and Italian, as
Greek and Latine; from whence moft of them have Stole
their Plots.

By GERARD LANGBAINE Efq;

Indice non opus eft noftris, nec vindice Libris:
Stat contra dicitq; tibi tua Pagina, Fures Mart.

LONDON: Printed for Nicholas Cox, and are to be Sold by him in
Oxford. M DC LXXXVIII.

FIGURE 3 Title-Page of Gerard Langbaine's *Momus triumphans*, London, 1688. Courtesy of the William Andrews Clark Memorial Library, University of California, Los Angeles.

a bit part. In 1687 Gerard Langbaine published his *Momus Triumphans: Or, The Plagiaries of the English Stage; Expos'd in a Catalogue.* In this first-ever catalogue on plagiarism he charts the borrowings of English authors from Greek, Latin, Italian, French, and other English authors. Exposing John Dryden's transgressions in this regard likely won Langbaine his enmity, such that Langbaine suspected that it was Dryden, who, on the sly, convinced the publisher of the *Plagiaries* to issue the book with the added title of *Momus triumphans* (Fig. 3).[145] Momus here is thus invoked as the malevolent critic exposing fraud. Langbaine held quite a different view of the critic, assigning Aristotle the role of the "Father of Criticism."[146] He is careful

[145] Pask, 2002, 728–29, 737–38.
[146] Langbaine, 1688, A2r and a3v.

222   *Doubting the Divine in Early Modern Europe*

to explain the difference between legitimate borrowings – by ancients such as Virgil or, among the moderns, by Shakespeare and Johnson – from the surreptitious ones to whom he assigns the "Cunning of a Jugler."[147] Though scholars have variously attributed the new concern with originality to the advent of the Copyright Statute of 1710, Pask sees this development as arising earlier and as reflecting a growing interest in property rights as reflected in Locke's *Second Treatise on Government* and a heightened respect for originality.[148] He portrays an emerging binary between the sacred "authority of origins" (in the Ancients and Scripture) and the secular "authority of originality" (the "true authors" to whom Langbaine hopes to restore their due ownership).[149]

Momus's role of exposing plagiarism was dramatized by Garzoni in the "Novel Prologue" of the *Piazza universale*. In his (weak) defense he has Minerva say that everyone (ancient and modern) does it, and in his chapter on "Writers of Books," not only does he not include it as a vice but he even praises it as a shortcut to fame – though his adding Annotations (or footnotes) in his 1587 second edition may have resulted from charges of plagiarism.[150] By the time of Langbaine, some writers, like Dryden, were still defending borrowing as part of the literary tradition, and thus Dryden – or a like-minded soul – apparently wanted to brand Langbaine with the epithet of Momus.[151] This charge reflects the sea change in Momus's persona from the time of Luther's accusation of Erasmus as an unbelieving, antireligious Momus.[152] Now Momus is a symbol of unbelievers

[147] Langbaine, 1688, a2v.
[148] Pask, 2002, 728–29; Wellek, 1941, 21, 25–26.
[149] Pask, 2002, 729; Langbaine, 1688, a2v.
[150] Garzoni, 1996, 489; McClure, 2004, 103.
[151] On Dryden's defense of Johnson's borrowings in his 1688 *Essay of Dramatick Poesy*, Dryden, 1956–2000, 17:57; Pask, 2002, 731–32.
[152] Interestingly, the suspicions regarding plagiarism even surface in Parnell's *Life of Zoilus*, where he depicts an incident of a poetic contest in Alexandria also described in Vitruvius (Vitruvius, 1934, 64–67). When Aristophanes (of Byzantium) exposed all but one of the entrants as plagiarists, he was rewarded by being named head of the famous library. Parnell embellished on Vitruvius to say that this exposing of plagiarism pleased Zoilus: "This

God of Modern Criticks

in authors and texts. And although Langbaine may have resented the publisher's taking this liberty with his title, *Momus triumphans*, it does reflect the culmination of Momus's role as Modern Critick challenging the originality of authors and battling traditional literary practice.

As Garzoni and Swift show, Momus became a useful trope in the emergence of a self-conscious art of literary criticism in the early modern period. Relative to Momus's role in Alberti's novel, in the satires of Franco and Doni, or in the religious tensions between Erasmus and Luther, his role generally shifts to the purely literary realm – and does so, coincidentally, alongside the literary professionalization accompanying the popular press. Momus also is variously useful as a vehicle for a type of "modernism." In Garzoni, this goal is accomplished by inversion: that is, Momus is depicted as a conservative critic of Garzoni's non-hierarchical, unorthodox *Piazza* – only to advertise these modern features of the work and to be rebutted by Minerva and Garzoni himself. The very self-conscious "modern" literary tactics Swift complains about and exemplifies in his *Tale* are already at play in Garzoni. Swift explicitly deputes Momus as the patron god of Modern Criticks, enlisting him as one who challenges the authority of the Ancients and reflects the hubris of the "new." Constantly submerging himself in the "nested boxes" of satire, Swift disguises his own voice – or rather is able to simultaneously mock the "Moderns," while himself acting the role of the freshest, newest Modern lampooning religious and literary controversies. Whether he truly deplores the Moderns or secretly relishes being one of them, his new mythology of Momus, spouse of Hybris and acolyte of uber-goddess Criticism, reflects the age's anxiety regarding cultural authority.

passage [from Vitruvius] ZOILUS often afterwards repeated with pleasure, for the Number of Disgraces which happen'd in it to the Pretenders in Poetry; tho' his Envy made him still careful not to name Aristophanes, but a judge in general" (Parnell, 1989, 78). For Momus's exposing plagiarism in later English works, see the anonymous 1775 *Sentence of Momus on the Poetical Amusements at a Villa Near Bath* (*Sentence of Momus* 10, 15).

224 *Doubting the Divine in Early Modern Europe*

In marking an increasing shift to challenging the authority of authors vs. the authority of gods, Momus's incarnations reflect larger currents in secularization. On the most literal level, this process is evident in the rehabilitation of Momus's human counterpart Zoilus, who now gains new dramatic, even demonic, stature. Even in that process, however, the residue of the sacred and sacrilegious subsists. Shared imagery suggests an occasional transference of authority from the divine to the worldly realm. When Garzoni depicts the trial of his book before the council of gods, his self-styled sacrilege is that, with all of his many criticisms of professions, he is indirectly insulting the gods who are patron deities of those professions. What Garzoni is actually doing, of course, is transferring the argument of apostasy against gods, which Minerva accuses him of, to the cultural and social world of learning and professions. The overlapping of imagery also assures that the sacral respect due the gods is being transferred to authors and texts, a process that, even when satirical, still elevates the cultural visibility, goals, and transgressions of critics. Thus, Pope in his *Essay on Criticism* depicts texts as "ancient altars" that should be immune to "reach of sacrilegious hands." Thus, Parnell's *Life of Zoilus* has Zoilus desecrating the temple of Homer and being burned as a heretic. And thus Swift – whether wittingly or unwittingly – depicts the goddess Criticism in terms recalling Milton's depiction of Sin in *Paradise Lost*. Pope completes this parody of Milton in the *Dunciad*, where Colley Cibber is deputed as "the Antichrist of wit" (2:1–16) and Dulness's (Satan's) realm of Chaos triumphs.[153] An overlapping set of binaries penetrate the porous boundaries of religion and literature. True and false gods, a particular concern of Lucian's Momus, have as an analogue true and false texts, a particular concern of the Modern Criticks. New and old gods are matched by the Ancient and Modern authors. "Momus triumphans" exposes plagiarists and pretenders, just as Lucian's Momus exposed the demigods as pretenders in the ancient pantheon. The insolent *parrhesia* Zeus endured from Momus now

---

[153] Pope, 1993, 459–60; A. Williams, 1955, 131–32, 155.

God of Modern Criticks

is enshrined in the title of Le Clerc's *Parrhasiana* on literary and scholarly critics.

If in fact it was Dryden who suggested the title *Momus triumphans* for Langbaine's work, Kevin Pask is astute in suggesting that it makes all the more meaningful Dryden's *Secular Masque* of 1700, in which Momus challenges the vocations of the more established gods: Chronos carrying the globe on his back, Diana sponsoring the hunt, Mars promoting "arms and honor," and Venus inspiring love.[154] Momus, who "enters laughing," disparages the worth of these traditions. His dark cynicism triumphs as all the gods, including Janus, who admits that a new age has arrived, sing:

> All, all, of a piece throughout:
> Thy Chase [Diana] had a Beast in View;
> Thy Wars [Mars] brought nothing about;
> Thy Lovers [Venus] were all untrue.
> 'Tis well an Old Age is out,
> And time to begin a New.[155]

"Momus triumphans" works his dark power here, as in Langbaine's catalogue of plagiarized texts, to announce the advent of change, the new, the modern.

[154] Pask, 2002, 738.
[155] Dryden, 1956–2000, 16:273.

7

Conclusion: Momus and Modernism

Momus passed a few centuries in Greece, where he specially dispensed his favours to the lively sons of Attica. He then crossed into Italy, where the monks' cowl so disgusted him that he quitted that country for France, and dwelt there till the return of the Bourbons, when to escape the thralldom of dullness, he took passage in a steam-boat for England. During the last seven years he has been frisking it between Bath, Cheltenham, Leamington, Brighton, Hastings … In these jaunts, however, he passed through London, Bristol, Liverpool … and other dens of care, and taking pity on the wretched inhabitants, his godship inspired two editors of the genius race of the Bulls to construct this work, to cheer and enliven the present gloomy existence of so many members of their family.[1]

Thus appeared a biography of Momus in an 1825 humor collection entitled *The Laughing Philosopher: Being the Entire Works of Momus, Jester of Olympus; Democritus, the Merry Philosopher of Greece, and Their Illustrious Disciples, Ben Jonson, Butler, Swift, Gay, Joseph Miller, Esq. Churchill, Voltaire, Foote, Steevens, Wolcot, Sheridan, Curran, Colman, and Others.* The work, appearing under the pseudonym John Bull (English Everyman), signals what largely became of Momus by the nineteenth century. Now, he is the "laughing philosopher," a symbol of wit and satire who was more court jester than heretic or critic.[2]

---

[1] *The Laughing Philosopher*, 1825, iv.

[2] An adumbration of this treatise appeared in the 1777 *Laughing Philosopher*, which at the start of its chapters is entitled *Momus: or, the Laughing Philosopher*, a droll survey of English society and manners (fashion, marriage, the military, court, theater, etc.). In the amiable tone of Erasmus's

Conclusion: Momus and Modernism   227

To be sure, the brief account of Momus's peregrinations reveals that his journeys were sometimes prompted by a saucy attitude – against the clergy in Italy, or the monarchy in France – but his playful persona is what dominates. The prologue explains how the two editors of the Bull family (in reality Charles Lamb and Thomas Hood), lacking a ready mortal satirist to help them, turn to Momus to "evoke a council of his deceased favourites from the shades," who were summoned forth to give the editors advice on the nature of humor. This parade of wits – including Cervantes, Swift, Voltaire and many others – offers a telling contrast to that parade of nefarious critics invoked by the monster in Isis' temple in Parnell's *Life of Zoilus*. This treatise is but one example of how the modern Momus becomes more the witty bon vivant and festive reveler than the forbidding scourge of gods and texts.[3] How did this transformation come about and how did this more fun-loving figure compare to the caustic one of Lucian, Alberti, Doni, Bruno, others? More broadly, what was the over-arching function of the Momus trope in Western culture and why was his reception in the early modern era so highly charged and controversial?

Momus's role as literary critic did not end with the generation of Swift. In fact, later in the eighteenth century in England he appears in the titles of works on literary and theatrical criticism. In 1767, the English actor George Saville Carey published *Momus, a Poem; or A Critical Examination Into the Merits of the Performers, and Comic Pieces, at the Theatre Royal in the Hay-Market*. This theater review appraises the likes of Carey's famous colleague David Garrick and admits that in some roles (Othello) even an Irish actor (Spranger Barry) is better.[4] A few years later

---

Praise of Folly, Momus associates himself with the actor/writer Samuel Foote (1720–77) (see, e.g., *Laughing Philosopher* [1777] 13). Even Momus's introduction of himself turns Hesiod's account in the *Theogony* to humorous ends: "I *Momus* am the laughing, merry, dissipated son of Madam *Nox* and Sam *Somnus* ... or, to be more plain, begot on Mrs. *Night* by Mr. *Sleep*; two heavy, dull, parental personages to give life to me, the Jester, the Caviller, the Wit, and the Satirist of the skies, and the earth" (1).

[3] Cast, 1974, 27.

[4] "In *Othello* must each actor yield, / There even *Garrick* must give up the field, / And own thee for the part, by nature fram'd, / We think of *Barry* when *Othello*'s nam'd" ([G. Carey], [1767], 13).

228 *Doubting the Divine in Early Modern Europe*

Momus starred in a critical exchange on a collection of some polite poetry composed at Bath. These literary pieces, including a few from Garrick, composed at the estate of Lady Anna Miller, were published in 1775 with the proceeds donated to the local Pauper-Scheme.[5] This benevolence did not deter critic(s) from immediately producing an anonymous *The Sentence of Momus on the Poetical Amusements at a Villa Near Bath*. When Venus is invoked to judge the offerings – bout-rimés on love, beauty, the death of Handel – she calls upon Momus, who appraises the pieces, more than once archly exposing plagiarism: "Ah Monsieur de Tems! I presume spick and span – / This sonnet is form'd on an elegant plan; / But my judgeship you must not expect to cajole – / Restore it to Lilly, from whom it was stole."[6] Momus's critiques provoked a satirical response in *Charity; or, Momus's Reward*, in which Charity complains of the forces of Vice, whose monstrous persona – resembling that of Criticism in Swift's *Battel of the Books* – stages his own literary contest in which Momus rehearses his attack on the Bath poets.[7] The harlot Contempt, Vice's reward for the best poet, is given to Momus. A chorus of 10,000 fiends sings an oration in Hell – reminiscent of Lucifer's followers in Milton's Hell – and Momus and Contempt repair to the couch of Oblivion. This exchange, along with Carey's Momus, illustrates that the Swiftian, demonic face of Momus the Critic commanded eponymous status in literary pieces in late eighteenth-century England.

In eighteenth-century France, as Dominique Quéro has shown, Momus achieved prominence as a buffoon figure in comedy, who

---

[5] [Miller], 1776, vi; Barbeau, 1904, 224–30.

[6] *Sentence of Momus* 10; also, cf. 15.

[7] Vice's attendants include Folly, Ignorance, Vengeance, Hatred, Avarice, Despair, Ambition, and Impiety (*Charity* 6–7). In introducing Momus, the poet says that it was "not that free-hearted, honest, jovial blade, / Whose harmless mirth, and humour, were his trade" (21), but rather the menacing Momus with the "defamatory libels" and "cruel and calumnious songs" (22–23). The poet thus clearly identified two personas of Momus: one light, one dark. As for Charity, presumably this figure is personified in part because the proceeds from the publication of the Poetical Amusements of Bath were to go to local poor relief.

Conclusion: Momus and Modernism 229

was the champion of laughter and happiness. In her exhaustive study of French theater and literature – from street fairs and satirical poetry to opera, ballet, *comédie française* and *comédie italienne* – she shows that Momus was often depicted in the guise of the court jester, complete with the marotte (the fool's scepter or baton).[8] Identified for the first time in an early nineteenth-century history of mythology as the "bouffon des Dieux," he became a figure closer to Erasmus's Folly than Alberti's Momus.[9] The buffoon of the gods even attached to the figure of the buffoon at court, as exemplified by the collection of humorous (but fictional) anecdotes associated with one of Louis XIV's courtiers, Gaston-Jean-Baptiste de Roquelaure, which appeared under the title of *Le Momus Français, ou les Aventures divertissantes du Duc de Roquelaure* in 1718.[10] As Quéro observes, Momus even acquired a "moral philosophy" as articulated in the 1750 *Momus philosophe, comédie in un acte et en vers*, which appeared from Claude-François-Félix Boulenger de Rivery.[11] This comedy purports to package Lucian's dialogues in a theatrical setting. In the foreword the author suggests that Lucian was the mocker of "pompeuses bagatelles" and created a "sistême di Philosophie morale" along that line.[12] At the play's opening, Mercury reports that Jupiter is weary of Momus's "profound malice" in banishing reason from the French stage. When Momus defends his goal of

[8] Quéro, 1995, esp. at 10.
[9] For instance, in the 1750 *Temple of Momus*, he is summoned as the "Aimable Dieu de la Satire" (in Quéro, 1995, 42–43) and is also the patron god of the "brevets de la Calotte," the satirical poetry emanating from military youth (12, 173–87). He could also, as in England, assume the role of theater critic (196–97).
[10] He is described as having a "Wit, satirical, merry and pleasant; his Conversation, civil, insinuating, free and noble, his Behaviour, or Deportment, lively and full of Fire; he had a fine piquant way of Raillery, a ready Wit, and a Tongue well hung; he was of a very amorous Disposition, and lov'd Pleasure to that degree, that sometimes he would Debauch himself ... his most prominent Vice was Satyr, which he would push so far sometimes, as to degenerate into Scandal" (Le Roy, 1718, vii–viii; Quéro, 1995, 25–26; Doran, 1858, 295).
[11] Quéro, 1995, 394–402, who entitles her own study *Momus philosophe* and describes another work with this title by Jacques Mague de Saint-Aubin (331–37, 497).
[12] Boulenger de Rivery, 1750, A3r.

230   *Doubting the Divine in Early Modern Europe*

tempering austerity and the "sovereign fire" of reason with a "light shade," Mercury accuses him of "bizarre novelty" and of always favoring satire. Momus embraces the charge of "*nouveauté*" – in effect, modernism – and claims that he shares (with love) "the empire of laughter and play."[13] When various archetypes then chastise Momus for his frivolous worldview, he responds by mocking a Philosopher, a Physician, and a Poet for their hubris and pomposity.[14] The lengthiest encounter is with the Poet, who enthuses about his divine inspiration and chides Momus for producing popular, low-brow culture that requires neither talent nor learning, so that "one has never seen so much frivolity, / So many Rhymers, so few Poets."[15] At the end, when the Poet again blames Momus for the rise of "shameful amusements," Momus proudly wears the badge and proclaims his credo: "The art that pleases is not sterile, / To amuse is to be useful, / It serves the happiness of society. / Mortals, who yearn after the supreme good, / You search in vain in pompous things. / If it is possible to find it, it is in the milieux of play (*jeux*), / Flee austerity, that extreme folly, / Wisdom is the art of being happy."[16] Boulenger de Rivery's Momus is thus not only a playful bon vivant, but also a cultural critic dethroning self-important professions and promoting an aesthetic revolution: namely, a *nouveauté* in which comedy unseats high art.

Quéro suggests that this comic and rather Epicurean persona of Momus in the eighteenth century coalesces to such a degree that by the early nineteenth century the term "Momusien" is a synonym for "Epicurean."[17] She also ties this face of Momus to

---

[13] Boulenger de Rivery, 1750, 18–20.

[14] Momus's cynicism, like that of Lucian toward his Cynics, even disabuses a like-minded Epicurean character Crispin of his carefree lifestyle, saying that "all pleasures pass like the wind" (Boulenger de Rivery, 1750, 35).

[15] Boulenger de Rivery, 1750, 40.

[16] Boulenger de Rivery, 1750, 51–52, my trans. Also, in a brief statement in the closing scene Momus condemns the arrogant poet who thinks his "art a mystery / that one ought never divulge to the masses" and "a Philosopher, [and] a Physician / [who] discuss their frivolous system" (52).

[17] She cites as an example a collection of poetry published in 1828 entitled *Les Momusiennes* (Quéro, 1995, 102–3) and includes in her bibliography another

Conclusion: Momus and Modernism

the emergence of the famous Café Momus, the gathering place of Henri Murger and his Bohemian friends whom Puccini portrays in *La Bohème* (Act 2 of which is set at the Café Momus).[18] In his *Scènes de la vie de bohème*, Murger recounts a gathering of the group at this café, identifying its patron god in terms virtually identical to those found in Boulenger de Rivery's *Momus philosophe*, where Momus proclaims his domain to be "l'empire des ris & des jeux": "Ils montèrent dans un café situé rue Saint-Germain-l'Auxerrois, et portant l'enseigne de *Momus*, dieux des Jeux et des Ris."[19] The collection of poor writers, artists, and musicians – so poor, they were "water-drinkers" – defined themselves in anti-establishment terms and thus Momus indirectly became the patron god of a counter-culture rebelling against bourgeois society.[20] This Epicurean and "café" Momus signals a notable departure from Lucian's scold of the pantheon, Alberti's purveyor of atheism, Garzoni's critic of texts, or Bruno's blasphemer of Christ. This general "lightening" of Momus to a more jocular character can be seen by comparing his grim depiction by Vincenzo Cartari in his 1556 *Imagini de i Dei* to Gabriel Jacques de Saint-Aubin's image of 1752 (Figs. 4 and 5).

Momus's modern festive role culminated when he migrated to America. In 1871 and 1872 parade groups called the Knights of Momus – a mash-up of popular classicism and the medievalism of Walter Scott – were formed in Galveston and New Orleans. In New Orleans the parade moved from New Year's Eve to the

> anthology from 1837 with a telling subtitle: *La Momusienne: chansonnier érotique, comique, bachique, joyeux, facétieux et grivois* (512).
>
> [18] For other accounts of the Café Momus, see the chapter "Le Café Momus" in Alexandre Schanne's *Souvenirs de Schaunard*, where he discusses the café "où en effet, de 1843 à 1848, se sont attablés quantité d'hommes de lettres devenus célèbres depuis" (Schanne, 1887, 200), a group that included "l'étrange, mais captivant Baudelaire" (202). Also, for an amusing story of how Champfleury caused the owner to sell the café, see *London Society*, 1867, at 183–84.
>
> [19] Murger, 1929, 19; Quéro, 1995, 103. The festive perception of Momus is also suggested toward the end of the *Scènes*, when two of the Bohemians encounters "joyeuses processions qui rentraient pour fêter Momus, Bacchus, Comus et toutes les gourmandes divinités en us" (Murger, 1929, 273).
>
> [20] On Murger's group, see Seigel, 1986, 31–58.

FIGURE 4 "Momus," from Vincenzo Cartari's *Le imagini de gli Dei de gli antichi*, Padua, 1608. Courtesy of the David M. Rubenstein Rare Book and Manuscript Library, Duke University.

Thursday before Mardi Gras in 1873. Four years later, when the celebration staged a parade entitled "Hades: A Dream of Momus" that satirized political figures, the authorities tried but failed to punish the revelers, whose names were kept secret. The political themes then disappeared, to re-appear only a century later in 1977, when the Momus Krewe targeted Governor Edwin Edward and Saddam Hussein; years later, another Krewe (Chaos) used the "Hades: Dream of Momus" motif to satirize the city's response to Katrina.[21] Although retaining this bit of

---

[21] Laborde, 2007a; Laborde, 2007b, 36–37, 75–77. The account of the 1872 revival of Momus cited Walter Scott as an inspiration for pageant themes. The identification of Momus depicts him as a now "kindlier" god than in his earlier days, but does so partly with the aid of garbled Latin (probably lifted from the Galveston group), which they do not seem to realize does

Conclusion: Momus and Modernism 233

FIGURE 5 "Momus," Gabriel Jacques de Saint-Aubin, 1752. Courtesy of the Pierpont Morgan Library, New York.

Momus's subversive nature, the Knights largely celebrated the fun-loving god, as can be seen in a float from the 1909 New Orleans parade.[22] The group's motto was "*Dum vivimus vivamus*" (while we live, let us live), a sentiment reflected in a

not have a "grim" message but rather one of *carpe diem*: "The sireless deity of raillery, who, in the old days of mith (sic), made gods the victims of his ridicule, and but hardly spared the matchless Aphrodite, daughter of the Foam, descends through the generous shadows of the centuries with a kindlier spirit, with a touch whose magic only beautifies, and the grim old motto 'dum vivitmis vivamus' (*read* dum vivimus vivamus) takes a better significance through the interpretation which his latter-day votaries have given it and gives us the right to welcome his advent with every sincerity and pleasure" (www.storyvilledistrictnola.com/mardigras_knights_momus.html; on the Galveston Knights, see www.knightsofmomus.com/history-html).

[22] See www.cointradingpost.com/Mardigras/M/Momus/1909/Momus1909Flt1.jpg.

234   *Doubting the Divine in Early Modern Europe*

poem by Ella Wheeler Wilcox (1850–1915) entitled "Momus, God of Laughter," which celebrates the gifts of Momus over those of all the other gods:

> Wisdom wearies, Love has wings –
> Wealth makes burdens, Pleasure stings.
> Glory proves a thorny crown –
> So all gifts the gods throw down
> Bring their pains and troubles after;
> All save Momus, god of laughter.
> He alone gives constant joy.
> Hail to Momus, happy boy.[23]

The literary and festive triumph of the libertine face of Momus in nineteenth- and twentieth-century Europe and America reveals a telling shift in Momus's ties to Epicureanism between the early modern and modern eras. In Alberti, Momus reflects the materialist, Lucretian dimension; in Boulenger de Rivery and the Knights of Momus, he embodies the (popular) libertine image. Among some other twentieth-century literary figures, however, Momus still commanded some higher mystery and meaning. In his 1914 poem "Momus," Sandburg depicts Momus as a cryptic, majestic, timeless figure aloof from the tragic follies of mankind.[24] Kafka inducts Momus into modern currents of Absurdism and existentialism. In *The Castle* (1926), Kafka depicts his main character as being completely at the mercy of a mysterious governor, whose secretary is Momus.[25]

---

[23] Laborde, 2007b, 82.

[24] Published in March, 1914, Sandburg's poem appeared just a month before the assassination of the Archduke Franz Ferdinand, making all the more relevant and prescient the last stanza of "Momus," where, addressing a majestic, bronze Momus, the poet says: "I wonder, Momus, / Whether the shadows of the dead sit somewhere and look with deep laughter / On men who play in terrible earnest the old, known, solemn repetitions of history. / A droning monotone soft as sea laughter hovers from your kindliness of bronze, / You give me the human ease of a mountain peak, purple, silent; / Granite shoulders heaving above the earth curves, / Careless eye-witness of the spawning tides of men and women / Swarming always in a drift of millions to the dust of toil, the salt of tears, / And blood drops of undiminishing war" (Sandburg, 1914).

[25] Kafka's use of Momus in *The Castle* inspired an avant-garde Scottish alt-rock artist/author, Nick Currie, to adopt this name as performer and writer.

Conclusion: Momus and Modernism 235

Momus here might be used to address the inexplicable higher powers that torment and befuddle mankind. In this role as assistant – and sole conduit – to the ultimate higher power, Momus approximates a perverse version of a mediator (priest or Christ figure) between humans and a distant God.[26]

Kafka's *The Trial* had spawned the title for the rock group "Joseph K," and Currie spun off from that group as "Momus." Once identifying himself as a "straight queen," he embodies a transgressive social ethos in the spirit of Murger's Bohemians. As for his role as political critic, his latest musical effort reacts to Britain's recent vote to exit the European Union: "*Scobberlotches* is Momus's post-Brexit record, recorded in the summer of 2016 against a backdrop of resurgent and often racist populism. Just as in the genre of the post-breakup album, there is a sense of anxiety, betrayal, and the *apportioning of blame running through the record*" (www.imomus.com, emphasis added). A 2014 satirical novel, *UnAmerica*, asserts that "America has forfeited God's love by becoming 'a machine for creating unpleasant people'" (ibid.).

[26] "K"'s encounter with Momus comes in ch. 9 (Kafka, 1969, 143–52), but is greatly extended in a fragment excised from the text (443–57). Max Brod, Kafka's associate and literary executor, and Edwin Muir, one of his translators, view the work in theological terms, Muir asserting that "the theme of the novel is salvation" (cited in Kafka, 1998, xiv). Others disagree (Kafka, 1998, xiv), but the encounter between Momus and "K" (initially written in the first person) strongly suggests that Momus is meant to represent an uncooperative mediator between a despairing human and a remote God. Momus insists that he acts "in the name of Klamm" (the Governor of the castle), and Momus is described as "the only road that will take you in the direction of Klamm. And do you intend to reject that road for nothing but pride?" To which "K" protests: "that's not the only road to Klamm, nor is it any better than the others" (Kafka, 1969, 145–46). In the excised fragment, furthermore, there is described a lengthy "protocol" against "K," which in effect is a survey of his guilt, a divine judgment he gains knowledge of only after much resistance (Kafka, 1969, 447–54). Other likely religious allusions include "K"'s surprise that the Governor really "trouble[s] himself about my affairs, then?" (Kafka, 1969, 145) and doubts that "anyone who believed he could, say, reach Klamm by taking a leap in the dark was after all seriously underestimating the distance separating him from Klamm" (Kafka, 1969, 444). This use of Momus certainly suggests at least one twentieth-century vestige of Momus's use to depict theological malice and human doubt. As for Kafka's interest in Greek mythology, he was elsewhere keen to debunk myths, depicting Poseidon as a petty bureaucrat who cannot even survey his whole domain and devaluing the Prometheus myth by discussing its several interpretations or versions (Gray, Gross, Goebel, and Koelb, 2005, 194, 198–99, 221–22, 230–31).

236   *Doubting the Divine in Early Modern Europe*

What is the cultural function of a Momus god? Hesiod's mythography was vague: along with Death, Woe, Strife, Nemesis, and others, Blame was but one of a matrix of gloomy forces besetting mankind. In that sense Momus could originally have been a response to the divine order, especially in regard to the ills attending the human condition. Aesop was the first to dramatize divine criticism by having Momus, a lesser god, criticize the creations and majesty of the greater gods. In the process, with Aesop's satirical edge, Momus became equally a god of criticism and mockery. An interesting theory regarding Momus's anthropological or psychological function appeared in the eighteenth century from George Lyttelton, who composed a dialogue between Lucian and Rabelais in his *Dialogues of the Dead* (1760). The subject of Momus arises when the two writers reflect on the constraints on freedom of thought in their respective eras, Rabelais explaining that the dangers for him were much greater than those for Lucian. When Lucian praises Rabelais as worthy to be seated on Olympus "at the right hand of Momus," Rabelais marvels that such a god could get a seat at the divine table: a king's fool is one thing, he argues, Jupiter's jester quite another.[27] Lucian's answer is astute, offering a theory regarding the function of Momus in Greek religion:

I think our priests admitted Momus into our heaven, as the Indians are said to worship the devil, through fear. They had a mind to keep fair with him. For we may talk of the *giants* as much as we please; but to *our gods* there is no enemy so formidable as he. *Ridicule* is the terror of all *false religion*. Nothing but *truth* can stand its lash.[28]

Lucian's Momus thus was a devil, an anti-god who was deified to be appeased, because his weapon – ridicule – is the most fatal to religion. Of course, Lyttelton's theory is only playfully couched in the fiction of the Olympian gods, but he does raise the question as to why authors (rather than gods) in either a polytheistic or monotheistic setting may have needed

---

[27] Lyttelton, 1797, 291; earlier, when Lucian identifies Rabelais as a likeminded soul, Rabelais adds Swift to their number (288).
[28] Lyttelton, 1797, 292, emphasis in original.

Conclusion: Momus and Modernism 237

a Momus figure. One theory, also invoking fear, is offered by Martha Bayless in her study of religious parody in the Middle Ages: namely, that "to laugh at God is to relax one's fear of him."[29] In the early modern period, however, Momus's humor signals temerity more than timidity.

The deification of rationalism in Momus is the literary and theological face of *parrhesia*. Foucault rightly suggests that "frank speech" may be hard-wired in the Western rational tradition. And although he does not incorporate Momus, this god completes the picture. Though Western and other cultures have a trickster god – the Greeks have Hermes, the Norse Loki, the Native Americans Coyote – a god of criticism is perhaps peculiar to the West.[30] Not surprisingly, when this god is invoked by writers to challenge belief, solid ground can become quicksand. Humor marries doubt in order to disguise, to deflect, or possibly even exorcise unbelief. Mockery is Momus's fellow traveler and protects writers *qua* writers and *qua* humans from the fate of Euripides' Pentheus, who was torn apart by the Bacchae for his contempt for Dionysus' rite. Momus, then, is the divine manifestation and comic face of frank speech.

Aesop's Babrius 59 offered the template for Momus's serio-comic challenge to the gods. His criticisms of the gods' creations – Zeus's man, Pallas' house, and Poseidon's bull – were mostly humorous but also, especially in the case of mankind, partly serious: mortals' true hearts do need to be more on display. Rather than declaring any of the gods the victor in the contest, he brashly judged them all deficient. When Lucian takes up the satirical mantle of Momus centuries later in *Zeus Rants* and *The Parliament of the Gods*, the calculus has shifted a bit more to the serious. In the guise of advising the Olympians about protecting their status, Momus gives voice to doubts about their justice, their behavior, and the porous boundaries

---

[29] Bayless, 1996, 202. She sees medieval parody as generally benign and undertaken for fun, agreeing with scholars who argue that religious parody became critical (rather than admiring) only starting in the nineteenth century (5–6). I would disagree; see McClure, 2010.

[30] On the trickster god, see Hyde, 1998.

238   *Doubting the Divine in Early Modern Europe*

of their pantheon. Lucian's Momus is equated with the mortal atheist Damis, the "god-hater." No wonder, then, that Byzantine theologians castigated Lucian as an atheist who was deservedly torn apart by dogs. During his time, however, Lucian's daring was not so dangerous: in their eighteenth-century dialogues, both Lyttelton and Voltaire comment that his era was safer for such speech than the sixteenth century of Erasmus and Rabelais.[31] And, in any case, in the second century CE, mocking the Greek pantheon was more an obituary than a rallying cry.

In the fifteenth century, however, when Alberti resurrected Momus in his fullest incarnation, religious orthodoxy was not so optional. This may explain the need for a coded message in his novel. Momus's promotion of atheism, the Lucretian currents, and the themes of irrational belief and hidden unbelief are all too present to see this work simply as a classical allegory or as a commentary on princely or papal rule. Not only is God framed in terms similar to Jupiter, but also Momus is more than critic and rebel. He is a hero and victim, ultimately vindicated by the end of the story, but only after being bound, like Prometheus, to a rock. Alberti has turned Momus to agnostic and possibly atheistic ends, even while disguising his goal in farce and diversionary declarations.

As the Reformation sharpened the religious climate, the use of Momus became far more explosive. Lucian's great translator Erasmus avoided the Momus dialogues, but even so a humorless Luther branded him an impious Momus once their reform agendas diverged. In France, the anonymous *Cymbalum mundi* (probably of Des Périers) likely borrowed the allegorical template of Alberti's *Momus*, using instead Momus's frequent colleague Mercury and two atheistic Lucianic dogs to stir condemnations from both Catholics and Protestants. By the mid-sixteenth century, the Spanish translator of Alberti's novel took pains to neutralize the blasphemous currents in the work and reassert its intention as only a political allegory. Around this same time in Italy, Anton Francesco Doni submerged Momic

---

[31] Lyttelton, 1797, 176; Voltaire, 1939, 146–47.

Conclusion: Momus and Modernism 239

doubts regarding divine justice within orthodox bookends affirming God and Christ – a strategy that still did not save the text from later excisions by censors uncomfortable with the juxtaposition of the sacred and the profane. By century's end, Bruno took the Momus trope to its most radical ends with too thinly veiled comparisons of Christ to a figure sent down to distract humans from Hermetic and naturalist truths. The result almost certainly helped lead to his execution, and more than one contemporary or near-contemporary saw the *Expulsion of the Triumphant Beast* as one and the same as the infamous *Treatise of the Three Impostors*. The latter work, in turn, was published initially as the *Spirit of Spinoza*, a figure who himself took Bruno's naturalist theology to its logical end.

The occasional interpenetration of the Momus and Lucifer myths – both involving courtiers who fell from grace – culminated, I argue, in *Paradise Lost*. Lucifer's powerful depiction as an antihero with deep recesses of interiority likely drew from Italian sources that Milton was definitely exposed to (in the case of Andreini) and likely exposed to (in the case of Alberti) during his months in Italy in 1638–39. Lucifer's proud and envious resentment of God and Christ, his searching soliloquies, and his sometimes piteous depiction recall the challenge Momus posed to Jupiter and the divine order in Alberti's *Momus*. Both Milton and Spinoza, just a few years apart, posed arguments regarding divine justice that harkened back to Job: Milton in his Christian epic that starred an anti-Christian hero, and Spinoza in his insight that the Adversary or Satan figure in the Book of Job was in fact Momus.

As the religious wars between confessions gradually abated in favor of the culture war between faith and reason in the Enlightenment, Momus's deployment became more relevant to matters of literary rather than divine authority. A process of secularization, already apparent in Garzoni in the late sixteenth century flowered in England with the codification of literary criticism in Dryden, Swift, Pope, Parnell, and others. The aesthetic dimension of Momus's role was present as early as Aesop's Babrius 59, as the three gods were depicted as competing to

240 *Doubting the Divine in Early Modern Europe*

create something *beautiful*. The tag line at some point added to Babrius 59 indicated that envy was Momus's particular impulse in criticizing the works of the gods. This association of Momus with envy continued in the ancient Greek world and fused with pride especially in the early modern era. The nexus of envy and pride that is the hallmark of Lucifer's sinful rebellion not coincidentally became the hallmark of the Critic's secular assault on ancient texts or contemporary authors. Authors, like gods, are creators and have their unrepentant critics.

Even as the use of Momus became increasingly secularized in the early modern and modern period – from an assault on gods (or God) to challenges to literary and professional hierarchy (in Garzoni), the ancient canon (in Swift), bourgeois society (in Murger's Bohemians), or political corruption (in the Momus Krewe) – one common thread is the challenge to authority.[32] *Parrhesia* (frank speech) is a correction to overbearing masters or tradition. This reaction to tradition, in turn, is one of the features of modernism that has confronted religious and cultural matters. Although this modernism would seem to have emerged most clearly in the literary and intellectual setting of, for instance, Garzoni and Swift, ironically it may have already been present in the ancient world, as new or lesser gods challenged older or dominant ones: as Aesop's Momus challenged Zeus, Pallas, Poseidon, and Apollo; or as Athena and Apollo, in turn, challenged the primeval Furies in Aeschylus' *Eumenides*. Even in the ancient world, modernism was characterized by the challenge of *logos* to *mythos*, as Aesop deployed it through "lower" and newer prose in opposition to "higher" and older poetry. In Swift, the Moderns challenged

---

[32] One other example of Momus's political use occurred during the student and labor revolt in France in 1968. A graphic novel appeared in May of that year from Maurice Lemaître entitled *Les aventures d'El Momo*, with the subtitle *Épisode de mai 1968: avec Apeïros* [presumably, the Greek "boundless"] *vers la création au pouvoir!* Momus identified as a legendary hero come to fight furor: "El Momo, héros légendaire, venu du fond des âges, aux côtés d'Apeiros ... pour combattre la fureur et le bruit" (Lemaître, 1968, 1). Momus presents various demands, including "La reduction des années du bagne scolaire," "Le crédit de lancement," and "La rotation au pouvoir" (4).

Conclusion: Momus and Modernism 241

the Ancients, and although the agon involved texts rather than gods, the dynamic may have been one and the same. As a modernist challenge to authority, Momus was a check on unquestioned authority. Whereas Lucian may have set him against the gods from a safe distance in the second century, writers in the fifteenth, sixteenth, and seventeenth centuries braved a greater danger. Momus was an ideal trope, since his essence and antics literally pertained only to a mythic world. By using him as a code for actual doubt or unbelief, writers could nip at the edges of orthodoxy, posing questions and doubts that asked for an airing. Whether religious or cultural in purpose, *parrhesia* has been a vital engine of Western rationalism and cultural change. No wonder this quality was deified in Momus – and no wonder this god became one of the classical tradition's most vexing and necessary gods.

Bibliography

Accetto, Torquato. *Della dissimulazione onesta*. Ed. Salvatore S. Nigro. Turin, 1997.

Adams, Robert M. *Strains of Discord: Studies in Literary Openness*. Ithaca, N.Y., 1958.

Aelian. *Historical Miscellany*. Ed. and trans. N. G. Wilson. Cambridge, Mass., 1997.

Aeschylus. *Aeschylus*. Vol. 1. Trans. Herbert Weir Smyth. Cambridge, Mass., 1922.

Agrippa von Nettesheim, Heinrich Cornelius. *De incertitudine et vanitate scientiarum declamatio invectivo*. n.p., 1542.

De occulta philosophia libri tres. Ed. V. Perrone Compagni. Leiden, 1992.

Dell'incertitudine e della vanità delle scienze. Trans. Ludovico Domenichi. Ed. Tiziana Provvidera. Turin, 2004.

Alberti, Leon Battista. *El Momo*. Trans. Agustín de Almazán. Madrid, 1553.

Opusculi inediti di Leon Battista Alberti: Musca; Vita S. Potiti. Ed. Cecil Grayson. Florence, 1954.

Opere volgari. Ed. Cecil Grayson. 3 vols. Bari, 1960–73.

I libri della famiglia. Ed. Ruggiero Romano and Alberto Tenenti. Turin, 1969.

De commodis litterarum atque incommodis; Defunctus. Ed., Italian trans., intro., and notes Giovanni Farris. Milan, 1971.

Dinner Pieces: A Translation of the Intercenales. Trans. David Marsh. Binghamton, N.Y., 1987.

On the Art of Building in Ten Books. Trans. Joseph Rykwert, Neil Leach, and Robert Tavernor. Cambridge, Mass., 1988.

244 *Bibliography*

Momus. Eng. trans. Sarah Knight. Latin text ed. Virginia Brown and Sarah Knight. Cambridge, Mass., 2003.

The Family in Renaissance Florence: Books 1–4, I libri della famiglia. Trans. and intro. Renée Neu Watkins. Long Grove, Ill., 2004; orig. Columbia, S.C., 1969.

Pontifex. Ed. Andrea Piccardi. Florence, 2007.

Alfredo, Serrai. *La biblioteca di Lucas Holstenius.* Udine, 2000.

Anderson, Abraham. Ed. The Treatise of the Three Impostors *and the Problem of the Enlightenment: A New Translation of the* Traité des trois imposteurs *(1777 Edition) with Three Essays in Commentary.* Lanham, Md., 1997.

Andreini, Giovan Battista. *Prologo in dialogo fra' Momo; e la Verità, spettante all lode dell'arte comica, da Lelio, et Florinda, comici del Sereniss. di Mantova.* Ferrara, 1612.

L'Adamo. Ed. Alessandra Ruffino. Trent, 2007.

Anselment, Raymond A. *"Betwixt Jest and Earnest": Marprelate, Milton, Marvell, Swift and the Decorum of Religious Ridicule.* Toronto, 1979.

Aquilecchia, Giovanni. "Scheda Bruniana: la traduzione 'Tolandina' dello Spaccio." *Giornale Storico della Letteratura Italiana* 92 (1975): 311–13.

Aristophanes. *Aristophanes.* Trans. Benjamin Bickley Rogers. 3 vols. Cambridge, Mass., 1924.

Arthos, John. *Milton and the Italian Cities.* New York, 1968.

Atkins, G. Douglas. *Swift's Satires on Modernism: Battlegrounds of Reading and Writing.* New York, 1913.

Augustine. *Confessions.* Trans., intro., and notes Henry Chadwick. Oxford, 1991.

Aulus Gellius, *The Attic Nights.* Trans. John C. Rolfe. 3 vols. London, 1927.

Babrius and Phaedrus. *Babrius and Phaedrus.* Ed. Ben Edwin Perry. Cambridge, Mass., 1975.

Bacchylides. *Complete Poems.* Trans. Robert Fagles. New Haven, Conn., 1998.

Bakhtin, Mikhail. *Problems of Dostoevsky's Poetics.* Trans. Caryl Emerson. Intro. Wayne C. Booth. Minneapolis, Minn., 1984.

Baldwin, Barry. *Studies in Lucian.* Toronto, 1913.

Barbeau, Alfred. *Life and Letters at Bath in the XVIIIth Century.* London, 1904.

Bayless, Martha. *Parody in the Middle Ages: The Latin Tradition.* Ann Arbor, Mich., 1996.

Bentley, Richard. *Dr. Richard Bentley's Dissertation Upon the Epistles of Phalaris, Themistocles, Socrates, Euripides, and Upon the Fables of Aesop.* Ed., intro., and notes Wilhelm Wagner. Berlin, 1874.

Berti, Domenico. *Vita di Giordano Bruno da Nola*. Florence, 1868.

Berti, Ernesto. "Alla scuola di Manuele Crisolora: lettura e commento di Luciano." *Rinascimento* 27 (1987): 3–73.

Berti, Silvia. "The First Edition of the *Traité des trois imposteurs*, and Its Debt to Spinoza's *Ethics*." In *Atheism from the Reformation to the Enlightenment*. Ed. Michael Hunter and David Wootton, 183–220. Oxford, 1992.

Bertolini, Lucia. *Grecus Sapor: tramiti di presenze greche in Leon Battista Alberti*. Rome, 1998.

Bietenholz, Peter G. *Encounters with a Radical Erasmus: Erasmus's Work as a Source of Radical Thought in Early Modern Europe*. Toronto, 2009.

Biow, Douglas. *In Your Face: Professional Improprieties and the Art of Being Conspicuous in Sixteenth-Century Italy*. Stanford, Calif., 2010.

Black, Christopher F. *The Italian Inquisition*. New Haven, Conn., 2009.

Blake, William. *The Complete Poetry and Prose of William Blake*. Ed. David V. Erdman. Rev. edn. Berkeley and Los Angeles, 1982.

Blanchard, W. Scott. *Scholars' Bedlam: Menippean Satire in the Renaissance*. Lewisburg, Pa., 1995.

Blum, Paul Richard. *Giordano Bruno: An Introduction*. Trans. Peter Henneveld. Amsterdam, 2012.

Boccaccio, Giovanni. *Il Filocolo*. Trans. Donald Cheney with the collaboration of Thomas G. Bergin. New York, 1985.

The Decameron. Trans., intro., and notes G. H. McWilliam. 2nd edn. London, 1995.

Genealogy of the Pagan Gods. Ed. and trans. Jon Solomon. Vol. 1. Cambridge, Mass., 2011.

Boschetto, Luca. "Ricerche sul *Theogenius* e sul *Momus* di Leon Battista Alberti." *Rinascimento*, ser. 2, 33 (1993): 3–52.

Bosman, Philip R. "Lucian among the Cynics: The *Zeus Refuted* and Cynic Tradition." *Classical Quarterly* 62 (2012): 785–95.

Boswell, Jackson Campbell. *Milton's Library: A Catalogue of the Remains of John Milton's Library and an Annotated Reconstruction of Milton's Library and Ancillary Readings*. New York, 1975.

Boulenger de Rivery, Claude-François-Félix. *Momus philosophe: comédie, en un acte et en vers*. Amsterdam, 1750.

Bowersock, Glen Warren. *Greek Sophists in the Roman Empire*. Oxford, 1969.

Boyle, Charles. *Dr. Bentley's Dissertation on the Epistles of Phalaris, and the Fables of Aesop, Examined*. 2nd edn. London, 1698.

Bracciolini, Poggio. *The Facetiae or Jocose Tales of Poggio Now Translated into English with the Latin Text*. Trans. anon. 2 vols. Paris, 1879.

246 *Bibliography*

Facezie. Intro., trans., and notes Marcello Ciccuto. Milan, 1983.

Branham, R. Bracht. *Unruly Eloquence: Lucian and the Comedy of Traditions*. Cambridge, Mass., 1989.

"Defacing the Currency: Diogenes' Rhetoric and the Invention of Criticism." In *The Cynics: The Cynic Movement in Antiquity and Its Legacy*. Ed. Marie-Odile Goulet-Cazé and Robert Bracht Branham, 81–104. Berkeley and Los Angeles, 1996.

"Cynicism." In *The Classical Tradition*. Ed. Anthony Grafton, Glenn V. Most, and Salvatore Settis, 247–48. Cambridge, Mass., 2010.

Brett, Thomas. *Discourses Concerning the Ever-Blessed Trinity*. London, 1720.

Brown, Alison. *The Return of Lucretius to Renaissance Florence*. Cambridge, Mass., 2010.

Bruno, Giordano. *Opere italiane*. Vol. 2: *Dialoghi morali*. Ed. Giovanni Gentile. Bari, 1927.

The Expulsion of the Triumphant Beast. Trans., ed., intro., and notes Arthur D. Imerti. Lincoln, Nebr., 1964.

The Ash Wednesday Supper. Ed. and trans. Edward A. Gosselin and Laurence S. Lerner. Toronto, 1995, orig. Hamden, Conn., 1977.

Bryson, Michael. *The Atheist Milton*. Farnham, 2012.

Budgell, Eustace. Entry in *The Spectator*. Vol. 4, no. 389, Tuesday, May 27, 1712. Joseph Addison and Sir Richard Steele. Repr., ed. Alexander Chalmers, 464–69. New York, 1853.

Bullard, Paddy and James McLaverty, eds. *Jonathan Swift and the Eighteenth-Century Book*. Cambridge, 2013.

Burckhardt, Jacob. *The Civilization of the Renaissance in Italy*. Trans. S. G. C. Middlemore. Intro. Peter Burke. Notes Peter Murray. London, 1990.

Burke, Peter. *Popular Culture in Early Modern Europe*. New York, 1978.

Callimachus. *The Poems of Callimachus*. Trans. Frank Nisetich. Oxford, 2001.

Cameron, Allan. "Doni's Satirical Utopia." *Renaissance Studies* 10 (1996): 462–73.

Camillo (Delminio), Giulio. *L'idea del theatro*. Florence, 1550.

Caponetto, Salvatore. *The Protestant Reformation in Sixteenth-Century Italy*. Trans. Anne and John Tedeschi. Kirksville, Mo., 1999.

Cardini, Roberto, with the collaboration of Lucia Bertolini and Mariangela Regoliosi. *Leon Battista Alberti: la biblioteca di un umanista*. Florence, 2005.

Carew, Thomas. *Coelum Britanicum: A Masque at White-Hall in the Banquetting-House, on Shrove-Tuesday-Night, the 18. of February, 1633*. London, 1634.

Bibliography

[Carey, George Saville]. *Momus, a Poem; or A Critical Examination Into the Merits of the Performers and Comic Pieces, at the Theatre Royal in the Hay-Market.* London [1767].

Carey, John. "Milton's Satan." In *The Cambridge Companion to Milton.* 2nd edn. Ed Dennis Danielson, 160–74. Cambridge, 1989.

Carr, John, trans. *Dialogues of Lucian, from the Greek.* Vol. 4. London, 1798.

Cartari, Vincenzo. *Vincenzo Cartari's* Images of the Gods of the Ancients: *The First Italian Mythography.* Trans. and annot. John Mulryan. Tempe, Ariz., 2012.

Cassirer, Ernst, Paul Oskar Kristeller, and John Herman Randall, Jr., eds. *The Renaissance Philosophy of Man.* Chicago, 1948.

Cast, David. "Martin van Heemskerck's *Momus Criticizing the Works of the Gods*: A Problem of Erasmian Iconography." *Simiolus: Netherlands Quarterly for the History of Art* 7 (1974): 22–34.

Caster, Marcel. *Lucien et la pensée religieuse de son temps.* Paris, 1937; repr. 1987.

Études sur Alexandre ou le faux prophète de Lucien. Paris, 1938.

Celenza, Christopher S. *Renaissance Humanism and the Papal Curia: Lapo da Castiglioncho the Younger's* De curia commodis. Ann Arbor, Mich., 1999.

Champion, Justin. "Toland and the *Traité des trois imposteurs* c1709–1718." At https://repository.royalholloway.ac.uk/file/99418 de1-2ae5-c62b-76bc-86c538c32a22/8/Champion_Spain3.pdf [1990?].

The Pillars of Priestcraft Shaken: The Church of England and Its Enemies, 1660–1730. Cambridge, 1992.

Chaney, Edward. "The Visit to Vallambrosa: A Literary Tradition." In *Milton in Italy: Context, Images, Contradictions.* Ed. Mario di Cesare, 113–46. Binghamton, N.Y., 1991.

Charity; or, Momus's Reward, A Poem. Bath, 1775.

Chasseneuz, Barthélemey de. *Catalogus gloriae mundi.* Lyons, 1546.

Cherchi, Paolo. *Enciclopedismo e politica della riscrittura: Tommaso Garzoni.* Pisa, 1980.

Cicero. *De natura deorum; Academica.* Trans. H. Rackham. Cambridge, Mass., 1951.

Citolini, Alessandro. *La tipocosmia.* Venice, 1561.

Cooper, Richard. "*Cymbalum Mundi*: état de la question." In *Le Cymbalum Mundi: actes du colloque de Rome (3–6 novembre 2000).* Ed. Franco Giacone, 3–17. Geneva, 2003.

Cordié, Carlo. "Nota introduttiva" and "Nota bio-bibliografica." In *Folengo – Aretino – Doni.* Vol. 2: *Opere di Pietro Aretino e di Anton Francesco Doni.* Ed. Carlo Cordiè, 571–96. Milan, 1976.

248   *Bibliography*

Craig, Harden. "Dryden's Lucian." *Classical Philology* 16 (1921): 141–63.

Damonte, Mario. "Testimonianze della fortuna di L. B. Alberti in Spagna: una traduzione cinquecentesca del *Momus* in ambiente Erasmista." *Atti della Accademia Ligure di Scienze e Lettere* 31 (1974): 257–83.

Damrosch, Leo. *Jonathan Swift: His Life and His World*. New Haven, Conn., 2013.

Davidson, Nicholas. "Unbelief and Atheism in Italy 1500–1700." In *Atheism from the Reformation to the Enlightenment*. Ed. Michael Hunter and David Wootton, 55–85. Oxford, 1992.

De Keyser, Jeroen. "Francesco Filelfo's Feud with Poggio Bracciolini." In *Forms of Conflict and Rivalries in Renaissance Europe*. Ed. David A. Lines, Marc Laureys, and Jill Kraye, 1–27. Göttingen, 2015.

Del Fante, Alessandra. "Note su Anton Francesco Doni: *Gli spiriti folletti*." *Atti e Memorie dell'Accademia Toscana di Scienze e Lettere (La Colombaria)* n.s. 27 = 41 (1976): 171–209.

"Note sui *Mondi* di Anton Francesco Doni." *Annali dell'Istituto di Filosofia* 2 (1980): 111–49.

Democritus Ridens, or Comus and Momus: A New Jest and Earnest Pratling Concerning the Times. London, 1681.

Des Périers, Bonaventure. *Cymbalum mundi or Satyrical Dialogues on Various Subjects. With A Letter to Mr. B, P; and G. Concerning the Book Entitled,* Cymbalum Mundi *by Prosper Marchand*. Trans. anon. London, 1723.

Cymbalum Mundi. Ed. Peter H. Nurse. Manchester, 1958.

Di Ceseare, Mario A., ed. *Milton in Italy: Contexts, Images, and Contradictions*. Binghamton, N.Y., 1991.

Di Stefano, Elisabetta. "Leon Battista Alberti e le immagini sacre." In *Il sacro nel Rinascimento. Atti del XII Convegno Internazionale (Chianciano Terme-Pienza, 17–20 luglio 2000)*. Ed. L. Secchi Tarugi, 517–31. Florence, 2002.

Dijkhuizen, Jan Frans van and Helmer Helmers. "Religion and Politics – Lucifer (1654) and Milton's *Paradise Lost* (1674)." In *Joost von den Vondel (1587–1679): Dutch Playwright in the Golden Age*. Ed. Jan Bloemendal and Frans-William Korsten, 377–405. Leiden, 2011.

Dobranski, Stephen B. and John P. Rumrich, eds. *Milton and Heresy*. Cambridge, 1998.

Doni, Anton Francesco. *La libraria*. Ed. Vanni Bramanti. Milan, 1972.

I mondi e gli inferni. Ed. Patrizia Pellizari. Intro. Marziano Guglielminetti. Turin, 1994.

Doran, John. *The History of Court Fools*. London, 1858.

Bibliography 249

Dryden, John. *The Works of John Dryden*. Ed. Edward Niles Hooker, H. T. Swedenberg, and Vinton A. Dearing. 20 vols. Berkeley and Los Angeles, 1956–2000.

Ehrenpreis, Irvin. *Swift: The Man, His Works, and the Age*. Vol 1: *Mr. Swift and His Contemporaries*. Cambridge, Mass., 1962.

Empson, William. *Milton's God*. Rev. edn. London, 1965.

Entzminger, Robert L. "The Politics of Love in Tasso's *Aminta* and Milton's *Comus*." In *Milton in Italy: Contexts, Images, Contradictions*. Ed. Mario di Cesare, 463–76. Binghamton, N.Y., 1991.

Erasmus, Desiderius. *The Colloquies of Erasmus*. Trans. Craig R. Thompson. Chicago, 1965.

    Collected Works of Erasmus. Vol. 2: *The Correspondence of Erasmus: Letters 142 to 297, 1501–1514*. Trans. R. A. B. Mynors and D. F. S. Thomson. Annot. Wallace K. Ferguson. Toronto, 1975.

    Collected Works of Erasmus. Vol. 4: *The Correspondence of Erasmus: Letters 446 to 593, 1516–1517*. Trans. R. A. B. Mynors and D. F. S. Thomson. Annot. James K. McConica. Toronto, 1977.

    Collected Works of Erasmus. Vol. 31: *Adages ii1 to iv100*. Trans. Margaret Mann Philips. Annot. R. A. B. Mynors. Toronto, 1982.

    Collected Works of Erasmus. Vol. 9: *The Corrrespondence of Erasmus: Letters 1252 to 1355 (1522–1523)*. Trans. R. A. B. Mynors. Annot. James M. Estes. Toronto, 1989a.

    Praise of Folly and Other Writings. Trans. and ed. Robert M. Adams. New York, 1989b.

    Collected Works of Erasmus. Vol. 76: *Controversies: De libero arbitrio, Hyperaspistes I*. Ed. Charles Trinkaus. Trans. Peter Macardle and Clarence H. Miller. Annot. Peter Macardle, Clarence H. Miller, and Charles Trinkaus. Toronto, 1999.

    Collected Works of Erasmus. Vol. 35: *Adages iiiiv1 to ivii100*. Trans. and annot. Denis L. Drysdall. Ed. John N. Grant. Toronto, 2005a.

    Collected Works of Erasmus. Vol. 84: *Controversies: Responsio ad epistolam paraeneticam Alberti Pii; Apologia adversus Rhapsodias Alberti Pii; Brevissima scholia*. Ed. Nelson H. Minnich and Daniel Sheerin. Toronto, 2005b.

    Collected Works of Erasmus. Vol. 78: *Controversies*. Historical ed. James. D. Tracy. General ed. Manfred Hoffmann. Toronto, 2011.

Eratosthenes and Hyginus. *Constellation Myths with Aratus's Phaenomena*. Trans. Robin Hard. Oxford, 2015.

Euripides. *Euripides*. In 4 vols. Vol 3: *Bacchanals, Madness of Hercules, Children of Hercules, Phoenician Maidens, Suppliants*. Trans. Arthur S. Way. London, 1912.

250   *Bibliography*

Bacchae, Iphigenia at Aulis, Rhesus. Trans. David Kovacs. Cambridge, Mass., 2002.

Evans, Willa McClung. *Henry Lawes: Musician and Friend of Poets*. New York, 1966.

Ewald Jr., William Bragg. *The Masks of Jonathan Swift*. New York, 1967; orig. Oxford, 1954.

Febvre, Lucien. "Origène et Des Périers ou l'énigma du *Cymbalum Mundi*." *Bibliothèque d'Humanisme et Renaissance* 2 (1942): 7–131.
The Problem of Unbelief in the Sixteenth Century: The Religion of Rabelais. Trans. Beatrice Gottlieb. Cambridge, Mass., 1982.

Ficino, Marsilio. *Marsilio Ficino: The* Philebus *Commentary*. Ed. and trans. Michael J. B. Allen. Berkeley and Los Angeles, 1975.

Filelfo, Francesco. *On Exile*. Ed. Jeroen De Keyser. Trans. W. Scott Blanchard. Cambridge, Mass., 2013.

Fish, Stanley. *Surprised by Sin: The Reader in* Paradise Lost. 2nd edn. Basingstoke, 1997.

Forsyth, Neil. *The Satanic Epic*. Princeton, N.J., 2003.

Foucault, Michel. *Fearless Speech*. Ed. Joseph Pearson. Los Angeles, 2001.

Franco, Niccolò. *Dialogi piacevoli*. Ed. Franco Ignatti. Manziana (Rome), 2003.

Frank, Joseph. "John Milton's Movement toward Deism." *Journal of British Studies* 1 (1961): 38–51.

French, J. Milton. *The Life Records of John Milton*. 5 vols. New York, 1966; orig. New Brunswick, N.J., 1950.

Friedman, Donald. "Galileo and the Art of Seeing." In *Milton in Italy: Context, Images, Contradictions*. Ed. Mario di Cesare, 159–74. Binghamton, N.Y., 1991.

Fubini, R. and A. Menci Gallorini. "L'autobiografia di Leon Battista Alberti." *Rinascimento*, ser. 2, 12 (1972): 21–78.

Gaddi, Jacopo. *De scriptoribus non ecclesiasticis, graecis, latinis, italicis*. Vol. 1. Florence, 1648.

Gadol, Joan; *Leon Battista Alberti: Universal Man of the Early Renaissance*. Chicago, 1969.

Gardner, Helen. *A Reading of* Paradise Lost. Oxford, 1965.

Garin, Eugenio. *Italian Humanism: Philosophy and Civic Life*. Trans. Peter Munz. New York, 1965.
"Erasmo e l'umanesimo italiano." *Bibliothèque d'Humanisme et Renaissance* 33 (1971): 7–17.
Rinascite e rivoluzioni: movimenti culturali dal XIV al XVIII secolo. Rome, 1975.

Garzoni, Tomaso. *La piazza universale di tutte le professioni del mondo*. Ed. Paolo Cherchi and Beatrice Collina. Turin, 1996.

Bibliography

Gauna, Max. *Upwellings: First Expressions of Unbelief in the Printed Literature of the French Renaissance*. Cranbury, N.J., 1992.

Gavin, Michael. *The Invention of English Criticism, 1650–1760*. Cambridge, 2015.

Giacone, Franco, ed. *Le Cymbalum Mundi: actes du colloque de Rome (3–6 novembre 2000)*. Geneva, 2003.

Giangrande, Giuseppe. "The Final Line in Callimachus' *Hymn to Apollo*." *Habis* 23 (1992): 53–62.

Giraud, Yves. "La lettre et l'esprit: problèmes textuels et éditoriaux autour *du Cymbalum Mundi*." In *Le Cymbalum Mundi: actes du colloque de Rome (3–6 novembre 2000)*. Ed. Franco Giacone, 23–39. Geneva, 2003.

Gordon, Walter M. *Humanist Play and Belief: The Seriocomic Art of Desiderius Erasmus*. Toronto, 1990.

Grafton, Anthony. *Forgers and Critics: Creativity and Duplicity in Western Scholarship*. Princeton, N.J., 1990.

Leon Battista Alberti: Master Builder of the Italian Renaissance. New York, 2000.

Gray, Richard T., Ruth V. Gross, Rolf J. Goebel, and Clayton Koelb. *A Franz Kafka Encyclopedia*. Westport, Conn., 2005.

Grayson, Cecil. *Studi su Leon Battista Alberti*. Ed. Paola Claut. Florence, 1998.

The Greek Anthology IV (Books X–XII). Trans. W. R. Paton. Cambridge, Mass., 1918.

The Greek Anthology V (Books XIII–XVI). Trans. W. R. Paton. Cambridge, Mass., 1918.

Greek Epic Fragments: From the Seventh to the Fifth Centuries BC. Ed and trans. Martin L. West. Cambridge, Mass., 2003.

Greenblatt, Stephen. *The Swerve: How the World Became Modern*. New York, 2011.

Grendler, Paul F. *Critics of the Italian World (1530–1560): Anton Francesco Doni, Nicolò Franco, and Ortensio Lando*. Madison, Wis., 1969.

The Roman Inquisition and the Venetian Press, 1540–1605. Princeton, N.J., 1977.

Guarino, Guido A. "Leon Battista Alberti's *Vita S. Potiti*." *Renaissance News* 8 (1955): 86–89.

Haan, Estelle. *From* Academia *to* Amicitia: *Milton's Latin Writings and the Italian Academies*. Philadelphia, 1998.

Hale, John. "The Multilingual Milton and the Italian Journey." In *Milton In Italy: Contexts, Images, Contradictions*. Ed. Mario di Cesare, 549–72. Binghamton, N.Y., 1991.

Bibliography

Hansen, William. *Classical Mythology: A Guide to the Mythical World of the Greeks and Romans*. New York, 2004.

Harris, Neil. "The Vallombrosa Simile and the Image of the Poet in *Paradise Lost*." In *Milton in Italy: Context, Images, Contradictions*. Ed. Mario di Cesare, 71–94. Binghamton, N.Y., 1991.

Harth, Phillip. *Swift and Anglican Rationalism: The Religious Background of* A Tale of a Tub. Chicago, 1961.

Hawes, Greta. *Rationalizing Myth in Antiquity*. Oxford, 2014.

Herman, Peter C. *Destabilizing Milton:* Paradise Lost *and the Poetics of Incertitude*. New York, 2005.

Hermetica: The Ancient Greek and Latin Writings Which Contain Religious or Philosophic Teachings Ascribed to Hermes Trismegistus. 4 vols. Ed. with Eng. trans. and notes Walter Scott. Vol. 1. Boulder, Colo., 1982; orig. Oxford, 1924–36.

Herz, Judith Scherer. "'For whom this glorious sight?': Dante, Milton, and the Galileo Question." In *Milton in Italy: Context, Images, Contradictions*. Ed. Mario di Cesare, 147–57. Binghamton, N.Y., 1991.

Hesiod. *Hesiod, the Homeric Hymns, and Homerica*. Trans. Hugh G. Evelyn-White. Cambridge, Mass., 1936.

Hewitt, Joseph William. "A Second Century Voltaire." *Classical Journal* 20 (1924): 132–42.

Hickes, Francis. *Certain Select Dialogues of Lucian: Together With His True History, Translated From the Greek Into English: Whereupon Is Added the Life of Lucian*. Oxford, 1663.

Hill, Christopher. *Milton and the English Revolution*. New York, 1977.

Hiltner, Ken. *Milton and Ecology*. Cambridge, 2003.

Hippocrates. *Pseudoepigraphic Writings*. Ed., trans., and intro. Wesley D. Smith. Leiden, 1990.

Huttar, Charles A. "Vallambrosa Revisited." In *Milton in Italy: Context, Images, Contradictions*. Ed. Mario di Cesare, 95–111, Binghamton, N.Y., 1991.

Hyde, Lewis. *The Trickster Makes This World: Mischief, Myth, and Art*. New York, 1998.

Jacob, Margaret C. *The Radical Enlightenment: Pantheists, Freemasons and Republicans*. London, 1981.

Jonson, Ben. *Pleasure Reconciled to Virtue: A Masque, As it Was Presented at Court Before King James, 1619*. In *The Works of Ben Jonson*. 3 vols. Ed. William Gifford, 3: 121–26. London, 1903.

Jones, C. P. *Culture and Society in Lucian*. Cambridge, Mass., 1986.

Kafka, Franz. *The Castle*. Trans. Willa and Edwin Muir. New York, 1969.

The Castle: A New Translation, Based on the Restored Text. Trans. and pref. Mark Harman. New York, 1998.

Kastor, Frank S. *Milton and the Literary Satan*. Amsterdam, 1974.

Kelley, Maurice and Samuel D. Atkins. "Milton's Annotations of Euripides." *Journal of English and German Philology* 60 (1961): 680–87.

Kircher, Timothy. *Living Well in Renaissance Italy: The Virtues of Humanism and the Irony of Leon Battista Alberti*. Tempe, Ariz., 2012.

Kirkconnell, Watson. *The Celestial Cycle: The Theme of Paradise Lost in World Literature with Translations of the Major Analogues*. New York, 1967.

Krapp, George Philip. *The Junius Manuscript*. New York, 1931.

Kurke, Leslie. *Aesopic Conversations: Popular Tradition, Cultural Dialogue, and the Invention Greek Prose*. Princeton, N.J., 2011.

Laborde, Errol. "Momus and the Rise of Satire." In *New Orleans Magazine*, February 2007a, www.myneworleans.com/New-Orleans-Magazine/February-2007/Errol-Labordes-Commentary-Momus-and-the-Rise-of-Satire/.

Krewe: The Early View of New Orleans Carnival: Comus to Zulu. Metarie, La., 2007b.

Lactantius. *Divine Institutes*. Trans., notes, and intro. Anthony Bowen and Peter Garnsey. Liverpool, 2003.

Langbaine, Gerard. *Momus Triumphans: Or, the Plagiaries of the English Stage; Expos'd in a Catalogue*. London, 1688 [1687], repr. Los Angeles, 1971.

The Laughing Philosopher. Printed for James Williams. Dublin, 1777.

The Laughing Philosopher: Being the Entire Works of Momus, Jester of Olympus; Democritus, the Merry Philosopher of Greece, and Their Illustrious Disciples, Ben Jonson, Butler, Swift, Gay, Joseph Miller, Esq., Churchill, Voltaire, Foote, Steevens, Wolcot, Sheridan, Curran, Colman, and Others. Trans. "John Bull" [Charles Lamb and Thomas Hood]. London, 1825.

Lauvergnat-Gagnière, Christine. *Lucien de Samosate et le Lucianisme en France au XVIe siècle: athéisme et polémique*. Geneva, 1988.

Le Clerc, Jean. *Ars critica*. London, 1698.

Parrhasiana; ou Pensées diverses sur des matiéres de critique, d'histoire, de morale et de politique. 2 vols. Amsterdam, 1699–1701.

Parrhasiana: Or, Thoughts Upon Several Subjects, as Criticism, History, Morality and Politics. Trans. anon. London, 1700.

Le Roy, Antoine. *The French Momus: or, Comical Adventures of the Duke of Roquelaure*. Trans. anon. London, 1718.

Leavis, F. R. "The Irony of Swift." In his *The Common Pursuit*, 73–87. New York, 1952.

Lemaître, Maurice. *Les aventures d'El Momo*. Paris, 1968.

Levine, Joseph M. *The Battle of the Books: History and Literature in the Augustan Age*. Ithaca, N.Y., 1991.

Lewalski, Barbara. *The Life of John Milton: A Critical Biography*. Malden, Mass., 2000.

Lewis, C. S. *A Preface to* Paradise Lost. London, 1942.

Libanius. *Selected Orations*. Vol 1: *Julianic Orations*. Trans. A. F. Norman. Cambridge, Mass., 1969.

Lodge, Thomas. *The Complete Works of Thomas Lodge*. 4 vols. New York, 1963.

London Society. "Coffee-House and Tavern Life in Paris." *Scott's Monthly Magazine* 3 (1867): 176–84.

Longo, A. "Anton Francesco Doni." In *Dizionario biografico degli Italiani*. Vol. 41, 158–67. Rome, 1992.

Lucian, *Part of Lucian Made English From the Originall in the Yeare 1638 ... To Which Are Adjoyned Those Other Dialogues As They Were Formerly Translated by Mr. Francis Hickes*. Trans. Jasper Maynes and Francis Hickes. Oxford, 1664.

    The Syrian Goddess: Being a Translation of Lucian's "De dea Syria," with a Life of Lucian. Trans. Herbert Strong. Ed., notes, and intro. John Garstang. London, 1913.

    Lucian in Eight Volumes. Trans. A. M. Harmon, K. Kilburn, et al. Cambridge, Mass., 1913–67.

Lucretius. *De rerum natura*. Trans. W. H. D. Rouse. Cambridge, Mass., 1937.

Luiso, F. P. "Studi su l'epistolario e le traduzioni di Lapo da Castiglionchio junior." *Studi Italiani di Filologia Classsica* 7 (1899): 205–99.

Luther, Martin. *D. Martin Luthers Werke: Tischreden (1531–1546)*. Vol. 1. Ed. Joachim Karl Fredrick Knaake. Weimar, 1912.

    Luther's Correspondence and Other Contemporary Letters. Vol 1: *1507–1521*. Trans. and ed. Preserved Smith. Philadelphia, 1913.

    D. Martin Luthers Werke, Kritische Gesamtausgabe: Briefwechsel. Vol. 7: *1534–1536*. Weimar, 1937; repr. 1969.

    Martin Luther: Selections from His Writings. Ed. and intro. John Dillenberger. New York, 1962.

    Luther's Works. Vol. 33: *Career of the Reformer III*. Ed. Philip S. Watson. Philadelphia, 1972.

Lyttelton, George. *Dialogues of the Dead*. Worcester, Mass., 1797.

McClure, George W. *Sorrow and Consolation in Italian Humanism*. Princeton, N.J., 1991.

    The Culture of Profession in Late Renaissance Italy. Toronto, 2004.

"Women and the Politics of Play Sixteenth-Century Italy: Torquato Tasso's Theory of Games." *Renaissance Quarterly* 61 (2008): 750–91.

"Heresy at Play: Academies and the Literary Underground in Counter-Reformation Siena." *Renaissance Quarterly* 63 (2010): 1151–207.

Machiavelli, Niccolò. *The Portable Machiavelli*. Ed. and trans. Peter Bondanella and Mark Musa. New York, 1979.

Mancini, Girolamo. *Vita di Leon Battista Alberti*. 2nd edn. Rome, 1971.

Manetti, Giannozzo. *Ianotii Manetti de dignitate et excellentia hominis*. Ed. Elizabeth Leonard. Padua, 1975.

Mansfield, Bruce. *Interpretations of Erasmus c1750–1920: Man on His Own*. Toronto, 1992.

Marchand, Prosper. *Dictionnaire historique, ou Mémoires critiques et littéraires concernant la vie et les ouvrages de divers personnages distingués, particulièrement de la République des lettres*. The Hague, 1758–59.

Marchetti, Valerio. *Gruppi ereticali senesi del Cinquecento*. Florence, 1975.

Marcus, Leah. *The Politics of Mirth: Jonson, Herrick, Milton, Marvell, and the Defense of Old Holiday Pastimes*. Chicago, 1986.

Marlowe, Christopher. *Doctor Faustus A- and B-Texts (1604, 1616)*. Ed. David Bevington and Eric Rasmussen. Manchester, 1993.

Marsh, David. *Lucian and the Latins: Humor and Humanism in the Early Renaissance*. Ann Arbor, Mich., 1998.

Martin, John. "Inventing Sincerity, Refashioning Prudence: The Discovery of the Individual in Renaissance Europe." *American Historical Review* 102 (1997): 1309–42.

Masi, Giorgio. "Echi Ficiniani dal dialogo *Torricella* di Ottone Lupano al *Mondo Savio/Pazzo* del Doni." *Filologia e Critica* 17 (1992): 22–72.

Mattioli, Emilio. *Luciano e l'umanesimo*. Naples, 1980.

Mercati, Angelo. *Il sommario del processo di Giordano Bruno*. Vatican City, 1942; repr. 1961.

Michelson, Emily. *The Pulpit and the Press in Reformation Italy*. Cambridge, Mass., 2013.

[Miller, Anna]. *Poetical Amusements at a Villa Near Bath*. Vol. 1. 2nd edn. London, 1776.

Millet, Olivier. "Le *Cymbalum Mundi* et la tradition lucianique." In *Le Cymbalum Mundi: actes du colloque de Rome (3–6 novembre 2000)*. Ed. Franco Giacone, 317–32. Geneva, 2003.

Milton, John. *Joannis Milton opera omnia Latina*. Amsterdam, 1698. *Prose Works*. Intro. Robert Fletcher. London, 1838.

256   *Bibliography*

The Works of John Milton. 18 vols. Ed. Frank Allen Patterson. New York, 1931–38.

The Complete Prose Works. 8 vols. General ed. Don M. Wolfe. New Haven, Conn., 1953–82.

Minois, Georges. *The Atheist's Bible: The Most Dangerous Book That Never Existed*. Trans. Lys Ann Weiss. Chicago, 2012.

More, Thomas. *Utopia*. Trans. and intro. Clarence H. Miller. New Haven, Conn., 2001.

Muir, Edward. *The Culture Wars of the Late Renaissance: Skeptics, Libertines, and Opera*. Cambridge, Mass., 2007.

Murger, Henri. *Scènes de la vie de bohème*. Paris, 1929.

Scenes from the Latin Quarter. Foreword James Naughtie. Intro. Anthony Lejeune. London, 2010.

Nagy, Gregory. *The Best of the Achaeans: Concepts of the Hero in Archaic Greek Poetry*. Baltimore, Md., 1979.

Nauert Jr., Charles G. *Agrippa and the Crisis of Renaissance Thought*. Urbana, Ill., 1965.

Novotný, Vojtěch. *Cur Homo? A History of the Thesis Concerning Man as a Replacement for Fallen Angels*. Prague, 2014.

Oliver, James H. "The Actuality of Lucian's *Assembly of the Gods*." *American Journal of Philology* 101 (1980): 304–13.

Omodeo, Pietro Daniel. "Heliocentrism, Plurality of Worlds and Ethics: Anton Francesco Doni and Giordano Bruno." In *Literature in the Age of Celestial Discovery: From Copernicus to Flamsteed*. Ed. Judy A. Hayden, 23–43. Houndmills, 2016.

Orgel, Stephen and Roy C. Strong. *Inigo Jones: The Theatre of the Stuart Court, Including the Complete Designs for Productions at Court, for the Most Part in the Collection of the Duke of Devonshire, together with Their Texts and Historical Documentation*. 2 vols. Berkeley and Los Angeles, 1973.

Origen. *Contra Celsum*. Trans., intro., and notes Henry Chadwick. Cambridge, 1965.

Ovid. *Metamorphoses*. Trans. Frank Justus Miller. 2 vols. London, 1921.

Palmer, Ada. *Reading Lucretius in the Renaissance*. Cambridge, Mass., 2014.

Paoli, Michel. *L'idée de nature chez Leon Battista Alberti (1404–1472)*. Paris, 1999.

Parker, William Riley. *Milton: A Biography*. 2 vols. Oxford, 1968.

Parnell, Thomas. *The Collected Poems of Thomas Parnell*. Ed. Claude Rawson and F. P. Lock. Newark, Del., 1989.

Pask, Kevin. "Plagiarism and the Originality of National Literature: Gerard Langbaine." *ELH* 69 (2002): 727–47.

Bibliography

Patey, Douglas Lane. "The Institution of Criticism in the Eighteenth Century." In *The Cambridge History of Literary Criticism*. Vol. 4: *The Eighteenth Century*. Ed. H. B. Nisbet and Claude Rawson, 3–31. Cambridge, 2005.

Petrarca, Francesco. *Petrarch's Remedies for Fortune Fair and Foul: A Modern English Translation of* De remediis utriusque fortune. Trans. and comm. Conrad H. Rawski. 5 vols. Bloomington, Ind., 1991.

Philodemus. *On Frank Criticism*. Intro., trans., and notes David Konstan, Diskin Clay, Clarence E. Glad, Johan C. Thom, and James Ware. Atlanta, Ga., 1998.

Pindar. *The Odes of Pindar*. Intro. and trans. John Sandys. Cambridge, Mass., 1937.

Plato. *The Collected Dialogues, Including the Letters*. Ed. Edith Hamilton and Huntington Cairns. Princeton, N.J., 1961.

Plutarch. *Plutarch's Moralia in Fifteen Volumes*. Trans. Frank Cole Babbit et al. Cambridge, Mass., 1927–2004.

Ponte, Giovanni. *Leon Battista Alberti: umanista e scrittore*. Genoa, 1981.

Pope, Alexander. *Alexander Pope*. Ed. Pat Rogers. New York, 1993.

Popkin, Richard H. *The History of Skepticism from Erasmus to Spinoza*. Berkeley and Los Angeles, 1979.

Quéro, Dominique. *Momus philosophe: recherches sur une figure littéraire du XVIIIe siècle*. Paris, 1995.

Quint, David. *Inside* Paradise Lost: *Reading the Designs of Milton's Epic*. Princeton, N.J., 2014.

Quintano, Ricardo. "Emile Pons and the Modern Study of Swift's *Tale of a Tub*." *Études Anglaises* 18 (1965): 5–17.

Rabelais, François. *Oeuvres de François Rabelais*. Vol. 3. Ed. Abel Lefranc. Paris, 1922.

Redfield, Robert. *Peasant Society and Culture: An Anthropological Approach to Civilization*. Chicago, 1956.

Relihan, Joel C. "Menippus in Antiquity and the Renaissance." In *The Cynics: The Cynic Movement in Antiquity and Its Legacy*. Ed. R. Bracht Branham and Marie-Odile Goulet-Cazé, 265–93. Berkeley and Los Angeles, 1996.

Renaissance Fables: Aesopic Prose by Leon Battista Alberti, Bartolomeo Scala, Leonardo da Vinci, Bernardino Baldi. Trans. and intro. David Marsh. Tempe, Ariz., 2004.

Revard, Stella Purce. *The War in Heaven:* Paradise Lost *and the Tradition of Satan's Rebellion*. Ithaca, N.Y., 1980.

Richards, Kenneth and Laura Richards, eds. *The Commedia dell'Arte: A Documentary History*. Oxford, 1990.

258 *Bibliography*

Ricottini Marsili-Libelli, Cecilia. *Anton Francesco Doni: scrittore e stampatore*. Florence, 1960.

Rinaldi, Rinaldo. "Momus christianus: altre fonti albertiane." *Lettere Italiane* 51 (1999): 197–252.

Robin, Diana. *Publishing Women: Salons, the Presses, and the Counter-Reformation in Sixteenth-Century Italy*. Chicago, 2007.

Robinson, Christopher. *Lucian and His Influence in Europe*. Chapel Hill, N.C., 1979.

Rowland, Ingrid. D. *Giordano Bruno: Philosopher/Heretic*. New York, 2008.

Saitta, G. *Il pensiero italiano nell'umanesimo e nel Rinascimento*. 3 vols. Bologna, 1949–51.

Salvini, Salvino. *Fasti consolari dell'Accademia Fiorentina*. Florence, 1717.

Sandburg, Carl. "Momus." *Poetry Magazine*, March 1914: 196–97.

Santinello, G. *Leon Battista Alberti: una vision estetica del mondo e della vita*. Florence, 1962.

Schanne, Alexandre. *Souvenirs de Schaunard*. Paris, 1887.

Seigel, Jerrold. *Bohemian Paris: Culture, Politics, and the Boundaries of Bourgeois Life, 1830–1930*. New York, 1986.

Seneca. *Ad Lucilium epistulae morales*. Trans. Richard M. Gummere. 3 vols. London, 1917.

Apocolocyntosis. Ed. P. T. Eden. Cambridge, 1984.

The Sentence of Momus on the Poetical Amusements at a Villa Near Bath. London, 1775.

Seznec, Jean. *The Survival of the Pagan Gods: The Mythological Tradition and Its Place in Renaissance Humanism and Art*. Trans. Barbara F. Sessions. New York, 1953.

Shelley, Percy Bysshe. *The Poems of Shelley*. Vol. 2: *1817–1819*. Ed. Kelvin Everest and Geoffrey Matthews. Harlow, 1989.

Simoncini, Stefano. "L'avventura di Momo nel Rinascimento. Il nume della critica tra Leon Battista Alberti e Giordano Bruno." *Rinascimento*, ser. 2, 38 (1998): 405–54.

Simonini, Ivan "Tomaso Garzoni, uno zingaro in convento." In *Tomaso Garzoni: Uno zingaro in convento: Celebrazioni garzoniane, IVo centario (1589–1989) Ravenna-Bagnacavallo, 9–25*. Ravenna, [1990].

Singleton, Ralph H. "'Milton's *Comus* and the *Comus* of Erycius Puteanus." *PMLA* 58 (1943): 949–57.

Smallwood, Philip. *Critical Occasions: Dryden, Pope, Johnson, and the History of Criticism*. New York, 2011.

Smith, Christine. "The Apocalypse Sent Up: A Parody of the Papacy by Leon Battista Alberti." *MLN* 119 Supplement (2004): 162–77.

Bibliography

Smith, Malcolm C. "A Sixteenth-Century Anti-Theist (On the *Cymbalum Mundi*)." *Bibliothèque d'Humanisme et Renaissance* 53 (1991): 593–618.

Sombart, Werner. *The Quintessence of Capitalism: A Study of the History and Psychology of the Modern Business Man*. Trans. M. Epstein. New York, 1915.

Spenser, Edmund. *The Works of Edmund Spenser*. Intro. Tim Cook. Ware, Hertfordshire, 1995.

Spinoza, Baruch. *A Theologico-Political Treatise and a Political Treatise*. Trans. and intro. R. H. M. Elwes. Bibliographical note Francesco Cordasco. New York, 1951.

Ethics. Ed. and trans. G. H. R. Parkinson. Oxford, 2000.

Spitzer, Wolfgang. "The Meaning of Bonaventure des Périers' *Cymbalum Mundi*." *PMLA* 66 (1951): 795–819.

Stampanato, Vincenzo. *Documenti della vita di Giordano Bruno*. Florence, 1933.

Swift, Jonathan. A Tale of a Tub, *to Which is Added* The Battle of the Books *and the* Mechanical Operation of the Spirit. Ed., intro., and notes A. C. Guthkelch and D. Nichol Smith. 2nd edn.Oxford, 1958.

The Essential Writings of Jonathan Swift. Ed. Claude Rawson and Ian Higgins. New York, 2010.

Symonds, John Addington. *Renaissance in Italy: Italian Literature in Two Parts*. 2 vols. London, 1898.

[Renaissance in Italy]: The Revival of Learning. Gloucester, Mass., 1967; repr. of 1877 edn.

Tafuri, Manfredo. "'Cives esse non licere': The Rome of Nicholas V and Leon Battista Alberti: Elements toward a Historical Revision. *Harvard Architecture Review* 6 (1987): 60–75.

Ricerca del Rinascimento: principi, città, architetti. Turin, 1992.

Tasso, Torquato. *Dialoghi*. Ed. Giovanni Baffetti. Milan, 1998.

Temple, William. *Five Miscellaneous Essays by Sir William Temple*. Ed., intro., and notes Samuel Holt Monk. Ann Arbor, Mich., 1963.

Tenenti, Alberto. "Le *Momus* dans l'oeuvre de Leon Battista Alberti." *Il Pensiero Politico* 7 (1974): 321–33.

Thompson, C. R. *The Translations of Lucian by Erasmus and St. Thomas More*. Ithaca, N.Y., 1940.

Tixier, Jean (Johannes Textor). *Theatrum poeticum atque historicum, sive Officina*. Basel, 1600.

Toffanin, Giuseppe. *History of Humanism*. Trans. Elio Gianturco. New York, 1954.

Trinkaus, Charles E. *In Our Image and Likeness: Humanity and Divinity in Italian Humanist Thought*. 2 vols. Chicago, 1970.

Bibliography

Ugolini, Aurelio. *Le opera di Giambattista Gelli*. Pisa, 1898.

Ullman, B. L. "Horace, Catullus, and Tigellius." *Classical Philology* 10 (1915): 270–96.

Valla, Lorenzo. *The Treatise of Lorenzo Valla on the Donation of Constantine*. Ed. and trans. Christopher B. Coleman. Toronto, 1993.

Vasoli, Cesare. "Riflessione sul 'problema' Vanini." In *Il libertinismo in Europa*. Ed. Sergio Bertelli, 125–67. Milan, 1980.

Vega, María José. "Traducíon y reescritura de L. B. Alberti: el *Momo* Castellano de Agustín de Almazán." *Esperienze Letterarie* 23 (1998):13–41.

Veyne, Paul. *Did the Greeks Believe in Their Myths? An Essay on the Constitutive Imagination*. Trans. Paula Wissing. Chicago, 1988.

Vitruvius. *On Architecture. Books VI–X*. Trans. Frank Granger. Cambridge, Mass., 1934.

Voltaire. *An Essay on the Civil Wars of France and Upon the Epick Poetry of European Nations, from Homer to Milton*. Dublin, 1760. *Dialogues et anecdotes philosophiques*. Ed. Raymond Naves. Paris, 1939.

Von Hutten, Ulrich. *Ulrich von Hutten: Schriften*. Vol. 4: *Ulrichi Hutteni equitis Germani opera quae reperiri potuerint omnia*. Ed. Edvard Böcking. Leipzig, 1860.

Waddington, Raymond B. *Aretino's Satyr: Sexuality, Satire, and Self-Projection in Sixteenth-Century Literature and Art*. Toronto, 2004.

Walker, D. P. *Spiritual and Demonic Magic: From Ficino to Campanella*. Notre Dame, Ind., 1975.

Walsh, Marcus. "Swift's *Tale of a Tub* and the Mock Book." In *Jonathan Swift and the Eighteenth-Century Book*. Ed. Paddy Bullard and James McLaverty, 101–18. Cambridge, 2013.

Watkins, Renée. "The Authorship of the *Vita anonyma* of Leon Battista Alberti." *Studies in the Renaissance* 4 (1957): 101–12.

"L. B. Alberti in the Mirror: An Interpretation of the *Vita* with a New Translation." *Italian Quarterly* 30 (1989): 5–30.

Weber, Max. *The Protestant Ethic and the Spirit of Capitalism*. Trans. Talcott Parsons. New York, 1958.

Weinberg, Bernard. *A History of Literary Criticism in the Italian Renaissance*. 2 vols. Chicago, 1961.

Weinbrot, Howard D. *Menippean Satire Reconsidered: From Antiquity to the Eighteenth Century*. Baltimore, Md., 2005.

Wellek, René. *The Rise of English Literary Theory*. Chapel Hill, N.C., 1941.

Bibliography

Werblowsky, R. J. Zwi. *Lucifer and Prometheus: A Study of Milton's Satan.* London, 1952.

Williams, Aubrey L. *Pope's* Dunciad: *A Study of Its Meaning.* London, 1955.

Williams, Harold. *Dean Swift's Library.* Cambridge, 1932.

Wind, Edgar. *Pagan Mysteries in the Renaissance.* New Haven, Conn., 1958.

Woodman, Thomas M. *Thomas Parnell.* Boston, Mass., 1985.

Wootton, David. "Lucien Febvre and the Problem of Unbelief in the Early Modern Period." *Journal of Modern History* 60 (1988): 695–730.

Wotton, William. *Reflections Upon Ancient and Modern Learning.* London, 1694; repr. Hildesheim, 1968.

Yates, Frances A. *The Art of Memory.* Chicago, 1966.

 Giordano Bruno and the Hermetic Tradition. New York, 1969; orig. London, 1964.

Zagorin, Perez. *Ways of Lying: Dissimulation, Persecution, and Conformity in Early Modern Europe.* Cambridge, Mass., 1990.

Index

Absurdism, 234

Academics (ancient school), 32

Accetto, Torquato, 58

Aeschylus, 75–76

Aesop, 2, 56, 57, 83, 146, 202, 206, 219

agnosticism, 23, 32, 66, 72, 179

Agrippa von Nettesheim, Heinrich
  Cornelius, 120, 124, 183, 187, 190–91

Alberti, Leon Battista, 47–48, 66
  "The Coin" (*Intercenales*), 50
  "The Cynic" (*Intercenales*), 50
  *De commodis litterarum atque
    incommodis*, 38
  De re aedificatoria, 46, 52, 64, 76
  Erumna, 44–45
  Intercenales, 44
  Momus, 52–81, 92–95, 113, 128, 129,
    156–76, 208
  On the Family, 39, 40, 42, 54, 158
  Philodoxeos, 44
  Pontifex, 51
  Profugiorum ab erumna, 46, 75, 77
  "Religio" (*Intercenales*), 50–51, 63
  Theogenius, 45, 46, 75, 76
  Vita S. Potiti, 48–49

Alembert, Jean Le Rond d', 213

Alexander of Abonoteichus, 27

Almazán, Agustín de, 92–95

Amsdorf, Nicholas von, 88

Andreini, Giovan Battista, 146
  L'Adamo, 151–56
  *Dialogo fra Momo e la Verità,
    spettante alla lode dell'arte
    comica*, 152–53

Anglicanism, 199, 208, 209

Apatisti (academy), 157

apistia (doubt), 10

Arethas of Caesarea, 11

Aretino, Pietro, 102, 148, 189, 190–91, 192

Arianism, 88, 124, 135, 172, 174–76

Ariosto, Ludovico, 158, 159

Aristophanes, 29, 209

Aristotle, 195, 206, 219

Arminianism, 170, 176

Asclepius, 130

atheism
  and Cicero, 31–32
  and *Cymbalum mundi*, 98–102
  and Desiderius Erasmus, 85
  and Epicureanism, 43
  and Étienne Dolet, 97
  and Giordano Bruno, 133, 136, 139
  and John Milton, 169, 170, 179
  and Jonathan Swift, 200
  and Leon Battista Alberti, 63–65, 66,
    68–72, 79, 93
  and Lucian, 14–20, 23, 26, 213

Augustine, 162

Babrius, 3

Bacchylides, 2

Barry, Spranger, 227

Bartoli, Cosimo, 158

Barzizza, Gasparino, 36

Bayless, Martha, 237

Bellarmino, Roberto (Cardinal), 137

Bentley, Richard, 202, 203, 204–05, 206,
  214

263

Index

Berni, Francesco, 192
Berti, Domenico, 137
Berti, Silvia, 137
Bible
  Exodus, 112
  Hebrews, 116
  Job, 140–41
  Matthew, 113, 131
  Numbers, 109
  Psalms, 105
  Romans, 101
Bietenholz, Peter, 92
blasphemy, 135, 143, 194, 218, 220
Boccaccio, Giovanni, 35, 137, 200
Boschetto, Luca, 77
Boswell, Jackson, 156
Botzheim, Johann von, 84
Boulenger de Rivery,
  Claude-François-Félix, 229–30
Boyle, Charles, 202, 206
Bracciolini, Poggio, 39, 63, 197
Brett, Thomas, 139
Brown, Alison, 43
Brown, Virginia, 75
Bruno, Giordano, 148, 212
Bryson, Michael, 169
Bucer, Martin, 97
Buchanan, George, 206
Burchiello (Domenico di Giovanni), 192
Burckhardt, Jacob, 36, 193

Caedmon, 146
Café Momus, 231
Callimachus, 8–10
Calvinism, 130, 170, 199
Camillo, Giulio, 186
Carew, Thomas, 102, 148–51
Carey, George Saville, 227
Carey, John, 145
Carnesecchi, Pietro, 103
Cartari, Vincenzo, 231
Cast, David, 122
Celsus, 98
censors, 116, 119
Cervantes, Miguel de, 227
Charity: or Momus's Reward, 228
Charles I (English King), 148
Charron, Pierre, 138
Chasseneuz, Barthélemey de, 188
Cibber, Colley, 216, 224
Cicero, 18, 31–32, 34, 35, 62, 174, 219
Citolini, Alessandro, 186

Civil War (England), 159, 166
clergy, 39, 42, 50, 51, 67, 68, 70, 71, 87,
  92, 107, 110, 169, 182, 199
Colonna, Vittoria, 103
comédie française, 229
comédie italienne, 229
Contarini, Gasparo (Cardinal), 103, 107
contemptus mundi, 65, 114, 117
Coornhert, Dirck, 122
Council of Trent, 107
Counter-Reformation, 93, 102, 116, 119
court jester, 229
courtiers, 53, 54, 78, 93, 95, 160, 164, 229
criticism (literary), 181–225
Cromwell, Oliver, 170
Crusca (academy), 157
Cymbalum mundi, 96–102
Cynicism, 10, 12–13, 28–29, 50, 100,
  126, 187, 219

Damonte, Mario, 93
Damrosch, Leo, 205
Dante, 73, 120
Dati, Carlo, 159
Deism, 200, 202
Demetrius of Phaleron, 3
Democritus, 70, 118, 187, 226
*Democritus Ridens: or Comus and
  Momus*, 150
Dennis, John, 203
Des Périers, Bonaventure, 96
Descartes, René, 206
Diagoras, 32
dignity of humankind, *topos*, 41
dissimulation, 4, 53, 54, 57–58, 73, 92,
  164
Dolet, Étienne, 97, 100
Domenichi, Ludovico, 187
Don Quixote, 202
Doni, Anton Francesco, 102–04, 108–21,
  195
  I mondi e gli inferni, 111–21
  Gli spiriti folletti, 109–11
Dryden, John, 176, 206, 221, 225

Edward, Edwin (Governor), 232
Egerton, Alice, 150
Egerton, John (Earl of Bridgewater), 149
Envy, 2, 3, 8–10, 220
Epicureanism, 10, 14–20, 27, 32, 43, 53,
  63–64, 70–71, 179, 230
Erasmus, Desiderius, 68, 82–92, 171

Index

265

Adages, 83–84
Colloquies, 89, 91
Freedom of the Will, 88
Julius Excluded from Heaven, 92
Praise of Folly, 85–86, 88, 92, 207, 212, 229
Eucharist, 134–35
Euclid, 206
Euhemerism, 68, 126, 174
Euripides, 18–19, 21–22, 101, 146, 170, 175
existentialism, 234

Fall (of mankind), 61, 145, 151, 161–62, 188
Faust, 162
Febvre, Lucien, 42, 98
Federico da Montefeltro, 40
Ficino, Marsilio, 124, 186
fideism, 134, 188
Fielding, Henry, 213
Filelfo, Francesco, 197
Fish, Stanley, 145
Florentine Academy, 109, 157, 158
Fontenelle, Bernard de, 202
Foucault, Michel, 13–14, 30, 237
Franco, Niccolò, 102–08, 115, 127, 192
Frank, Joseph, 174
Froben press, 84

Gaddi, Jacopo, 157–58
Gadol, Joan, 40, 41, 52
Galileo, 159, 177–78
Garin, Eugenio, 44, 46, 52, 55, 70, 77, 86, 92
Garrick, David, 227
Garzoni, Tomaso, 120, 182–98, 222
Gavin, Michael, 198, 213
Gelli, Giambattista, 109
Gellius, Aulius, 100
Gelosi (acting company), 152
Gonzaga, Giulia, 103
Gonzaga, Ludovico, 40
Grafton, Anthony, 67
Grayson, Cecil, 55
Greek Anthology, The, 8
Greenblatt, Stephen, 43
Grendler, Paul, 102, 103
Grotius, Hugo, 146, 154
Grub Street, 217
Guicciardini, Francesco, 206
Guthkelch, A. C., 206

Harth, Phillip, 199
Heemskerck, Maarten van, 122
Heraclitus, 187
Hermeticism, 61, 124, 129–30
Herodotus, 15, 206
Hesiod, 1, 8, 146, 147
Hill, Christopher, 170
Hippocrates, 206
Hippocrates, Ps.-, 118
Hobbes, Thomas, 138
Homer, 146, 206, 215, 218, 219
Homer, Ps.-, 218
Hood, Thomas, 227
Horace, 203
humanism, 39, 41, 42, 49
Hussein, Saddam, 232
Hutten, Ulrich von, 87
Huttich, Johann, 84

Ibn Ezra, Abraham, 141
iconoclasm, 68
Iliad, The, 14, 18, 208, 218, 219
d'Illiers, René (Bishop), 85
Index of Forbidden Books, 103, 108
Interregnum (1649–60), 159

Job, 104, 116, 171–73
Johnson, Samuel, 201
Jones, Inigo, 148
Jonson, Ben, 150, 222
Juan de Valdés, 103
Julius II (Pope), 92

Kafka, Franz, 234–35
Karlstadt, Andreas, 68
Knight, Sarah, 75
Kore Kosmou, 61, 77, 124, 128, 132
Kurke, Leslie, 4

L'Esprit de Spinoza, 139
La Bohème, 231
Lactantius, 11
Lamb, Charles, 227
Lando, Ortensio, 111
Langbaine, Gerard, 221–23
Lapo da Castiglionchio, 39
Lawes, Henry, 149
Le Clerc, Jean, 217
Le Roy, Antoine, 229
Lefranc, Abel, 98
Leonello d'Este, 40, 45, 54
Letters of Phalaris, 202, 220

266 Index

Levine, Joseph, 204
Lewalski, Barbara, 171
Lewis, C. S., 145, 169, 176
Libanius, 8
Life of Aesop, 4
Linguardo, Francesco, 109, 119
Locke, John, 222
Longinus, 219
Louis XIV (French king), 229
Lucian, 10–33, 85, 91, 146, 201, 209
  Alexander the False Prophet, 17, 26–27,
    84, 85
  Banquet, 84
  *The Dead Come to Life, or the
    Fisherman*, 12
  Gallus, 85
  Hermagoras, 17
  Hermotimus, 14, 83
  How to Write History, 31
  On Sacrifices, 26, 51, 84
  Parliament of the Gods, The, 20–23,
    68, 84, 108, 125, 128, 132, 175
  Passing of Peregrinus, The, 11, 28–29,
    175, 176
  Philosophers for Sale, 12
  Prometheus, 75
  Syrian Goddess, The, 140
  Zeus Rants, 14–22, 63, 64, 79, 84, 99,
    108, 114, 125
  Zeus Refuted, 16, 25–26, 62, 99, 100,
    108, 125, 126, 174
Lucifer, 56, 74, 109–10, 144–80.
  see also Satan
Lucretius, 32, 43, 63, 70, 79, 126, 129,
    146, 200, 209, 211
Lull, Raymond, 124
Lupano, Ottone, 140
Luther, Martin, 82–92, 97
  Address to the German Nobility, 88
  On the Bondage of the Will, 88
  Table Talk, 83
Lyttelton, George, 24–25, 236–37

Machiavelli, Niccolò, 64, 127, 138
magic, 129, 130, 136
Marchand, Prosper, 101–02, 138
Mardi Gras (New Orleans), 150,
    231–34
Marguerite of Navarre, 97
Marlowe, Christopher, 146, 162
Marsuppini, Carlo, 75
Massa, Lorenzo, 197

materialism, 64, 70, 79, 93, 118–19, 129,
    138, 139–40
Mayne, Jasper, 176
Medici, Duke Cosimo I, de', 108
Menippus, 12, 87
Miller, Lady Anna, 228
Millet, Olivier, 96
Milton, John, 206, 216
  and Alberti's Momus, 156–76
  Areopagitica, 169–70, 177, 179
  Comus (or *Masque at Ludlow
    Castle*), 149–51
  *Defense of Himself Against Alexander
    More*, 147
  On Christian Doctrine, 170, 175, 180
  Paradise Lost, 144–80, 206, 207, 219
  Paradise Regained, 164, 172
  Prolusions, 147–48, 212
  *Reason of Church Government Urg'd
    Against Prelaty*, 169, 171
  Samson Agonistes, 172–74, 179
  Second Defense of the English People,
    157, 170
Minois, Georges, 137
miracles, 97
Mirandola, Pico della, 127
mnemonists, 186
Mocenigo, Zuan, 124
modernism, 191, 208, 210, 230, 240–41
Molin, Biagio, 48
momos (blame), 2
Momus Krewe (Mardi Gras), 232, 240
More, Alexander, 147
More, Thomas, 84, 85, 92, 111
Morin, Jean, 96
Murger, Henri, 231

Nauert, Charles, 187
Neoplatonism, 124
Nesi, Giovanni, 112
Niccoli, Niccolò, 63
Nicholas V (Pope), 37, 39, 67, 167

Ochino, Bernardino, 103
oracles, 15
Origen, 98
Ovid, 100, 113, 146

Palaephatus, 30
Palmer, Ada, 43
Palmieri, Matteo, 158
Pandolfini, Agnolo, 158

Index

Pandolfini, Filippo, 158
pantheism, 93
Paolini, Fabio, 197
Parker, William, 169
Parnell, Thomas, 218–20, 227
parrhesia (frank speech), 10, 12–14, 57–58, 72, 101, 170, 218, 220
Pask, Kevin, 220, 222, 225
pasquinades, 102, 189, 192, 195–96
Pausanias, 30, 214
Perrault, Charles, 203
Petrarca, Francesco, 127
Phaedrus, 3
Philippus of Thessalonica, 8
Pignatti, Franco, 107
Pindar, 2, 206
Pio, Alberto, 90
plagiarism, 186, 191, 221–23
Plato, 6–7, 206
Pliny, 186
Pole, Reginald (Cardinal), 103
poligrafi (polygraphs), 102, 182, 187
Poliziano, Angelo, 186
Pope, Alexander, 208, 214–17
    Dunciad, The, 215–17, 218
    Essay on Criticism, An, 214–15
popes, 55, 136
predestinarianism, 170–74
princes, 54, 78, 93, 94, 189
professions, 113, 120, 182–89
Prometheus, 1, 26, 53, 56, 63, 74–76, 78, 141, 145, 177–78
Protagoras, 32, 41
Ptolemy Philadelphus, 219
Puccini, Giacomo, 231
Puritans, 200, 208
Pyrrho of Elis, 187

Quéro, Dominique, 228–29, 230–31
Quint, David, 146, 165, 168, 177

Rabelais, François, 24–25, 42, 91, 100, 148
Ramponi, Virginia, 152
religious impostors, 17, 28
religious relativism, 137
Restoration (England), 159, 166, 170
Riccobono, Antonio, 197
Rittershausen, Konrad, 136
Roman Inquisition, 103, 124, 137, 139, 177
Rubeanus, Crotus, 87
Rymer, Thomas, 203

Sadoleto, Jacopo (Cardinal), 103
Saint-Aubin, Gabriel Jacques de, 231
Salvini, Salvino, 158
Sandburg, Carl, 234
Satan, 58, 141, 219. *see also* Lucifer
Schoppe, Caspar, 136
Scott, Walter, 231
Scriblerus Club, 215, 218
Sentence of Momus on the Poetical Amusements at a Villa Near Bath, The, 228
Shakespeare, William, 146, 222
Shelley, Percy Bysshe, 145, 177
Sidney, Philip, 123, 126, 128, 135, 148, 212
Simoncini, Stefano, 58
skepticism, 2, 88, 91, 125, 134, 138, 140, 174, 187
Smallwood, Philip, 213
Smith, Christine, 58
Smith, D. Nichol, 206
Smith, Malcolm, 100
Socrates, 7, 122
Sombart, Werner, 41
Sozzini, Camillo, 103, 109
Sozzini, Fausto, 103
Sozzini, Lelio, 103, 109
Spinoza, Baruch, 64, 129, 138, 139–41
spirituali (or Evangelists), 103
St. Peter's basilica, 167
Stobaeus, 61, 124
Stoicism, 14, 17–20, 32
Suda, 11, 34, 100
Svogliati (academy), 157
Swift, Jonathan, 198–213, 215, 227
    "Apology", 199
    Battel of the Books, The, 205–09, 218
    Discourse on the Mechanical Operation of the Spirit, 202
    Tale of a Tub, A, 199–205
Symonds, John Addington, 42

Tafuri, Manfredo, 67
Tasso, Torquato, 58, 158, 159, 206
Temple, Sir William, 199, 202, 205, 206, 209
Terence, 102
theodicy
    Antoii Francesco Doni, 114–16, 117–18, 119–20
    and John Milton, 174
    and Leon Battista Alberti, 62, 64–65, 79
    and Lucian, 15, 16, 18
    and Niccolò Franco, 104–07

Index

Thompson, Craig, 85
Tixier, Jean, 185, 192, 193
Toffanin, Giuseppe, 42
Toland, John, 138, 216
transubstantiation, 136
Treatise of the Three Impostors, The,
    137, 138, 139, 142, 200
Trinkaus, Charles, 42

Valla, Lorenzo, 197
Vanini, Giulio Cesare, 138
Vega, María José, 94, 95
Venegas, Alejo de, 95
Vergerio, Pier Paolo, 103

Veyne, Paul, 31
Virgil, 146, 216, 222
Voltaire, 24, 91, 151–52, 227
Vondel, Joost van den, 146, 154, 159

Weber, Max, 41
Weinbrot, Howard, 199, 208
Wilcox, Ella Wheeler, 234
Wotton, William, 201, 202, 203, 204, 206

Yates, Frances, 130

Zoilus, 189, 191–92, 203, 215, 218–20
Zwingli, Ulrich, 68